differently wired

Raising an Exceptional Child in a Conventional World

DEBORAH REBER

WORKMAN PUBLISHING ▪ NEW YORK

//

TO MY INCREDIBLE BOY, ASHER

But *of course* I am dedicating this book to you, the reason for it all. I love you with everything I am.

//

Copyright © 2018 by Deborah Reber

All rights reserved. No portion of this book may be reproduced—mechanically, electronically, or by any other means, including photocopying—without written permission of the publisher. Published simultaneously in Canada by Thomas Allen & Son Limited.

Library of Congress Cataloging-in-Publication Data is available.

ISBN 978-1-5235-0212-7

Design by Galen Smith / Cover by Janet Vicario

Workman books are available at special discounts when purchased in bulk for premiums and sales promotions as well as for fund-raising or educational use. Special editions or book excerpts can also be created to specification. For details, contact the Special Sales Director at the address below, or send an email to specialmarkets@workman.com.

Workman Publishing Company, Inc.
225 Varick Street
New York, NY 10014-4381
workman.com / tiltparenting.com

WORKMAN is a registered trademark of Workman Publishing Co., Inc.
DIFFERENTLY WIRED is a registered trademark of Deborah Reber

Printed in the United States of America

First printing June 2018

10 9 8 7 6 5 4 3 2 1

Contents

A Differently Wired World

*Normality is a paved road: It's comfortable to walk,
but no flowers grow on it.*
—Vincent van Gogh

A few weeks ago, my twelve-year-old son, Asher, was having trouble getting off his computer and coming to the dinner table. I don't remember why, exactly—likely he'd gotten caught up in an expedition in *Subnautica* or experienced a critical launch failure in *Kerbal Space Program*, two of his passions du jour. I finally heard him close his laptop, toss his headphones aside, and release a lengthy, dramatic sigh.

"I'm sorry," he muttered in a low voice, head down, slowly shuffling over to his chair.

"That's okay, honey," I said as he sat down and began to eat. "You didn't do anything wrong. Let's just try to learn from this so we can figure out where you're getting off track, yeah?"

Before I go any further, this would probably be a good time to tell you that Asher is what's known as "twice exceptional" or "2e," with the trifecta diagnoses of attention deficit hyperactivity disorder (ADHD), Asperger's, and a ridiculously high IQ. He's *really* good at hyperfocusing. And losing track of time. And tuning everything out. And he's not so good at transitions, switching gears, follow-through… that sort of thing.

"I'm sorry," Asher repeated before shoving a forkful of buttered noodles into his mouth.

"Sweetie . . . seriously. You don't have to apologize. It's totally fine."

I refilled my glass of sparkling water and was just about to ask him a question when he interjected. "I think I've just been conditioned to apologize for everything because I had to do it all the time in school."

Well, *that* got my attention. "What do you mean you had to do it *all the time* in school?" Though I homeschool him now, Asher had spent kindergarten through second grade in a handful of different public and private schools.

"Yeah. Every time I did anything wrong that was related to my ADHD, I had to say 'sorry.' Like if I fidgeted. Or I forgot to raise my hand. Or I interrupted somebody. Or I got upset."

"How often did *that* happen?" I said, trying to calmly absorb this news flash.

"All the time," he said matter-of-factly before picking up his Kindle and immersing himself in a book, his way of signaling that the conversation was over.

My husband, Derin, was out of town, so he'd missed this Asher insight, another paper-thin layer of the onion peeling off to reveal a clearer picture of how our boy had become the person he is today.

> People apologize for things they've done wrong. Things they regret. My son apologized for who he is.

I'm not sure why I was surprised by this revelation, but I was. I mean, I was well aware of the fact that school hadn't been a smashing success for Asher. In traditional classrooms he'd been anxious and by all accounts the exact opposite of thriving. It's why we'd decided to homeschool him in the first place.

But this new bit of information Asher nonchalantly dropped on me chipped away another piece of my heart. Because what I know about apologies is that they're what people say to take responsibility for things they've done that are wrong. Things they regret. Things they could have made better choices about if they'd been more thoughtful or conscientious or *good*.

I thought of Asher, at the tender ages of six, seven, eight—my little guy with the too-long hair falling over his big brown eyes, his rail-thin body laboring under the weight of an oversize shark-themed backpack overflowing with library books—going back and forth to school every day ready to learn, grow, play with his friends, and be a kid.

And apparently, regularly apologizing for who he is.

I had to wonder—*How many times in his short life has Asher gotten the message that he's wrong or broken or rude or bad?*

I don't know about you, but I'm not okay with *any* part of this story, and it's indicative of a massive tragedy playing out in schools and communities and homes everywhere. We live in a world where children who are in some way neurologically atypical, or what I describe as "differently wired"—a term I use to refer to the millions of people with neurodifferences such as ADHD, giftedness, autism, learning disorders, and anxiety, as well as those with no formal diagnosis but who are clearly moving through the world in a unique way—are being told day in and day out that there is something wrong with who they inherently are.

As you likely know all too well, parenting an atypical kid in a conventional world is an often lonely and difficult journey, with our families paying the price for the intolerance, misinformation, and lack of support that exists in today's society. Fueled by a desire to shift the way difference is perceived and experienced by exceptional kids like Asher and the parents raising them, I founded TiLT Parenting in 2016 to change the conversation surrounding neurodiversity—and to help parents find more peace, confidence, and joy along the way.

Initially launched as a weekly podcast featuring interviews and conversations to inspire and inform parents like us, TiLT has developed into a thriving global community of people committed to embracing and supporting who our kids are, no matter what. My highest goal is to ensure that parents walking this unmarked path never feel alone again—and have what they need so their extraordinary children can thrive.

Differently Wired won't give you a step-by-step formula for magically ending your daughter's months-long regressions or fixing your son's organizational challenges. I'm not going to share the secret to eliminating your child's anxiety or explain how to create a positive behavioral support chart so you can finally end screen-time battles. And this is not a book specifically geared toward any one diagnosis. Plenty of good books are already available for every developmental difference—many of them sit well worn on my bookshelf; they will give you tactical strategies for specific challenges. Many of you may not even have a formal diagnosis for your child. The truth is, dividing us into diagnostic buckets, although helpful when searching for specific tools to address specific challenges, also has the side effect of keeping us separate and secluded. The way I see it, difference is difference is difference. Though the symptoms and behaviors of our kids may vary, so many of our challenges as their parents are actually the same. And we are much more powerful together.

> It's time to say *no* to trying to fit square-peg kids into round holes, and *yes* to the gifts of their uniqueness.

We need one another because I'm looking to tackle something big. And, I hope, something revolutionary. Because the übergoal of *Differently Wired* is to redefine how neurodiversity is perceived in the world, and shift the parenting paradigm to one that acknowledges and includes our experiences. At its heart, this is a book about saying *no*—*no* to trying to fit these square-peg kids into round holes, *no* to educational and social systems that don't respect and support how they move through the world, *no* to frustration and isolation—and saying *yes* to the gifts of these unique children and everything that goes along with who they are.

Differently Wired lays out a vision for starting with us—parents—and shifting our thinking and actions in a way that will not only change our family dynamic, but allow our children to fully realize their best selves. The best part? By making these shifts in our own world, we are rejecting what's broken in the status quo and demanding a new, inclusive, supportive paradigm. And that, my friends, means we're actually moving the world closer to a place where difference is genuinely seen and valued.

It's time for things to change for today's atypical generation and the parents raising them. I'm thrilled you're reading this book, and I hope you connect with its vision for launching a shift that will have far-reaching implications. Because when these kids have the chance to let their gifts flourish, there is no limit to what's possible.

I hope you'll join me.

PART ONE

A Rallying Cry

CHAPTER 1

//

An Unmarked Path

//

When did you first know there was something different going on with your child? If you're like most parents raising an atypically developing kid, there probably wasn't a pivotal aha moment neatly wrapped up with classic symptoms, an easy-to-peg label, and a clear course of action. More often than not, the realization that a child is different happens slowly and unevenly, like a head-to-toe Band-Aid being yanked off one hair at a time over a period of years. That's because when they're little, kids with no obvious diagnosis or visible difference tend to fly under the radar. Sure, some might be colicky or more sensitive or less cuddly than other babies, but those traits can all easily fit into the range of normal baby behavior. After all—aren't all babies difficult? All parents sleep deprived? All new families making it up as they go along?

That's what my husband, Derin, and I figured, anyway. Asher was colicky from day one. Nothing could settle him, his sleep patterns were hellish, and he seemed generally, for lack of a better description, *pissed off.* I viewed him as an old soul, annoyed for having been thrust back into such a tiny body and into a life where he'd have to wait a good, long time to get to the juicy stuff. So we read the baby books, tracked feedings and soiled diapers on a spreadsheet, and sought advice from seasoned parents about how to get our boy to sleep through the night. As first-time parents, we assumed our experience was no different from anyone else's. *Mostly.*

Shortly after Asher was born, we joined the Program for Early Parent Support (PEPS), a Seattle organization connecting new parents for community and support. New to the city and with no social circle to speak of, Derin and I were hungry for camaraderie and hoped to glean some wisdom about how this whole parenting thing was going to work. I remember getting together that first night, six couples sitting cross-legged on the floor cradling infants bundled up for the fall weather, nervously sharing our birth stories. Back then, we were all on equal footing—our babies blank slates, differentiated only by the number of hours they slept or how severely they reacted to breast milk soured by the curry in the previous night's meal. As time went by, these families would become the first control group in our ongoing, high-stakes research project—figuring out how to parent a unique kid.

We survived year one, grateful to be on the other side of the colic and ready for things to get easier. But instead, things stayed hard, just in new and different ways. In our PEPS group, we witnessed our children evolving from helpless blobs into little people with distinct personalities, temperaments, and senses of humor. By the time he was two, we felt certain Marques was destined to be a pro athlete. Campbell was clearly the artist of the group, Ella a natural dancer. And Asher? Asher was the precocious one. The kid was intense. Stubborn. Sensitive to loud sounds. Fairly accident-prone. And also fascinating, delightful, and super-chatty.

By his second birthday, Asher was regularly turning heads with his rich vocabulary, along with his propensity for engaging in complex conversations with any willing adult. He could recite a book verbatim after hearing it read only once or twice. His focus for solving puzzles was remarkable. We knew enough toddlers to know his intellect wasn't typical, and Derin and I frequently found ourselves exchanging looks of both disbelief and pride at something Asher said or did.

Another thing Asher turned heads with? His apocalyptic conniptions. The kid had lungs, not to mention an iron will. Whereas most two-year-olds work from the same tantrum playbook—arched backs, flopping to the ground, red-faced screaming—Asher's tantrums just seemed somehow... *bigger*. When other parents witnessed an Asher conniption, I noted the shock and awe in their eyes. Not wanting to make me feel worse than I already did, these parents would often confide in me about a recent meltdown they'd had to endure, the message being that this was a normal part of raising a kid.

But if the intensity of Asher's tantrums was so normal, why were none of my friends regularly bailing halfway through dinners out because their child was disrupting the whole restaurant? Why hadn't they had an uncomfortable exchange with the woman in the moss-green house on the corner, the one who stepped outside one afternoon because Asher's screaming apparently led her to believe he was being abducted or abused, the one who eyed me suspiciously as she asked, "Is everything *okay* here?" And then there was the day our mother's helper—warm, loving, experienced—carried my rigid, hysterical child upstairs, passed him back to me like a store clerk handing over a sack of potatoes, and quit.

> Holy crap. We were *that* family. With the kid who drives the nanny to quit.

"I can't do this anymore." She was crying, her arms raised in defeat. She mumbled apologies as she retreated down the stairs, grabbed her things, and bolted out the door. It was her fourth day on the job.

I stood there on the landing, a hapless mother in a Judd Apatow film, trying to process what had just happened. And all I could think was *Holy crap. We're* that *family. The family with the kid who drives the nanny to quit.*

Suffice it to say that by the time Asher was two, Derin and I knew we were engaged in a more extreme form of parenting than most. We knew Asher was intense and challenging, or as one parenting book labeled him, "spirited." We were discovering he was freakishly smart. And we knew he didn't respond to the parenting tools spelled out by the books our friends were relying on (*The Happiest Toddler on the Block, Positive Discipline, How to Talk So Kids Will Listen and Listen So Kids Will Talk*).

We didn't have a clue as to what we were dealing with. We didn't know how to differentiate between your standard "terrible twos" fare and what was happening inside our home. Our only frame of reference was what we saw in our community, in Asher's drop-in preschool, and on TV. One day I'd see a child shut down the supermarket aisle with a tantrum while Asher quietly sat in our cart flipping through a book, and I'd think, *See? We're all good here.* Then the next day Asher would stage an hour-long protest about getting into his car seat and I'd once again be bewildered. As the evidence mounted, the Band-Aid slowly peeled away, revealing small patches of red, irritated skin underneath. I began having dark moments of doubt, when I'd be convinced there was something seriously wrong, and then I'd read an article online that would convince me otherwise, or a pediatrician would chalk it up to normal three-and-a-half-year-old behavior and send us on our way with an "Everything looks fine to me."

But things didn't *feel* fine. Derin and I began distrusting ourselves and our experience. Was there something "going on" with Asher or not? Were we just overbearing parents with ridiculous behavioral expectations, or were we in denial about something everyone around us already knew? The fact that our friends frequently normalized Asher's behavior added to our bewilderment. In retrospect, I'm sure they were trying to allay our fears, but back then, it just made us feel even worse.

By the time Asher turned four, Derin and I had accepted that our son was atypical. We just didn't know how to figure out what that meant or what to do about it. Isolation set in. Other than my sister, my best friends, and our parents, no one knew how difficult things were at home. I longed for someone or something to help us fit Asher and his behavior neatly into a box so I could get busy fixing whatever was wrong. I'm a resourceful person and a researcher by nature, but I was floundering. Where was the community of families like us? The concrete strategies? The path? And why did my husband and I constantly feel like we were the only parents struggling with these issues?

And then there was school. Notes home from preschool teachers about problems in class, on the playground, with other kids, and with authority became a regular experience. Tried-and-true strategies used by seasoned educators were proving futile when it came to my kid. I felt like I was raising a child Method actor preparing for the roles of Jekyll and Hyde in an upcoming Broadway production. I mean, the kid was committed, especially to his anger, which seemed to be the prevailing emotion during that first year of school. After a string of bad weeks in which I received a phone call, note, or email from the school detailing yet another incident almost every day, I asked a friend, not for the last time, "Is it possible they would kick him out of preschool?"

We searched for clues about what was behind his anger, which was beginning to feel unpredictable and unsafe. More than once he'd whipped off his shoe and thrown it wildly in the car while I was driving, hitting the dashboard. I occasionally got calls from the preschool about dangerous things he'd done on the playground, wielding sticks or throwing small stones. The apology letters, dictated by Asher, written by me, and delivered to classmates before school, mounted up. Though the school worked tirelessly with us to help Asher, nothing improved things. I couldn't help but feel I was failing as a parent.

About midway through the year, a friend mentioned the words "sensory processing disorder," and something in me clicked. She jotted down the name of a must-read book, *The Out-of-Sync Child*, and I left her house feeling an instant sense of relief. *Yes. Out of sync! Finally we have our answer!* Within a week I had tracked down the go-to occupational therapy clinic for kids with sensory processing challenges and added our name to the waiting list. A few months later, Asher began seeing an incredible therapist named Kris, with whom he ended up working for the next four years.

Finally—we had our answer. We were taking the right action, and I expected the intense and disruptive behavior to fizzle out pretty soon. It would totally work. Any... day... now...

But as Asher entered his second year of preschool, things continued to grow more difficult. Emotionally, I was a wreck, experiencing some form of embarrassment, shame, anger, or confusion on an almost daily basis, mostly stemming from pressure I placed on myself to handle everything in the "right way."

At the urging of a friend, we did a more thorough assessment with Asher that spring. The results: provisional diagnoses of pervasive developmental disorder not otherwise specified (PDD-NOS), which we were told is akin to "mild autism," and attention deficit hyperactivity disorder (ADHD). The diagnoses were provisional because he was only five and over time might outgrow certain behaviors. But I was skeptical about *all of it*. In my mind, the testing procedures were too subjective, and all of Asher's diagnoses—giftedness, the sensory issues, the ADHD, the PDD-NOS—shared nearly identical "symptoms." So what exactly was what? And what, if anything, would actually "work"?

It was also time to figure out the plan for kindergarten. Derin and I had assumed Asher would go to the neighborhood public school, yet the general consensus among people who knew him was that smaller classrooms and a more individualized curriculum were his best bet. So we reluctantly turned our attention to private schools.

The following fall, we sent him off to a private school for highly gifted kids. We crossed our fingers and, miraculously, Asher made it through that first year—thanks to a seasoned teacher who shared his love of engineering and cats. I did have weeks at a time in that first year when I allowed myself to stop worrying and warily consider that maybe Asher had found his place. But two months into first grade, things fell apart. I began having concerns about the way some of his classmates, as well as his teacher, were "shaming" Asher for things he was doing his own way (read: wrong) or that were tied to his challenges. His self-esteem was taking a serious hit.

Then, in an after-school meeting with Asher's entire teaching team, the head of the lower school announced that she'd never encountered a child as intense as Asher in all her thirty-plus years working in education. I nervously laughed and called her bluff.

"I find it hard to believe that Asher is the *most* intense child. I mean, *seriously.*"

Without missing a beat, she curtly replied, "It's true."

But they were just getting warmed up. For the next half hour, I sat there and listened to a chorus of teachers relay tales of daily outbursts. Here I'd shown up to the meeting with a journal and pen in hand, ready to capture notes about our new plan, but those props were completely unnecessary. When the art teacher, who I knew was one of Asher's favorites, began listing off his offenses in the studio, it hit me. This wasn't a meeting to brainstorm how to meet Asher's needs at all. It was an ambush.

That's when it hit me. This wasn't a meeting to brainstorm how to meet Asher's needs at all. It was an ambush.

I sat in that dimly lighted classroom, my body uncomfortably wedged into a chair meant for a six-year-old, and listened to the guidance counselor tell me other kids were beginning to fear Asher, that they didn't want to partner with him because of his unpredictable outbursts. My face grew hot and tingly. I was embarrassed. I said all the things someone in denial says about support mechanisms and getting ahead of the problem. But as I walked back to my car, their parting words kept running through my mind: *Maybe this school isn't the right fit for Asher. We need to see a significant change if he is to continue here next year.*

Over the next two weeks, I organized meetings, brought in experts, and created colorful "zone charts" and scripts to help the teachers support Asher's dysregulation. But the thought of Asher normalizing the way he was being treated made me dizzy. I felt like I was feeding him to the sharks when I dropped him off each morning, gritting my teeth, hoping I wouldn't run into anyone as I walked back to the parking lot. As soon as I was safely inside my car, I'd sink back into the seat and cry tears of frustration, trying to reach Derin, my sister, or my mom on my cell phone for moral support. I was slowly falling apart, heartbroken over the possibility that my son's beautiful spirit was being permanently damaged, and outraged at the way things were playing out. And so, the day before winter break, we walked out of those double doors for the last time and never looked back.

Operation Elementary School, take two.

We started fresh that January at a lovely private school whose focus was emotional development, critical thinking, and social justice. While I adjusted to the new drop-off and pickup drill, Asher did what he always does—be himself no matter what. As was his style, in class he blurted out his opinion freely, let his frustration flag fly when anything happened that he perceived to be unfair, and found creative loopholes that enabled him to turn any school project into something squarely centered on his area of interest, which, at the time, happened to be origami. Within six weeks, Asher had spearheaded the Origami Frog Olympics, an idea that had classmates obsessively folding paper frogs and apparatuses. (Asher's inspirations are nothing if not infectious.)

After a brief honeymoon period, things started to deteriorate. By May, Derin and I were sitting in the school director's office listening to their concerns about meeting Asher's intellectual needs as well as how much teacher time his disruptions were costing the rest of the class. The bottom line: If we chose to return the following year, we would need to bring in a part-time paraprofessional, at our expense, to support Asher. It was another situation of "it's not us, it's you." Another goodbye. Another loss. For us, and for Asher.

Operation Elementary School, take three.

This time we opted for a full-time gifted program in public school with classroom accommodations outlined in an individualized education plan (IEP). I joked to friends who were empathizing with our plight, "At least they can't kick him out!"

As Asher adjusted to life in his third school in as many years, I adjusted to what was beginning to feel like my new full-time job— educating Asher's teachers about how to manage his behavior in the classroom and advocating for him when things went south. It was clear to me he was bored, disengaged, and unmotivated—from what I could tell, the only thing Asher was learning in school was how to sneak-read his Kindle and build a successful side business selling origami Pikachus (at ten cents apiece, they were a steal). And although it was nice that Asher was bonding with the kind principal because of the sheer amount of time he spent in her office, I came to realize that his IEP wasn't enough, concluding that most mainstream schools just aren't designed to meet the needs of kids who think differently.

It had been three years since Asher's first assessment, so that year Derin and I added our name to a five-month-long waiting list, eventually getting him evaluated at the University of Washington's Autism Center, a two-week process that involved controlled observations, teacher evaluations, written tests, and parenting interviews. The process was both eye-opening and painful, because although I craved concrete answers, I didn't necessarily want the ones we got— autism spectrum disorder, ADHD, and disruptive behavioral disorder not otherwise specified. Derin and I digested the final report, feeling overwhelmed and uncertain about what it all meant in the long run. Eventually, we concluded that Asher's diagnoses were just another piece of the puzzle, insight to be folded into our growing picture of Asher's unique way of being.

By the end of second grade, it was clear Asher was striking out on the school front. On top of that, I was exhausted—from our crazy therapy schedule (four sessions at four different places per week), from the social pressures . . . from all of it. Asher was perpetually anxious—his poor little fingernails and the skin around them were gnawed into oblivion. At home, his intensity meant living in what sometimes felt like a war zone—explosions were big, frequent, and unpredictable. We knew Asher deserved more than being shoved into a system that wasn't designed for him, and that by continuing on this path, our actions (or perhaps inaction?) would likely lead to even more dysregulation, anxiety, insecurity, bullying, and challenges for our family. Something had to give.

Desperate for a solution, Derin and I put it out to the universe that we wanted a big change. And in a case of karmic conspiracy, the universe answered with a resounding *yes* when Derin's company asked us to move to Amsterdam. Leaving everything behind and starting from scratch in the lowlands of the Netherlands, a place I'd never even visited, was more than a little terrifying, but by that point, we figured we didn't have much to lose. (Our other thought: *If it's going to be hard, it might as well be hard in Europe!*)

So shortly after the school year wrapped up, we painfully extricated ourselves from our life in Seattle—sold our house, lost our dog to cancer, made the choice to homeschool, and did our best to support a certain eight-year-old boy who was furious we'd made the choice to move without consulting him.

The next year was one of intense adjustment. Finding our footing took a while and was easily one of the hardest transitions I've ever gone through. But slowly, over time, things got better. Although I felt (a lot of) resistance about the idea of homeschooling Asher, over that first year I gradually found my groove, eventually realizing I was better equipped for the role than I had previously believed. Together, Asher and I fostered a new relationship while I grappled with my own insecurities about what it meant for him to follow an unorthodox educational path.

Don't get me wrong. Even as things were improving, I still struggled—a lot—mostly with things like jealousy of my friends raising "normal kids" or panic over what the future would look like. I also struggled with truly accepting that we weren't screwing Asher up if his childhood looked different from that of his peers. Still, there was no denying that this forging of our own path, this questioning-everything approach, was working. Because Asher? He was *thriving*. The kid was happy. Joyful. Light. He loved school. And his anxiety was gone. I'm talking *I had to cut his fingernails*.

The most important thing I learned that year was that my biggest source of conflict in parenting Asher was my relationship with myself—more specifically, my thinking about what my life as a mom "should" look like. That realization was a biggie. Because once I figured that out, I could surrender to what my momhood actually *did* look like. And how our child was. And what *his* life could look like. It was only after I started

> My biggest source of conflict was my own thinking about what my life as a mom "should" look like.

the hard work of surrendering that my energy began to shift. More remarkably, and I'm sure as a direct result, Asher's did, too.

In many ways, making the choice to adapt our life to support who Asher is sparked a renaissance in our family. And today, five years later, we are continuing to create our new, perfect "normal." Instead of being at odds with one another, together we're mostly in flow. Today, Asher is anxiety-free, and his tantrums are rarer-than-rare occurrences. Over time, he's become more and more present. With presence has come connection. And because he's no longer in chronic fight-or-flight mode—because he is able to just be the awesome person he is without being told he's bad or screwing up or doing it wrong—his beautiful qualities such as empathy and compassion and a dogged desire to stand up against inequality are flourishing. He's secure and confident. And it's been the most incredible thing to witness.

When people ask me how we've gotten to a place where our family is thriving, I tell them this: We embraced and accepted who Asher is while exploring alternative ways of being as a family. More than anything, we let go. Of control. Of what other people thought of our child or our parenting techniques. Of what the future "should" look like. We started truly living in the now, noticing the gifts that are here every day.

· · · · · ·

I've talked with enough parents to know that my family's story isn't even close to unique. I know parents like me are literally everywhere, all moving through the unmarked journey in their own way, grappling with the unexpected detours and the roadblocks that emerged on the path they assumed they'd be on when they first brought their children into the world.

Parents like Amy, who presumed her son would start kindergarten at the neighborhood charter school in Atlanta where she herself was a teacher, until she finally admitted to herself it wouldn't meet his sensory needs. "There was a little bit of mourning as I saw people he played with go off to the school I helped build, but I also knew it wasn't the right thing for him." A move across the country, a few more diagnoses, and a handful of schools later, Amy once again finds herself at a crossroads, as their most recent school in Portland, Oregon, has closed its doors and she's left trying to figure out what's next. But Amy is relentless in her quest to understand her boy's unique needs and find the right environment where he'll be seen for who he is. As she said to me during a recent conversation about raising atypical kids, "It's just what you do."

Jill, a speech pathologist by training who works with high school students with disabilities, didn't recognize what was going on with her son until she went to a professional development class on sensory processing disorder. As the instructor rattled off the characteristics of children with sensory issues, she realized the instructor was describing her four-year-old son to a T. "For some reason, I hadn't put two and two together. But in that moment, it was like a wave washed over me. I had chills over my entire body, and I just started weeping."

Bari, a psychologist by training, found herself in uncharted territory when she learned about the challenges stemming from asynchronous development in her two gifted children, both of whom have received a diagnosis of ADHD, auditory processing disorder, and executive functioning issues. But she leaned in to who they are and tapped into her gifts to become their most powerful advocate. A few years ago, Bari and her husband made the decision to pull their kids out of private school and (reluctantly) moved to the suburbs so their kids could attend a public school. Bari says things there are working out "okay," though she never stops questioning their choices, looking for the opportunities that will help her kids thrive, and educating the school about the needs of different types of learners. As she explains, "I'm full of ideas, but my advocacy has come more in the form of trying to change our immediate family and educational milieu and raising awareness and understanding. Because I think that that kind of shift and awareness can benefit all children, not just ours."

In conversations with parent after parent about raising differently wired children, I've heard about the same challenges: uncertainty about a child's neurodiversity; lack of school fit; tough behavior; families, friends, and educators who don't get it; and difficulty getting the information, resources, and tools we need. The details differ about who our kids are, but the common experiential thread is the same—frustration, confusion, sadness, and a pervasive sense of being overwhelmed.

Because differently wired kids can often "pass" as "typical kids," it's not always easy for teachers, other parents, and sometimes even our own families to recognize or respect the challenges we're going through. Our kids can be super-intense. Strong-willed. *Tricky*. The usual parenting approaches simply don't work for us. Every decision about our child involves just a little more consideration, stress, and anxiety than what other parents might experience. It's no cakewalk. Yet those with the energy, resources, and time continue to show up every day with no map and a dull blade to hack at the brush in search of a viable path. It's difficult, lonely work; our only markers are occasionally helpful therapists and self-help books offering disorder-specific tools that serve as a constant reminder: There is "something wrong" with our child. For those families who are overworked, underpaid, and without the flexibility to devote the time it can take to advocate and fight for the support their child needs, the situation can often feel hopeless.

The stigmas of raising different kids drive us underground to suffer in secrecy.

The stigmas associated with most neurological differences are enough to drive us underground to suffer in secrecy, lest anyone know what's really going on. Raising different kids in a parenting culture that thrives on sameness and conformity doesn't leave room for us to openly share the reality of our experience. So instead, we soldier on, fielding frequent emails from frustrated teachers, ignoring the glares of other parents when our kids do something "off" in public, and pretending we're not hurt when playdates aren't reciprocated. We want to figure out where and how to fit our kids in so everything doesn't have to feel so hard. We want them to have access to the same kind of life success as everyone else.

To be clear, I'm not talking about a handful of kids here. According to the latest estimates, approximately one in five school-aged children is in some way neurologically diverse, meaning that how their brains function is "atypical" from what's considered "normal." In reference to this statistic, author John Elder Robison wrote on his *Psychology Today* blog *My Life with Asperger's*, "That makes neurodiversity (in total) more common than being six feet tall, or having red hair."

It's obvious to me that being differently wired is no more an aberration than being left-handed, yet here we are at a crisis point, where 20 percent of today's kids are struggling to fit in at school and in society because the way they think, learn, and show up is inconvenient or presents challenges to the status quo. Their neurological differences are treated like deficits instead of part of the essential fabric that makes up these creative, complicated, awesome beings.

I don't believe there is any one way to be okay or typical or "normal" in today's world. (And who came up with the definition of "normal" anyway? Since when is normal what we're striving for?) How many people have to receive diagnoses of "disorders" before we start realizing that maybe there's something else going on here... an influx of children with creative gifts who have the capacity to positively change the world? If anything, our uniquely wired children, with their sensitivities and gifts, *are* the new normal.

It's time society stopped looking at our kids' neurodifferences as things in need of "fixing" and instead considered the possibility that today's increasingly large population of atypical children may actually be a modern-day evolution. It's time for our children to be seen and celebrated for who they truly are. It's time for our families to thrive.

But to change everything for our kids, and for us, we're going to have to throw out the current parenting paradigm. It just isn't practical anymore, and it's doing more harm than good. We need to lead in the creation of a new one, one that embraces difference and uniqueness in children, rejects fear- and guilt-based messaging, authentically reflects our families' realities, and provides options for us to access or design the ideal education for our child's needs.

Listen, I know this isn't easy stuff. I know that sometimes you might wish you could wave a magic wand and become a member of the other club, the one full of neurotypical families, the one whose manual is so much more straightforward. I know that many people, from educators to parents of neurotypical kids, might be afraid to consider a new definition of "normal" because it would require them to question their own status quo. I know that staring convention and fear in the face and forging ahead in your own way can be harrowing.

But I also know we can do it. I believe that we—you and I and every other parent raising an atypical kid—have the capability to truly change this paradigm from the inside out. Even more than that, we're the only ones who *can* do it. When we voice our reality, educate others, and stand up for what we and our family need from a place of compassion, strength, confidence, and peace, the whole outdated, ineffective, intolerant parenting paradigm that we've lived with for decades is going to come tumbling down.

Are you with me?

CHAPTER 2

The New Normal

A few months ago, I ordered the book *Neurotribes: The Legacy of Autism and the Future of Neurodiversity*. I'd heard an interview with the author, Steve Silberman, on Terry Gross's radio program *Fresh Air*, and appreciated what he had to say about shifting the conversation surrounding autism and neurodiversity to one focused on true acceptance and understanding. A package from Amazon UK arrived as I was making lunch one day, and between the time I placed the book on the dining room table and five minutes later, when I gave Asher a sandwich, cashews, and some sliced pears, he was already engrossed.

Asher's a much faster reader than I am, so I took my place in line, curious to hear his take on the book, since, after all, he is part of the core population Steve writes about. More than that, I love that Asher is showing so much interest in learning about his own tribe—I see it as part of the self-identity journey he's enthusiastically embraced in recent years. Over the next two days, Asher devoured the book, occasionally pausing to share something that struck him or to email me a quote that particularly resonated with him.

One night as we were doing our usual good-night squeeze—me on tiptoes and him leaning over the railing of the top bunk—Asher said he was feeling creeped out. When I pressed him, he told me he'd read a section in *Neurotribes* earlier that day describing how children with neurological disabilities such as autism had been murdered by the Nazis because they were judged to be a burden to society. We'd been studying World War II all year, so Asher was well read on the Holocaust and the related horrors of that time. But this bit of information came without warning and had understandably hit him hard. So I joined him in bed and we fell into a long conversation about ignorance and hate and misunderstanding, all the while my heart breaking, knowing that my thoughtful boy had learned that in another time and another place, he might have met the same fate.

We lay there quietly for a moment, his face buried in the pillow, me staring at the ceiling, and then he suddenly popped up his head, his mood all at once animated and proud.

"There was this awesome quote in the book from an autistic writer though, about what if things were totally reversed and *we* were the normal ones and everybody *else* was wrong," he said.

"Oh really? What was the quote?" I knew he'd likely committed it to memory as he so often did with concepts that clicked.

"It said, 'Neurotypical syndrome is a neurobiological disorder characterized by preoccupation with social concerns, delusions of superiority, and obsession with conformity.'" He paused and chuckled before dramatically delivering the last line in the exaggerated voice of a TV announcer: "'There is no known cure.'"

"Yep . . . pretty much!" I responded with a laugh, appreciating how comfortable he already was in his differently wired skin. Sensing he would be able to settle into sleep now, we hugged one last time, and I climbed down the metal ladder, hit the Play button on his audiobook, and quietly exited the room, wondering to myself what it would take for neurodiversity, and kids like my son, to stop being perceived by society as a problem.

Us Versus Them

For as long as people have existed, society has been drawing lines, placing the people who are "normal" on one side and those who are not—those with some sort of physical, mental, or neurological difference—on the other. The "normal" side is flush with challenges and discrimination related to race, ethnicity, religion, sex, sexual orientation, and/or gender identity. Yet, as the gold standard of human experience, the "normal" side is where most people want to be, because it comes preloaded with the expected ingredients that make up a "typical" life—access to a decent education, and the ability to choose a career path, earn a living wage, get a driver's license, and live independently.

In contrast, the "other" side is on the periphery, unable to fully participate in the same way as the "normal" folks because society doesn't accommodate and support those outside the norm. Whether it was intended to be this way or not, it has become an us-versus-them kind of thing. Right and wrong. Whole and broken. But there's no room for that kind of thinking anymore—it's becoming increasingly clear that different ways of being are more normal than most people realize, and that is truer with each passing year. As educator and parent coach Alison Bower told me, "The more and more children I see, and the more and more parents I see, the more and more I know that there are not that many typical kids. If everyone were to raise their hands saying, 'Yeah, I have a typical kid,' there wouldn't be so many hands up."

In truth, millions of kids today are moving through the world "differently" from their same-age peers as a result of the way they're wired, yet for some reason these kids are still considered outliers—aka the "other"—in our conventional world. I believe one reason for this outsider status is that society often divides neurodifferences into separate categories based on how challenging, desirable or undesirable, or "fixable" they are, along with whether the special needs can be easily accommodated or supporting them is especially inconvenient or disruptive. Breaking differently wired kids into separate groups—kids with learning differences, gifted kids, kids with ADHD (and within that label the delineation of inattentive type, hyperactive, and more), autistic kids, and so on—makes it easier for educators and society to go about business as usual. *You are different in this way. . . . You belong there* (or perhaps more accurately, *You* don't *belong here*). The bottom line is, when divided by diagnosis and difference, children can be more readily pushed aside (or out of the picture) and neatly placed into "other" status. (A boy with whom Asher attended summer camp even tried to convince other kids in the group that his diagnosis of attention deficit disorder [ADD] wasn't "as bad" as Asher's diagnosis of ADHD.)

But when we start to look at these neurodifferences as a collective whole, this population is not nearly so easy to dismiss. Because... *20 percent.* One in five. An average of four to five children in your son's or daughter's class. These are not insignificant numbers. So at what point does the *other* become accepted and embraced for who they are? What's the magic number that will tip the scales to a place where these kids get their full invitation to participate in society? Twenty-five percent? Thirty? I don't know about you, but I don't want to sit around waiting for the statistic to hit some arbitrary number. And I know for sure that our kids don't have that kind of time.

Difference Is Difference

A few years ago on an unseasonably warm day, Asher, Derin, and I set up a picnic lunch in Vondelpark, a few blocks from our apartment. Earlier that morning, I'd read an article about new research on autism rates, and I brought it up over tuna wraps and a bag of Bugles.

Asher, who up until this point had had his head buried in his Kindle, heard the word "autism" and immediately looked up with interest. "What are you talking about?"

"I was just telling your dad about an article I read. It said that the risks of having an autistic child—"

Asher cut me off. "The *risks*? What do they mean 'the *risks*'?! What do they think it is . . . some kind of *disease*?"

Um, *right.* Point for Asher. We decided the word "chances" would have been a better choice, as in, the *chances that a child would be autistic*, and then continued with the conversation. But that moment got me to thinking about the many messages Asher had already internalized and would continue to internalize as a neurodiverse person. Unfortunately, the way difference is typically discussed in the mainstream tends to have negative undertones and associations, sometimes in the subtlest of ways. But the effect is real.

When I first started imagining the revolution that eventually became my podcast and community, TiLT Parenting, the phrase I found myself using over and over in my creative notes, the mission, and the manifesto was "differently wired." As that conversation with Asher reminded me, words matter. And the phrase "differently wired" is not only more accurate when defining this population of neurodivergent people, but it's free of the harmful stigmas that come along with words like "disorder." It's time we break down the divisions between alternative ways of being wired so these kids (and us as their parents) can stop feeling isolated and like anomalies, and start feeling like they're part of a big, brilliant tribe of creative, unique thinkers.

When we consider atypical people as a whole, the lines of division between neurodifferences aren't so distinct after all. Just ask someone who diagnoses conditions in kids for a living—it's complicated. There's plenty of overlap and there are plenty of shades of gray. The way I see it, difference is difference is difference. Anything beyond that in the way society chooses to perceive and think about the way another human being is wired—that's on us. And it can be changed.

Is Your Child Differently Wired?

"Differently wired" isn't a scientific or diagnostic term—there are no specific criteria to determine which kids fall under this label and which don't. So how can you know if your child is differently wired? Both for the purposes of this book and how I define this phrase within my community at TiLT Parenting, here's how I suggest you approach this question: *If you believe your child is differently wired, then he or she probably is.* Really, we're a self-selected bunch. We may or may not have a diagnosis (or multiple diagnoses) for our child. We may simply recognize that some aspects of our child's life appear to be *more* than that of our child's peers (more intense, more emotional, more intelligent, more difficult . . . just *more*). We may have noticed a disconnect between our child's performance at school and what we know they're capable of. We may recognize that our child struggles where other kids sail through with confidence. And most if not all of us would be challenged to say our kids are truly thriving—we recognize that at least one aspect of who they are means their path to adulthood is going to come with more than its fair share of twists and turns.

I often define the kids in our community as those caught in a kind of limbo, since many are living with "invisible differences" that aren't so easily perceived or recognized from the outside or out of context. Unlike a child who has a neurodifference such as cerebral palsy or is severely affected by autism or another disorder, many kids in the TiLT community slip through the cracks. The underlying reasons for their social or academic struggles or the full picture of why they behave as they do are often missed or misdiagnosed, and as a result, they are wholly misunderstood. This misunderstanding often leads to these kids being punished or disciplined instead of supported. It leads to frustrated students being held back or unchallenged as a result of poor academic performance rather than given accommodations and strategies to help them learn the way they need to. It means parents face constant criticism for their child's "inappropriate" behavior or milestone delays rather than receive understanding. And that just scratches the surface.

> The kids in our community are caught in a limbo. They slip through the cracks. They are misunderstood.

But who exactly are these kids? And what exactly about their wiring is keeping them stuck? Here's a look at some of the broader diagnostic buckets and invisible differences often seen in these kids.

ADD/ADHD

I'll be honest—when we did that first round of assessments for Asher when he was five and the results included a provisional diagnosis of ADHD, I bristled. Based on the one child I knew who had ADHD, the diagnosis equated to out-of-control hyperactivity. I pictured disheveled boys running around with dangerous unpredictability, unable to slow down and connect. And I thought, *ADHD? No way*. My *kid is not one of* those *kids*.

Now, seven years later, it's abundantly clear to me that oh yes indeedy, Asher does have ADHD, and it's hard to remember why I felt such a palpable resistance to the label. As Ann Douglas, author of *Parenting Through the Storm*, said to me about the stigma tied to diagnoses like ADHD, "It seems there are some acceptable disorders and some that people are still struggling with." ADHD was definitely one of those for me, and apparently is for a lot of people.

ADHD and its close cousin ADD are perhaps two of the more maligned diagnoses today, in part because there are so many myths and untruths circulating about what exactly they are, not to mention the fact that there's no shortage of articles insinuating that they aren't real disorders but are actually the result of things like permissive parenting or too much sugar. Um, *yeah*.

One such article in *Psychology Today* went viral in 2013. Titled "Why French Kids Don't Have ADHD: French Children Don't Need Medications to Control Their Behavior," the article explained that ADHD doesn't exist in France because French parents are clearly in charge. The piece highlighted the strict disciplinary philosophy the French embrace, as if that is all it takes. The author of the article, Marilyn Wedge, PhD, wrote, "As a therapist who works with children, it makes perfect sense to me that French children don't need medications to control their behavior because they learn self-control early in their lives. The children grow up in families in which the rules are well-understood, and a clear family hierarchy is firmly in place." It should be noted that two years later, *Psychology Today* published a follow-up article disputing the original piece, aptly titled "French Kids Do Have ADHD: And It's Not All About Parenting," explaining that because ADHD isn't very well understood in France, French children with ADHD are "clinically invisible" and therefore many struggling children are simply being overlooked. Though I'm happy the rebuttal piece was published, it didn't come close to receiving the more than two million likes the original article garnered on Facebook. There seem to be *a lot* of people out there who want to believe ADHD is not real.

Another viral article popped up in a mompreneur group I'm in on Facebook, posted by a mother who, though not personally touched by ADHD, felt compelled to share a piece that claimed ADHD doesn't exist. It referred to an interview with Harvard psychologist Dr. Jerome Kagan in which he flat-out declared ADHD a fraud. "[ADHD] is an invention. Every child who's not doing well in school is sent to see a pediatrician, and the pediatrician says: 'It's ADHD; here's Ritalin.'" The problem? Kagan's assertion is based on his opinion, not science. In fact his study ignores all scientific evidence showing distinct differences in the size of frontal lobes in the brains of people with ADHD. The bigger problem in my opinion? People see "Harvard PhD" and suddenly with the mindless click of the Share or Like button, misinformation, stigmas, and judgments about ADHD are perpetuated. And around and around we go.

So let's get real about ADHD and what it is. According to Understood.org, the excellent online resource for kids with learning and attention issues, ADHD is a common childhood condition involving the brain. The 2014 annual report from the National Center for Learning Disabilities (NCLD) places the number of kids in the United

States who have received a diagnosis of ADHD at 6.4 million, with more than twice as many boys as girls diagnosed. As is the case with autism, it's becoming increasingly apparent that ADHD presents differently in girls. As a result, ADHD is still less likely to be diagnosed in girls, even though it's now believed to affect as many girls as boys.

In addition to the "classic" ADHD marker of hyperactivity, a number of other "negative" characteristics are common among children with ADHD, including trouble focusing, daydreaming, being disorganized, being impulsive, having a short fuse, constantly interrupting, trouble reading social cues, and feeling the need to fidget or constantly move.

Put all these traits together and it's easy to understand why kids with ADHD present a challenge in the classroom. I totally get it. Yet treating these kids like ill-behaved children who can be punished or suspended out of their behavior, as many schools do, doesn't just do them a huge disservice—it's undeniably harmful. In addition to causing children to sink into the shame, guilt, and low self-worth that comes with being targeted as the "bad kids," treating kids this way ignores the amazing gifts that come with ADHD, intense creativity and passion being at the top of the list. One need only look at phenomenally successful people with ADHD, such as Michael Phelps,

> Endless ideas and energy come with an ADHD diagnosis. So does passion.

Justin Timberlake, Michael Jordan, Emma Watson, Lisa Ling, and Richard Branson, to see what can result from the endless ideas and energy that come with an ADHD diagnosis.

Despite this evidence, ADHD, more than any other neurodifference I write about in this book, carries with it not only a plethora of stigmas and invites skepticism from teachers, friends, and family alike, but also what appears to be a refusal among educators and society at large to accept its characteristics. A comment on Asher's report card from his disastrous first-grade experience says it all: "Asher is constantly moving, be it his entire body, his hands, playing with an object, etc., which gets in his way of focusing on the task at hand for extended periods of time." As Asher or anyone with ADHD will explain, it is through movement that he's actually *able* to focus. For most kids with ADHD, surviving traditional school is possible only by taking one of the many available medications such as Ritalin or Adderall. As Yafa Crane Luria, an ADHD parenting coach who herself has ADHD, says, "If you think about it, people with ADHD are the only people who are asked to change who they are. Kids in special education aren't asked to change their learning differences but instead to learn additional skills. But we are asked to change. We are wrong."

Giftedness

When I first launched TiLT Parenting, I received numerous emails from parents thanking me for including giftedness as one of the neurodifferences we're committed to supporting. And I understand why they felt compelled to reach out: The plight of highly gifted kids is often ignored or completely left out of conversations surrounding challenges related to neurodiversity, as if being supersmart can't have any downsides—the thinking being *These kids already have a leg up, so why would they need extra support?*

One of my best friends, Alice Wilder, educational psychologist and expert in all things preschool, was the first to use the word "gifted" in relation to Asher. He was probably eighteen months old at the time, and although it was obvious to anyone who knew him that he had a lot going on upstairs, I remember telling her that I'd rather not use the word "gifted"—it made me uncomfortable, and I didn't want to be one of "those" parents. You know, the ones who've already mapped out their child's path to Harvard by the time he turns three. But Alice insisted that giftedness isn't a subjective thing—it's a true neurological difference that needs to be acknowledged and supported.

Our parenting coach Julie Ross had a similar point of view when we explained the challenges we were facing with Asher a few months later. "I've never had a parent come see me and excitedly exclaim that their child is gifted. If they do, then I know that child probably isn't actually gifted. Because highly gifted children are typically very challenging. In fact, being highly gifted is actually a special need in its own right," she explained.

So, what exactly is giftedness? I wish I could give you a simple answer, but unfortunately there is no one agreed-upon definition. The National Association for Gifted Children defines gifted people as "those who demonstrate outstanding levels of aptitude (defined as an exceptional ability to reason and learn) or competence (documented performance or achievement in top 10% or rarer) in one or more domains. Domains include any structured area of activity with its own symbol system (e.g., mathematics, music, language) and/or set of sensorimotor skills (e.g., painting, dance, sports)." In terms of IQ, what qualifies as "gifted" varies by state, although Hoagies Gifted, a popular online resource that shares information on all aspects of giftedness for parents, educators, and other professionals, offers a breakdown of the rate of giftedness based on generally accepted scores depending on the IQ test. For example, for the Wechsler Intelligence Scale for Children (WISC-IV) or Wechsler Preschool and Primary Scale of Intelligence (WPPSI-III) exams, the following Full Scale IQ scores correspond with the different definitions: gifted or moderately gifted, 130–138; highly gifted, 138–145; profoundly gifted, 145–152; and exceptionally gifted, 152–160. I should also note that IQ specifically relates to academic giftedness and doesn't touch upon or recognize artistic giftedness, and most IQ tests don't account for neurodifferences such as autism or slow processing speed that may negatively affect the score. Confused yet?

When thinking about gifted children, many people assume that their only issue is perhaps boredom in school. They therefore expect that the "problem" can be fixed with extra math worksheets or leveling them up in one or two subjects or perhaps even a grade. But although accelerated work may benefit some gifted children, pushing them ahead academically doesn't address the challenges many highly gifted kids face, including asynchronous development and "overexcitabilities." Think of an eight-year-old who's reading at a college level, yet is emotionally in line with, if not lagging behind, her same-age peers. The disconnect between those two extremes—an incredibly high intellect and a lower level of maturity—can create a ton of problems, because emotionally she's just not ready to process what she's capable of reading. As a result, she feels out of place, is extremely intense, has big reactions and meltdowns, and feels overwhelmed much of the time. Likewise, overexcitabilities, defined by the advocacy group Supporting the Emotional Needs of the Gifted (SENG) as "inborn intensities indicating a heightened ability to respond to stimuli," are thought to be another reason for the often-amplified experience of highly gifted people.

> The disconnect between an incredibly high intellect and a lower level of maturity can create a ton of problems— big reactions and meltdowns, anxiety, and feeling out of place.

Just as there are stigmas associated with ADHD, gifted kids can get hit from all sides. There are the teachers and parents who place high demands on them to meet their capabilities while neglecting to support their emotional development; those who don't respect the challenges gifted children face and equate a parent's declaration that their child is gifted with that parent thinking their child is "better" than others; and the kids themselves, many of whom are, at their core, perfectionists, plagued by anxiety and feeling like misfits among their peers. Plainly put, gifted kids are kids who think differently, and like their other differently wired peers, many are stuck in a system that doesn't meet their unique needs. These children and their extraordinary minds deserve to be nurtured and supported so they can reach their full potential.

Learning Differences

Back when I was a kid, learning styles and academic potential were cut-and-dried—you were either "smart" or you weren't. You either kept up or you got left in the dust. And the kids who did fall behind in reading or writing or math were, for the most part, written off as less intelligent, or "slow," and moved into lower-level, less-challenging classes, end of story. Knowing what I know now about the many types of learning differences and the ways they present in children, it pains me to think about how many kids were simply labeled as unintelligent and pushed aside, society's expectations for what they would achieve all but gone.

Heidi Nord, a former teacher and reading specialist, and an expert on dyslexia, told me about this lack of awareness twenty and thirty years ago. After teaching for several years and noticing that some of her students were struggling to learn how to read even though they were all getting the same instruction, Heidi went back to school to get her reading specialist credentials and a master's degree in reading. "Ironically, at the time I graduated, in 1994, *nothing* about dyslexia was said in that program," she said. Yes, that's right, folks. Dyslexia wasn't even mentioned in a reading graduate program.

Things are better today, but only just. Most teachers are ill prepared for understanding not only how to recognize learning disabilities, but also how to support the students who have them. According to a 2017 article in the *Atlantic* titled "How Teacher Training Hinders Special-Needs Students," "Many teacher-education programs offer just one class about students with disabilities to their general-education teachers, 'Special Ed 101,' as it's called at one New Jersey college. It's not enough to equip teachers for a roomful of children who can range from the gifted to students who read far below grade level due to a learning disability."

So what exactly is a "learning difference" or "learning disability"? According to the Learning Disabilities Association of America, learning differences are "neurologically based processing problems" that can interfere with everything from learning how to read, write, and do math to planning and organizing, abstract reasoning, memory, and attention.

Of course, when people think of learning differences, the one that most often comes to mind is dyslexia, a difference resulting in difficulty with reading and fluency, which also happens to be the most common learning difference, thought to affect between 5 and 10 percent of the population (though many experts believe this number is much higher). Less familiar are learning differences such as dysgraphia (difficulty with writing), dyscalculia (difficultly with math), executive functioning issues, slow processing speed, nonverbal learning disorder, auditory processing disorder, and visual processing issues—differences that can be mysterious and hard to nail down and, as a result, often go unrecognized and unsupported in schools.

Slow processing speed can result in even the brightest of students crashing and burning on, for example, timed math tests or written exams. When a teacher knows a child is more than capable, the poor showing may be misattributed to laziness or lack of preparation, and the child is told to just "work harder" or "apply yourself." On the flip side, when an educator assumes a student isn't competent, the child isn't taught to their potential. Talk about frustrating.

Nonverbal learning disorder makes it difficult for kids to recognize and interpret nonverbal information that is communicated in relationships, concepts, or patterns. Some children may struggle to understand facial expressions or hand gestures and other nonverbal social cues, and others may have difficulty making sense of circumstances in their day-to-day life, from following multistep instructions to dealing with changes in routine.

Deficits in executive functioning skills can lead to all kinds of challenges for students, and again, unless an educator is highly tuned in, there's a good chance they'll chalk up the challenges to laziness, sloppiness, or a poor work ethic. Think of the child who repeatedly forgets to turn in his assignments (even when he did them the night before), the student whose locker is so messy that the contents spill out onto the floor every time she opens it, or the student who struggles to begin even the most straightforward writing assignment, perpetually runs late, or has poor impulse control. These are all indicators of poor development in executive functions—sometimes referred to as the brain's "command central"—but many parents and educators are unaware of this underlying cause, and therefore the child never gets support in strengthening these skills. In fact, I'd venture to say that unless processing problems or executive functioning deficits have affected them or their family, most people have never even *heard* of these brain differences and don't understand what they are or how they affect the children who have them.

According to the most recent statistics from the NCLD, 5 percent of American school-aged children (2.4 million) are identified as having learning disabilities such as those listed above, and Understood .org says the number may be as high as 10 percent. Yet despite this prevalence, the lack of awareness of how to recognize and support these kids is shocking, and the cost to them (and to society) is high. As James H. Wendorf, former executive director of the NCLD, said, "The data in this 2014 report reveal that, left unaddressed, as many as 60 million individuals risk being left behind, burdened by low self-esteem, subjected to low expectations, and diminished in their ability to pursue their dreams."

But do learning differences have to be liabilities? This assumption is up for dispute the instant the context changes. Sure, in a classroom setting, processing differences can present significant challenges for students, especially in the areas of reading, writing, and math, but in other contexts, their differences may actually give them an advantage.

For example, as dyslexia coach Heidi Nord explains, "Let's say a student is writing a three in reverse. That is one of the warning signs of dyslexia, but what that really means is that the student is able to flip and rotate shapes in their mind. Now, that's amazing! That's a really important skill for engineering, for architecture, for design, for art. And it's something that many see as a negative, but really it's a positive when you look at that capability."

Asperger's/Autism/PDD-NOS

I had just graduated from high school when the movie *Rain Man* came out. Like most other Gen Xers, I was first introduced to autism through Dustin Hoffman's portrayal of Raymond Babbitt, an autistic savant with a penchant for counting cards. (Thanks, Hollywood!) Thirty years later, society has caught up *a bit* when it comes to awareness and understanding of autism, but with the exception of people who know an autistic person, public perceptions are still largely framed by high-profile media portrayals. In other words, there's still plenty of misunderstanding to go around.

High-functioning/low-functioning, nonverbal/verbal, brilliant/average/low intelligence—as the saying goes, "If you know one person with autism, you know one person with autism." Although no two presentations are alike, autistic people are typically identified as having some degree of social, communication, and behavioral differences. For example, some autistic people may struggle with making eye contact, and others may engage in repetitive behaviors or movements. Many autistic people have deep areas of interest; they may crave structure, routine, and order. And because autism is truly a spectrum with no rigid definition, a wide range of behaviors may or may not fall into the diagnosis. The closer a person is to the edge of this spectrum, meaning they aren't so severely impacted that it's readily apparent that they are autistic, the more subjective a diagnosis becomes.

Until 2013, the widely used label for people with "mild autism" was Asperger's syndrome, which was named after Viennese pediatrician Hans Asperger. In the 1940s, Asperger noticed that some boys in his practice had normal language development and intelligence but demonstrated some "autistic tendencies" in the areas of social skills and communication. Today, the *Diagnostic and Statistical Manual of Mental Disorders* (*DSM-5*) no longer recognizes Asperger's syndrome as its own classification, and instead lumps everyone into the diagnosis of autism spectrum disorder (ASD), a decision that has been met with mixed results. Although some people welcomed the loss of distinction, others, especially many with the Asperger's diagnosis who proudly relate to their tribe of "Aspies," felt as if their identities had been stripped away.

Today, many people still use the term "Asperger's," although another phrase—"high-functioning autism"—has recently joined the lexicon, sparking controversy. When Stephen Borgman ran a poll on his blog *My Aspergers*, he found that many readers with Asperger's thought the label was apt, since they "'blend in' with neurotypicals to a large extent." In contrast, many are offended by the term, including author John Elder Robison, who wrote on his blog, "It's not accurate, and it's degrading to us 'high and low functioning people.' Suggesting that 'you're a real high functioning autistic' feels to me a lot like 'you talk pretty good for a retard.' People say the former to me all the time today, and they said the latter to me quite a bit 50 years ago. I didn't like it then and I don't like it now. Both phrases imply I (and all others like me) am pretty good even though we are the

> To use the term "Asperger's" or "high-functioning autism"? It's a controversial question that has sparked debate.

'other'; some lesser class of human. How would you feel about that, if it were you?"

This is obviously a contentious topic, and although I want to recognize the divide, I don't feel it's my place to choose a side. I tend to use the term "Asperger's," since that's the term Asher goes with most of the time, though he's using "autism" with more and more frequency. But for the purposes of this book, I want to acknowledge the controversy, because it's the kids whose autism isn't as noticeable as those more severely affected who often find themselves the most stuck or inadequately supported in school, not to mention highly misunderstood by society. Because their differences aren't so obvious, at least to an outsider looking in, their behavior is often viewed with intolerance and confusion.

Just as with other neurodifferences, the gifts that come with autism are many. There's no shortage of examples of innovators whose contribution to society is a result of the way they think differently, including many of history's most influential scientists and creative geniuses who are believed to have been on the autism spectrum. Luckily, today, businesses are waking up to the many advantages that come along with being autistic. For instance, 75 percent of software company ULTRA Testing's team is on the autism spectrum. Founded by Rajesh Anandan and Art Shectman, two graduates of the Massachusetts Institute of Technology, ULTRA has set out to prove that neurodiversity is a competitive advantage, and the results have powerfully confirmed their belief. How cool is that?

Twice Exceptional

In 2014, a documentary called *2e: Twice Exceptional*, about a group of high school students from Bridges Academy in LA, made the rounds of the film festival circuit. For the majority of viewers, the movie was their introduction to the term "2e" or "twice exceptional," which refers to intellectually gifted people with at least one neurological difference.

Twice-exceptional kids often find themselves in an especially tricky spot. In some cases, a child's giftedness masks their neurodifference—they're so bright that they're able to compensate for their deficits. They may struggle for years in certain areas without knowing why, but because they're performing above average, their deficits, especially processing differences or learning disorders such as dyslexia and dysgraphia, simply aren't seen. But inevitably, their deficit catches up with them, and often it's at a point when some aspect of school has become incredibly frustrating and their self-confidence has taken a significant hit.

More common, though, are the kids whose neurodifference masks the giftedness. Think about it: If a child is reading below grade level or is constantly bombing on math or written assignments, most people's first thought isn't going to be *Oh, this child must be gifted!* Because we live in a society that dwells on deficits rather than strengths (more on that later), educators and even parents tend to focus on what's *not* working. And so these kids plod through the education system with their gifts and talents largely ignored. And we know that when gifted kids are bored or aren't engaged, they frequently act out or check out, which can lead to behavioral challenges in the classroom and then... well, you can see where this is going.

The third category for twice-exceptional kids is cases where the child *has* been identified as 2e, a distinction that, although helpful, doesn't necessarily solve anything, primarily because 2e learners are some of the most challenging children to educate. As Dr. Devon MacEachron, a psychologist specializing in providing neuropsych and psychoeducational assessments for twice-exceptional kids in New York City, told me, "There is rarely going to be a good school fit, because you might find a good school for gifted kids that doesn't address the weaknesses or a school for kids with autism or dyslexia that doesn't address the giftedness. There are very few schools in the world that attempt to address both sides of the equation." When I asked her why this was the case, she described the challenges even schools specifically designed for 2e learners face in adequately meeting the needs of all their students, because their needs differ so vastly. A gifted kid with ADHD is going to need something different from what a gifted kid with Asperger's needs, and the gifted kid with Asperger's is going to need something different from what a gifted kid with dyslexia needs.

Anxiety

Ask any parent raising a child with an anxiety disorder and you'll invariably hear stories of intolerance and lack of awareness by teachers, other parents, and even their own family members. It seems that anxiety, not unlike depression, is one of those neurodifferences people have a hard time wrapping their head around unless they've experienced or witnessed firsthand the disruption it can cause in a person's life. Because there's so little understanding, highly anxious kids are often expected to "just deal" or "stop being so sensitive," while parents shielding these kids from anxiety-inducing situations or swooping in when they have an anxiety attack frequently find themselves defending their parenting choices to people who just don't get it. You know, the people who make flip comments like "Doesn't *everybody* have anxiety these days?" and suggest we stop making such a big deal out of our child's challenges. Talk about exhausting.

> Deadlines, exams, competitions—they can completely derail a child with anxiety.

According to the Anxiety and Depression Association of America, anxiety disorders affect one in eight children, either as a stand-alone condition or linked to another neurodifference. For example, ADHD and anxiety often appear together, as do autism spectrum disorders and anxiety. Because anxiety manifests in different ways, it can be hard to recognize. Kids with anxiety disorders may feel regulated and calm some days and completely shut down on others. Situations that stress out even the chillest of students—big deadlines, high-stakes exams, school competitions—can completely derail a child with anxiety. Some anxious kids might break down and cry or withdraw into their shells, and others will act out, unable to make sense of the powerful anxiety in their system. But however anxiety presents in a child, the potential long-term negative ramifications are equally damaging, including poor school performance, low self-esteem, challenges with social interaction, depression, suicidal tendencies, and more.

Sensory Issues/Highly Sensitive Kids

Remember when my friend first suggested sensory processing disorder (SPD) to me as a possible explanation for Asher's intensity and sometimes hypersensitivity? I was relieved to discover there was a name that captured the essence of what we were experiencing, and immediately consumed the bible for parents raising kids with SPD, *The Out-of-Sync Child* by Carol Stock Kranowitz. At the same time, I was confused to discover that SPD, sometimes also referred to as sensory integration disorder, isn't formally recognized among all members of the medical community as an actual disorder. A 2014 article in *Slate* magazine discussing the legitimacy of SPD opened with this line: "Sensory processing disorder is one of those peculiarly modern diseases caught in the purgatory between legitimacy and quackery."

SPD may not be part of the *DSM*, but that doesn't change the fact that millions of parents are raising kids who are out of sync. And these parents *know what they know*. They know that their kids experience certain aspects of their lives—emotions, physical sensations, senses, and/or an inner or spiritual world—more intensely than most. Whether they're sensory seeking (hyposensitive), sensory avoidant (hypersensitive), or a mix of the two, the unique way they process sensory information can cause challenges in everyday situations, frequently and without warning. Getting their hands muddy might lead to a meltdown. They might need to don headphones at the movies because the sound is just too much. They may relish the way lying under a weighted blanket or wearing a weighted vest makes them feel more grounded and calm. Children who've been identified as "highly sensitive" might cry for days after mistakenly stepping on a beetle. Their overly empathic nature might lead to them feeling troubled for weeks after an interaction with a homeless person.

Having sensory processing differences or being a highly sensitive kid often leads to heightened experiences, which can be tricky to navigate as a child but which potentially give them a unique perspective and advantage as they grow, especially if they're able to develop coping skills in areas where their sensory issues most negatively affect them. Still, the lack of awareness, understanding, and even tolerance for many sensory processing issues means that SPD remains a challenging diagnosis for many families to navigate in a conventional school system and in society at large.

A Growing Population?

Of course, there are many more ways to be neurodiverse than those I've described in this chapter. The list of neurological and mental differences goes on to include conditions such as Tourette's, bipolar disorder, cerebral palsy, obsessive-compulsive disorder, synesthesia, and more. And because humans are magnificently complicated, rarely are neurodifferences singular, nor are they concrete in their presentation. Of the parents I've connected with through TiLT Parenting, the majority have children whose neurodifferences incorporate two or more distinct differences: ADHD with giftedness, giftedness with dyslexia, autism with anxiety and obsessive compulsive disorder, non-verbal learning disorder with SPD, and on and on. Beyond that, many differently wired children don't even have a specific diagnosis, either because their differences don't fall neatly into one of these categories or because their parents, although knowing intuitively that their child is atypical, are more interested in addressing this child's symptoms than they are in labels. Whatever the neurological makeup, I see all of them fitting under the big umbrella of "differently wired."

It's clear that neurodiversity isn't a trend. It's a reality that isn't going away anytime soon. And although most scientists believe the increases in autism diagnoses in the past twenty years can be largely attributed to growing awareness and expanded diagnostic criteria (rates of diagnosis have been growing exponentially), that still leaves us with the fact that today one in forty-five children in the US is autistic (2.2 percent), and likely the number is much higher when taking into account the growing understanding of the ways autism presents differently in girls. Similarly, according to the Centers for Disease Control, ADHD diagnoses have increased an average of 5 percent per year between 2003 and 2011 (and again, girls are thought to be significantly underdiagnosed). And as parents and educators become more adept at recognizing learning and processing differences, as well as identifying and supporting gifted kids in populations that are typically underrepresented, such as children living in poverty and children of color, it's becoming increasingly clear that to be "typical" is less and less, well, *typical*.

As Steve Silberman wrote in an article for *Wired* magazine, "In forests and tide pools, the value of biological diversity is resilience: the ability to withstand shifting conditions and resist attacks from predators. In a world changing faster than ever, honoring and nurturing neurodiversity is civilization's best chance to thrive in an uncertain future." I couldn't agree more. Not only are these differences not going away, but we as a society need the millions of neurodiverse children in the world today, with their powerful gifts, talents, and abilities, to flourish. Because they are the future.

CHAPTER 3

//

Square Pegs in Round Holes

//

If you've ever run a marathon, you've likely experienced "hitting the wall," the metaphor for reaching a point in the race, usually between miles eighteen and twenty-two, when your body suddenly rebels against what you're putting it through. Fatigue sets in, and any forward momentum you had comes to a screeching halt.

This same thing happens to parents raising differently wired kids, except instead of our wall being caused by nutritional depletion or muscular exhaustion, it stems from butting up against the many limitations of the status quo for our children and families.

Lisa, mother of a differently wired eight-year-old on the autism spectrum, hit the wall when her son got kicked out of preschool. "He would just spin out and do things that were really distracting and troublesome for the other people in the school and for the teacher. And I was just like, 'Oh my gosh, we're in a six-child, in-home Waldorf preschool and my kid's been kicked out. What are we going to do next? We're going to have to try something really different.'"

For Jill, the wall came in the form of a conversation with her twice-exceptional ten-year-old son on the way home from school one afternoon. "He'd been telling us for months that [school] wasn't working, but we just kept trying to make it work. Then one day I picked him up from school and he looked at me and said, 'Mom, the kids at school are killing my dreams,' and it was like a punch to my gut. I told my husband what happened and asked him, 'When are we going to listen to our son?'"

As was the case for Lisa's and Jill's children, for most atypically developing kids, it's the first few years of schooling when the proverbial crap hits the fan. Their typically developing peers have mostly outgrown less-than-lovely behaviors such as tantrums or intense defiance or unsafe and overly physical play, while differently wired kids may not have. Typical peers are generally reaching educational milestones as expected or are on track with their fledgling social skills, while again, atypical kids may not be. As atypical kids struggle to fit into a construct—aka school—that wasn't designed to accommodate them, what's already hard gets amplified.

Not long after I became pregnant with Asher, while in the midst of packing up our life in Los Angeles for a move to Seattle, I grabbed lunch with a friend I'd worked with at Cartoon Network. Jay was already dad to two kids—a third would be on its way within the year—and over Mongolian stir-fry we talked about how different life was about to become for Derin and me. I was thirty-four years old, having very consciously conceived the baby growing in my womb, and feeling as ready as I could be for what was coming next. I'll never forget Jay's parting words: "If I could sum up parenthood in one word, it would be 'relentless.'" At the time, I had no idea how spot-on he was.

To be clear, I know this is the case for most *every* parent, regardless of their kid's wiring or how "born to be a parent" they may be. Bringing a child into the world or into your home truly changes everything, and until you find yourself responsible for another human being's survival, it's impossible to fully appreciate, understand, or prepare for the ways in which your reality will forever be altered.

With that being said, and with full acknowledgment that this is not a competition, those of us raising differently wired kids are engaged in a more extreme form of child-rearing. I like to think of us as the base jumpers or wingsuit flyers of parenting. It's messier, less predictable, more intense, and, to use Jay's word, more relentless.

Even as I write that, I'm aware that honestly talking about the experience of parents raising differently wired kids is in and of itself controversial. Within a week of launching TiLT, I received an email from a woman skeptical of what I was up to. One of her concerns was that my home page says, "Differently wired isn't a deficit . . . it's a difference." She herself was differently wired and was concerned my language minimized the challenges faced by people like her.

She went on to write, "It's a huge problem in disability circles; parents talk to each other but not to adults who share their children's disabilities, and that really does promote stigma and misunderstanding and all the other stuff we need to get rid of."

I've since read more than one article on the harms of parents raising differently wired kids talking about how hard it can be. In one such piece that went viral in 2015 after *Sesame Street*'s introduction of an autistic character (the first-ever autistic character on a children's television show), blogger Erin Human wrote of the show's online parent support videos, "Parenting is hard sometimes, yes. But this narrative of suffering only strengthens the stigma that autistic people face in the world. It helps NO ONE. Not even the person complaining. And certainly not their child."

I don't want this book to be a complaint. But complaining and acknowledging the differences in parenting requirements aren't the same thing. Countless parents raising neurologically atypical kids are struggling with and feeling overwhelmed by their reality. And I believe we can't positively shift our experience until we acknowledge and name what's going on. It's important that we talk, out loud, about what's hard so our experiences can be validated. In getting real about how the day-to-day reality negatively affects our kids and our families, we can become empowered to know that changing it isn't a question of *if* but *when*. So let's get real.

Isolation and Stigma

Shortly after launching TiLT Parenting, I received this email from the parent of a differently wired second grader:

I have a hard time talking about what has been going on in our family with most people I know. It all seems to shine a really negative light on my daughter, and I guess us as her parents, too. I want to be open and help people see that you can take charge and manage your situation, but I feel like I can only talk about the dark times euphemistically without feeling like I'm throwing my wonderful and amazing daughter under the bus. Except for a few people who also have very challenging children, it seems hard to be honest with others. On the one hand I feel like being open helps to break the stigma of differently wired people, but on the other hand I guess I want us to seem normal?

Many of us experience this same sense of isolation, fear of judgment from others, and not knowing where we fit into our schools, neighborhoods, and communities, and as a result, we feel left out of the party, cut off from the cool parenting club. Because our experiences aren't validated or understood by much of society, we're left with high levels of worry, loneliness, insecurity, guilt, and sadness. As Rita Eichenstein writes in her 2016 book *Not What I Expected*, "Having an atypical child will trigger emotions that are hard-wired in all of us—denial, fear, bargaining with fate, isolation, and depression—along with hope, optimism, and joy."

Many of us turn to Facebook for comfort, connecting with a handful of parenting support groups filled with strangers bonded by our shared experience of navigating what sometimes feels like an endless onslaught of obstacles. And when we have those *really* bad days—the ones where we fear we won't survive one more meltdown or shaming look—we reach out in desperation, wanting more than anything to know that we're not alone, that we're not crazy… that it will get better. We share lurid details of a public tantrum or an embarrassing showdown with a teacher or a frustrating conversation with an unsympathetic relative, and cry tears of gratitude for the virtual hugs and words of support that come streaming in.

The thing is, there are thousands of these Facebook groups. Because parents like us? We're everywhere. So then why are we on the fringes? Huddling in private? Trying to figure out how to fit ourselves and our kids into the world when the world isn't willing to meet us halfway? The struggle, as they say, is real. And it's hurting us—emotionally, mentally, and spiritually.

Behavioral Challenges

A few years ago, I met a friend for coffee one Saturday morning. I knew she wasn't in a great space mentally and emotionally, primarily because she was sharing her home with an extremely angry six-year-old and over the previous several months had unwittingly become the main target of her son's rage and hostility. We made small talk, catching up on work, mutual friends, and politics before I asked her how things were going at home.

Her face instantly fell as she began describing the war zone she was living in. Her son had been acting out in anger more than ever, frequently hitting her, kicking her, and lobbing objects at her. Just the night before, my friend had caught the corner of a book on her upper arm, and she had the bruise to prove it. As I gave her a hug in solidarity, I let her know it wasn't always going to be that hard. That over time, her son would outgrow these extreme behaviors and settle in. I know she believed me, but I also recognized that envisioning a more peaceful future is little comfort when you're in the thick of it.

Not all differently wired kids act out in inappropriately physical ways, but many do, especially when they're younger and don't know how to manage their big emotions. For Anne, mother of a five-year-old on the spectrum, the most challenging behavioral issue has been her daughter's aggression toward others and, as she describes it, "a general sort of belligerence." Michelle, a mother raising an eight-year-old with ADHD and Asperger's, wore long sleeves for an entire summer to cover up the scratches left on her arms by her differently wired son.

There's a reason the metaphor of a volcano is so frequently used to help differently wired kids understand what's going on inside. Their emotions bubble up until the inevitable explosion occurs. Although it's hard to be on the receiving end of these physical manifestations, we also know it's not a conscious choice—it's a reaction to their intense internal state. And because of the way they're wired, their ability to stop this process once it has begun is for the most part nonexistent, at least until they've developed the coping skills necessary to help them move through emotional upheavals in a more positive way.

Yet despite the fact that big emotional responses are not only normal in atypical kids but are to be expected, they're mostly perceived as unacceptable by the outside world. And I get why that is. After all, people could get hurt, and intense reactions can be scary. A child who manifests his anxiety or intensity in the form of tears and breakdowns feels manageable—crying is an "acceptable" reaction to adversity, or at the very least, one that can be dealt with in a compassionate way. Yet a child who responds to the same situation with unpredictable anger is a whole other story. Which is why so many parents feel uncomfortable sharing the truth about the physical behavioral challenges they're facing. I mean, *why would anyone want to talk about it?*

> Society has decided that anger isn't acceptable, even though it's a completely normal emotional response for atypical kids.

One of the scariest behavioral challenges affecting some families is having children who are physically unsafe in public, such as those who "bolt" with no warning and/or run out into traffic. This behavior is so common, especially among autistic children, that it has a name (actually two)—"wandering" or "elopement." A recent study by the Interactive Autism Network found that nearly 50 percent of kids on the spectrum between ages four and ten have done this. Talk about terrifying.

Of course, not all behavior challenges are physical. It takes a lot of energy to cope with another person's big emotions such as anger or defiance or end-of-the-world-level despair, and when emotions like those are children's go-to reaction to anything that dysregulates them, it can feel overwhelming. I mean, how should a parent respond when their child flat-out refuses to do something they need to do, like get into the car, go to school, finish their homework, or go to bed? One mother wrote to me explaining that although her daughter's tantrums have, fortunately, eased up, their biggest challenge now is a lack of follow-through. "She can't seem to focus long enough to complete anything. She can get distracted and delayed even just walking down the stairs. It drives me nuts when she finishes her homework and then forgets to turn it in. Her homework feels like my second job."

> Rearing atypical kids is arduous and tiring. It wears us down. We end up feeling incompetent, judged, and shamed.

These are perplexing behaviors, and unfortunately the strategies our friends with neurotypical kids use are inadequate for us. Parents of typical kids might threaten to take away an iPad to secure compliance or guide a child through the logical process of understanding how their behavior negatively affects others. But punishments are essentially penalizing a differently wired child for being who they are. And logical conversations that don't address what's at the root of a child's behavior won't yield results.

It's for all these reasons and more that the behavioral challenges of differently wired kids remain some of the biggest difficulties parents will face. And the way in which these challenges play out and affect us? It's complicated. On the one hand, we have our own challenges with how the behavior impacts us. Because the not knowing what to do all the time? It's arduous and tiring. We feel incompetent and would pay just about any amount of money for Supernanny, someone skilled in rearing atypical kids, to come and live in our house for a few months to get things under control. We are in serious need of strategies for tough behavior. It's wearing us down. In some cases, it may even be dangerous, especially as our kids get older and bigger. And it's hard to know where to start, because how exactly to get help isn't so clear.

On top of that, it's difficult to deal with judging and shaming from people who see only our child's behavior and are missing out on getting to know the creative, complicated person who lies inside it all. The urge is strong to hide what's really going on, because we don't want others to prejudge or dislike our child. We want people to see only the good, not the bad. And who can blame us?

Strain on the Family

Raising kids, even in the very best of circumstances, requires dedication, commitment, and the ability to keep many balls in the air. Throw in a differently wired child or two—or more—and suddenly there's an inordinate strain on the family unit and the relationships between partners, siblings, and even extended family. How can partners raising a neurodiverse child—or more than one—take care of their personal needs and their children's needs while also nurturing their relationship with each other? How can parents meet the needs of a differently wired child who takes up extra resources such as time, money, and energy while ensuring their typical child gets what he or she needs?

One mother shared with me that her biggest challenge comes with trying to protect the relationship between her older, differently wired son and her younger, neurotypical son. Her younger son idolizes his big brother, but most of the time her older son responds with annoyance and anger. So this mother is left stuck in the middle, feeling protective of her differently wired son, whom she knows doesn't mean it, while simultaneously feeling protective of her younger child's emotional life and physical well-being.

I've heard similar stories from many other families—parents concerned about their typical child getting shortchanged; parents who worry that, though their typical child doesn't seem to mind now, there may be a negative, long-term effect on their children's relationship with each other. Many parents in the TiLT community have two or more differently wired children, but their neurodifferences are unique, which obviously creates its own challenges, such as having to research, identify, and implement completely different strategies and solutions for each child. For my friend Tia, this looks like sending her three kids to three different schools, each designed to meet that child's distinct needs. (It also looks like *a lot* of running around.)

Likewise, because of the emotional stresses placed on parents of differently wired kids, each experienced in a very personal way, the health of our relationship with our partner (if we have one) often suffers, if for no other reason than the fact that the sheer mental exhaustion leaves us depleted, with nothing left for our partner, who may be feeling the same way. As one parent wrote to me, "Sometimes after my son has a meltdown, I don't even want to talk to my husband. When we finally put him to bed, we just can't even speak. I mean, we're just so exhausted."

Some families move away from relatives, just when they need help most, to escape their judgment.

Family strains sometimes include our extended families, too. Let's just say misunderstandings and judgments from our own parents and other relatives who question the veracity of our children's challenges and how we're addressing their behavior can lead to some uncomfortable conversations over Thanksgiving dinner. I know of families who've literally moved across the country to lessen the amount of time spent with relatives who just don't get it, which is unfortunate, because it's when we're tapped out and dealing with the really tough stuff that we could most use the support of family.

Lack of Choice

One of our primary jobs as parents is making choices—about everything from diet and clothing to schooling and beyond—that will enable our child to be healthy, stay safe, and thrive. But for many of us, "choice" is a complicated concept. Because most every child-related decision parents raising differently wired kids make requires just a little more consideration.

The most significant place we feel this lack of choice is our child's education. Whereas many families send their child to their neighborhood school without a second thought or consider private school possibilities like they would main dishes on a menu, school options for differently wired kids are often extremely limited. For starters, many private and charter schools simply don't accept children with learning disabilities like dyslexia or neurodifferences such as ADHD, with the explanation that they don't have the resources to properly support these students. Highly gifted children may not have access to accelerated programs in their school district where they may find like-minded peers or the kind of individualized learning programs that would allow them to fully tap into their gifts. Circumstances, such as financial constraints or a child's plummeting emotional and mental health because of poor school fit, lead many families down the road of homeschooling, frequently as a last-ditch effort to cobble together a solution the family can live with.

Extracurricular activities present similar challenges. Depending on what's going on with our child—say they're supersensitive or they fall apart if things don't go their way or their poor social skills make team sports a disaster—we can't just sign them up for an athletic or enrichment activity and assume things will be fine. Unfortunately, this reality is often a lesson we learn painfully, over time, as the negative experiences for our kid and our family add up.

I remember being excited the summer Asher was four, because he was finally old enough to participate in many of the area's summer day camps. I had my color-coded spreadsheet filled out and deposits in by mid-March, eight weeks of back-to-back fun and adventure lined up. I registered for all those camps well aware of Asher's intensity, but honestly, back then it didn't occur to me that he couldn't just head off to camp like the rest of his friends.

Sometimes things worked out, especially at camps where the counselors were college students or where he was particularly engaged. But other camp experiences were miserable failures. Inevitably, staff members would call me to come in for an early pickup or I'd be pulled aside at the end of the day for a rundown of every problematic occurrence. Sometimes we'd come up with a plan to get Asher through the week; sometimes that conversation marked the end of the road.

This is how things went for the next few summers. I'd seek out camps to match Asher's interests, and every week I'd drop him off with a book (or three) in his backpack in case he needed to "reregulate," and hope for the best. It wasn't until our fourth season of summer camp that it struck me that I should be calling ahead to ensure a camp could adequately support Asher's participation. (Sometimes I can be slow to catch on to the obvious.) But invariably those were difficult calls for me. When I did get someone on the line, I would vaguely explain things that could be difficult for Asher and paint a general picture of his intensities. I tended to mention only the ADHD, perhaps because that seemed somehow more "acceptable" than his other challenges. And though I don't remember my exact words, I'm sure I downplayed how tough he could be, so desperate was I for him to have a "regular kid" experience and worried that if the camp staff knew the reality of the situation, they'd say, *Sorry—this probably won't work out.*

Looking back, it's clear I was still in denial, my own emotions surrounding Asher's neurodiversity a jumble of shame, embarrassment, confusion, and fear. These are emotions I'm super-familiar with, and they're the ones I know contribute to the daily reality for parents like me as we learn that some experiences or opportunities available to neurotypical kids just might not be in the cards for ours, or if they are, may come with a side dish of formidable snags.

The reality is, whether our child is gifted, has learning or attention problems, is on the autism spectrum, or has another or multiple neurodifferences, there will be times when we'll need to overthink things, ridiculously plan ahead, make peace with the fact that we may have to drop everything at a moment's notice when the phone rings, and deal with a lack of awareness, understanding, and tolerance. And we'll be doing these things while trying to figure out how to advocate without burning out, and grappling with our own insecurities about how we and our kids are being judged.

Financial Strain

Ruth, the mother of a child with learning disabilities, told me that more than any other challenge she and her family faced, it was the financial implications that were the most daunting, because interventions for learning differences aren't typically covered by insurance. As she explained, "My son was diagnosed with learning differences prior to actually failing in school, and in our public school district, if your child isn't classified as needing their help (yet), you are left with the choice of doing nothing, waiting for the school to acknowledge the need for intervention and potentially watching your child fall further behind, or taking matters into your own hands (and your own wallet) and finding private interventions."

Ultimately, Ruth and her husband made huge financial sacrifices, paying out of pocket for private occupational therapy, private reading tutoring, and private psychotherapy. On top of that, she resigned from her full-time office job so she could manage her son and his needs full-time. Although Ruth says this was the right choice for her family, she acknowledges it hasn't been an easy road, and even so, it's a luxury many families can't afford.

Getting our child the support he or she needs isn't just a difficult quest—it often comes with a hefty price tag, one that creates significant burdens on countless families. As a 2016 article in the *Atlantic* titled "The Special Education Charade" said of the challenges for parents navigating the daunting task of getting their child tested and securing services at school, "Testing is expensive and time-consuming, campus psychologists are spread very thin, and schools are under pressure to put fewer kids in special education, in the name of 'mainstreaming,' not more. So the parents often end up resorting to private testing, which can run as high as $2,000 and is seldom covered by insurance." Frequently, testing isn't covered by insurance providers because it's considered to be "educational," not "medical," in nature, and they'll cover only the latter. At the same time, a diagnosis is necessary to be reimbursed for therapy, and therefore many families feel they have no choice but to fork over the money for the initial assessment.

> Raising differently wired kids comes at a cost that some families can't afford.

Spending large amounts of money for an essential assessment can be a genuine hardship. For many families, it's simply not a possibility. The costs are prohibitive enough that it might mean delaying the assessment if they're able to afford it at all, and, as a result, losing valuable time when it comes to getting a child help. Even when a child does have a diagnosis, only certain types of support are covered by insurance, and only for a certain amount, and only until a child reaches a certain age. For instance, Asher's social skills class—a nine-month program in Seattle that I credit with his learning how to "be" with other kids—wasn't covered by insurance. (Oh, and we also waited a year to get in the door.) When we left Seattle in 2013, he was nearing the age when the occupational therapy that helped him make so much progress with his sensory issues would no longer be covered by insurance.

The bottom line: The decisions many families raising differently wired kids feel they have no choice but to make—leaving a job or cutting back on hours so they can homeschool their child, bringing in tutors or other instructors to support a child's growth or keep them on track academically with their peers, paying for additional testing—come at a cost. And one that's felt deeply.

No Clear Path

When the therapist who assessed Asher at the University of Washington gave Derin and me the lowdown on his diagnoses of ADHD, autism spectrum disorder, and disruptive behavioral disorder not otherwise specified, she threw in a few closing remarks that I wasn't too keen to hear. Specifically, she said, "Helping Asher develop his executive functioning skills is critical if he's going to live independently as an adult." I left that meeting in tears, the phrase "if he's going to live independently" looping through my mind. Up until then, I had just wanted to get him through elementary school, but suddenly the stakes felt much higher.

One of the first things I learned when I began my own therapy in my midtwenties was that "there are no guarantees." At the time, I had a fair amount of anxiety about things I couldn't control, and even when I was feeling happy and content, part of me was waiting for the other shoe to drop. My therapist Jamie, a twentysomething intern at the Albert Ellis Institute, would gently remind me that I could get hit by a bus on my way home. (Nice, right?) But I saw her point: No matter how much I planned, managed, and gripped everything around me tightly in an attempt to control the outcome, *there were no guarantees*. Anything could happen. I couldn't predict the future any more than I could ensure a happily ever after.

It's these same words that I still have to meditate on anytime I start to spiral into worry about what the future for Asher will look like. I'll be straight with you—it's a hard concept to fully embrace, and not just for me. I know anxiety about future unknowns is a reality for many parents of differently wired kids, because all around us, we see other kids whose futures seem to be paved with possibility from the time they're toddlers. As I wrote earlier, when parents get to choose things such as where their children will go to school or which sports they'll participate in or which musical instrument they'll take up, it looks to the rest of us as if there actually *are* guarantees . . . we just don't have any of them ourselves. Rather, we're stuck wondering what size kids' Velcro shoes go up to or when (or if) our child will ever be able to safely cross the street by himself. We can't imagine our child turning in a homework assignment on time without a dozen reminders, let alone juggling a handful of classes at university and having a "typical" college experience. We worry about what will happen to our children when they're adults and we're no longer around. Will they be able to hold down a job? Cover a mortgage? Have a family of their own? Fulfill their dreams?

I know we're not alone in this worry. I understand that neurotypical kids' paths can and do diverge at many points along the way. I know *all* parents are concerned their child may not live up to his or her potential, and they'd do anything to ensure their best possible outcome. And I never forget that there are no guarantees. But still, this is a hard one. We want to know we're on the right track—that if we do all the right things and get all the right therapies and do everything in our power to help our child discover their strengths while also sorting out their challenges, they can ultimately live as fulfilled adults. We read articles on websites such as My Aspergers Child that say things like "Approximately 80 percent of grown-ups with Aspergers and High Functioning Autism (HFA) do not have full-time jobs—not because they can't do the work, but because they often have difficulty being *socially acceptable* while they get the work done," and we feel paralyzed. Our eyes are drawn to headlines like "Scary New Statistics About ADHD" by Mama MD on Boston.com, and we skim the article to find this nugget: "People who had ADHD as children were more likely to suffer from other problems such as alcohol or drug abuse, anxiety, depression or other mental health problems. They are also more likely to try to commit suicide." And we have to suppress a sudden, overpowering wave of nausea.

Because there is no playbook and there are very few mentors to show us and our kids how it's done and what moving down this road with confidence, grace, and optimism looks like, fears of future unknowns will continue to be a tremendous source of stress for parents raising atypical kids.

. . . . . .

As parents of neurodiverse children, we spend much of our life pushing through these daily challenges, often on the outside looking in when it comes to parenting and securing what we need to set up our children for success. But this reality isn't circumstantial, accidental, or a case of bad luck. Rather, the challenges are pretty much guaranteed—and exacerbated—by an entrenched system and set of norms that weren't designed with our children in mind. Our daily challenges may discourage and exhaust us, but the system is what's keeping us stuck.

CHAPTER 4

What's Keeping Us Stuck

Every parent wants their child to be appreciated for the unique being he or she is. We know how special they are, and we want everyone else to see it, too. Yet as much as we want our children to be perceived as extraordinary, it's equally true that there is immeasurable value in simply *fitting in*. At the end of the day, parents can confidently make choices about their child's experiences because their child fits in to the definition of what is considered "normal." Normal is good. Normal ensures doors are open.

But how did we get here in the first place? What factors have ensured this status quo where sameness, fitting in, and conformity are so highly prized and embraced? How has this current parenting paradigm—one that encourages labels, medications, and quick fixes for anything outside the "norm"—been able to flourish? I know one thing for certain: It's being perpetuated and reinforced every day by a culture and a system that don't want to make room for anything else.

The Neurotypical Parenting Experience

Last year, a meme was circulating on Facebook, and it was only because it was shared in so many groups I'm in, as well as the fact that it showed up on at least a dozen friends' time lines, that I took notice. The item featured a photograph of a sign, presumably posted at a venue for children's athletics. Here's what it said:

> *Your child's success or lack of success in sports does not indicate what kind of parent you are. But having an athlete that is coachable, respectful, a great teammate, mentally tough, resilient, and tries their best IS a direct reflection of your parenting.*

I have this bad habit of scrolling through my Facebook news feed in the mornings while lying in bed, which admittedly doesn't always result in the best start to my day. The morning I read that post was no exception, and my blood began to boil even before I got through the first comment, my mind conjuring up memories of failed attempts at organized sports with Asher. As lifelong athletes—I'm a runner and Derin is a soccer player—we, like many other parents, assumed our child would participate in some type of sport throughout his life. We had Asher in gymnastics by age three, soccer from ages four through six, and cross country when he was six and seven. Suffice it to say that none of them went particularly well. Hyperaware of where he stood in relation to his peers when it came to athletic ability, Asher would often get frustrated when others performed better than he did, as well as when things didn't go the way he expected, which (no surprise here) was most of the time.

If Asher was having an off day during a soccer practice or game, any little thing could spark a tantrum, which might look like yelling, stomping the ground, wildly kicking the ball off the field, and/or storming away. In other words, pretty much the exact opposite of "coachable, respectful, a great teammate, mentally tough, and resilient." According to the aforementioned post, Asher's inability to handle the emotional, mental, and physical demands of organized sports meant I was failing as a parent.

Perhaps what hurt the most was how many friends shared and

liked this particular post, which from my point of view reeked of shaming, judgment, and self-righteousness. I imagined millions of sharers and likers around the world proudly raising their hands in unity over their well-adjusted children with a silent cheer of *Yeah!* followed by *That's my kid!* I instantly went on the defensive, commenting on a few friends' posts that the meme was omitting an important last sentence: "Unless your child is developing differently due to his or her brain wiring and struggles with competitive situations and unpredictability, is overly anxious or a perfectionist, and/or has executive functioning deficits that make certain tasks required in team sports extraordinarily challenging." But I guess that's not as catchy. Or perhaps we're just supposed to keep our differently wired kids out of organized sports altogether for everyone else's sake?

More recently, another meme made the rounds on social media, aimed at a different community but equally as judgmental. Perhaps you've seen it, too:

> *We need to care less about whether our children are academically gifted and more about whether they sit with the lonely kid in the cafeteria.*

Widely shared, and often with generous commentary, this meme sparked a different kind of fury, pitting parents of neurotypical children and gifted children against each other and shining a spotlight on the intolerance and misunderstanding that abound. Although I don't believe this was the intention, the post suggested that being academically gifted is something parents can "will" their children into being—that it's a quality overly ambitious parents strive for and prioritize above all else. But as we know, giftedness isn't a choice—it's a neurological difference. It can't be forced, and it can't be helped. And it's certainly no ticket to a charmed and easy life. Even more, the meme seemed to say that kindness and giftedness are mutually exclusive. What's *that* all about? If anything, when we consider the challenges faced by profoundly and exceptionally gifted children, there's a high probability that *they* are the lonely kids in the cafeteria.

These two examples are emblematic of the ways parents raising neurotypical kids unwittingly perpetuate and reinforce a status quo that is harmful to differently wired children everywhere. Messages like these, and the somewhat ignorant sentiment behind them, are indicative of the privilege parents with neurotypical kids enjoy without even realizing it. Their experience is the norm, and if the rest of us can't adapt and conform accordingly, we're simply out of luck.

An example of what this looks like for thousands of parents every day comes from Bari, whose son has ADHD, auditory processing disorder, and executive function challenges. Bari hoped that being proactive and talking to coaches, teachers, and program directors ahead of time would get everyone on the same page and allow her son to have a successful experience like the rest of his friends, but it rarely worked out that way. "It took many painful partings of ways with places where he felt a sense of community but where they just couldn't support or understand someone who might have an outburst or burst into tears out of frustration. It was very painful to navigate through that. And so we've had to create our own solutions."

Although, admittedly, accommodating the needs of differently wired kids in such activities may involve more effort, time, and resources than many organizations can afford, that doesn't make the outcome any less harmful or unfair for an entire generation of exceptional children. Some people call it ableism, a type of discrimination defined by StopAbleism.org as "a set of practices and beliefs that assign inferior value (worth) to people who have developmental, emotional, physical or psychiatric disabilities." In its simplest form, it boils down to *normal equals good* and *abnormal equals bad.*

Perhaps what makes this such a difficult obstacle to overcome is the fact that this sentiment is incessantly strengthened by the world around us and the books we read, the television shows we stream, and the articles we scroll through in our newsfeed. Just as negative stereotypes about, for instance, people of color, members of the LGBTQ community, single parents, immigrants, people living in poverty, and overweight people are perpetuated through the media (when and if these groups are represented at all), differently wired people are another marginalized group getting the shaft.

Consider this: Despite the fact that in the "real world" one in five people is wired differently, neurodiverse characters are few and far between in the majority of mainstream media, especially as primary characters. On occasions where a neurodiverse character *is* included, their different wiring is typically the focal point, such as in the Netflix original series *Atypical*, about an autistic teenager coming of age; the popular novel *The Rosie Project*, which tells the story of differently wired professor Don Tillman's comical quest for love; and the show *Parenthood*, which included a couple raising an atypical child. Although portrayals like those are clearly a step in the right direction, the neurodiverse experience is almost always viewed through the lens of or in relation to a "normal" way of being. Fictional portrayals of neurodifferences such as ADHD are often humorous; a character's hyper energy or inability to focus are the punch line of many a joke. Highly gifted people are often portrayed as one-note savants—quirky, socially awkward, walking encyclopedias. Learning differences such as dyslexia and dysgraphia are rarely portrayed at all. As a result, the experience of "typical atypical" people—one-fifth of the population—are for the most part invisible. As the saying goes, *We don't know what we don't know*. And when inaccurate portrayals of neurodifferences are what's available, these fictionalized representations steeped in stereotypes and stigmas become the baseline for those who don't have any context.

The plethora of books, magazines, blogs, and podcasts aimed at parents present another challenge, because these media are overwhelmingly aimed at the "typical" parenting experience. Parenting philosophy books almost always use neurotypical kids in their examples, which reinforces the notion that there is a standard. Many don't even mention alternative ways of being in the strategies they present. Likewise, popular parenting websites, in their quest to get traffic, regularly feature headlines that rely on fear, blame, and guilt as clickbait while simultaneously

> Parents are driven by wonder and by curiosity—and they are fueled by fear.

promoting a "normal" way of being. Essentially, the media is the key spokesperson for reinforcing neurotypical privilege, which negatively affects parents on all sides.

Lastly, we have the news media, featuring coverage that frequently latches onto story angles that highlight different ways of being. For instance, when covering a tragedy, a reporter might mention that the perpetrator has Asperger's or an anxiety disorder, as if their neurodifference is the reason for their actions. And just like that, a negative association with neurodifference becomes a little more firmly entrenched in the minds of people everywhere. Whether they're doing it to try to make sense of a story or because we live in a world of twenty-second sound bites, highlighting neurodifferences in news coverage can do genuine harm, especially when the story is a negative one.

So what do all of these elements standardizing a neurotypical experience in the world have in common? The way I see it, they're all rooted in one thing: *fear*.

When children first come into the world, they are essentially blank slates. Parents have no idea how their bundles of joy will develop, who they'll become, and what their ultimate lot in life will be. They're driven by wonder and curiosity as they hit each milestone. *When will she take her first step? What will his first word be? When will her first tooth come in?*

At the same time, they're fueled by fear. *Is she gaining enough weight? Is he allergic to nuts? Is her fever too high?* Beneath these smaller, common concerns are underlying causes for bigger worry. Aware of the ages at which children are frequently identified as having developmental and neurological delays and differences, parents everywhere breathe sighs of relief when they realize they're past the age when autism is easily recognized. *Dodged that bullet.* They notice a child in their son's preschool who dramatically falls to pieces at the slightest inconvenience or discomfort and, while giving empathetic looks to the child and his mother, say a little prayer. *Thank goodness my kid can handle adversity.* Their child learns to read without difficulty by kindergarten, and they silently celebrate the lack of any apparent learning disabilities such as dyslexia. And on and on it goes, through elementary school, middle school, high school, and beyond.

So here's the deal. I recognize that parenting is an individualized sport. Children are a parent's top priority, as they should be. And I understand being relieved when a child develops "normally" and it becomes apparent that there are no pervasive deficits that could create more hardship and challenge for them. *But* (you knew there was a but, right?) there's a part of the status quo that needs to be fixed. Because right now, parents of typically developing kids are focusing only on themselves and leaving everyone else to fend for themselves. *It's not my problem... I have my own kid to worry about.*

> We need to educate parents of neurotypical kids and convince them to stop supporting systems that exclude so many.

The same parenting paradigm that is broken for the rest of us has remained in place for so long because it (mostly) works for parents of typical kids. That's not to say that these parents don't have genuine gripes, but for the most part, what exists for them is good enough. The current paradigm is one in which these parents feel safe and secure—they know how and where their child fits into the world, and because it's a system where "normal" prevails, they don't have any incentive to make any noise. After all, if they truly considered the notion that the current paradigm is flawed, where would that leave them? They would have to call everything that feeds their sense of belonging into question.

When you consider the amount of influence they have in their children's schools, among their peers, and within their communities, it's evident that parents of typical children are one of the biggest contributors to keeping the current paradigm in place. To change that, part of our big work in the world needs to involve patiently and compassionately educating those who are unwittingly supporting systems and norms that are excluding so many of us.

The Traditional Educational Model

From the age of four or five on, kids usually learn in some sort of institutional setting—a public school, a charter school, a private school—and through the framework of any number of educational philosophies such as Montessori, Waldorf, Maker schools, Democratic and Free schools, and so on. In the United States, children formally enter the education system for kindergarten, and it's assumed they'll work their way up into middle school or junior high, and then high school. Not all kids may make it to graduation, but by law, every child has the right to have access to all thirteen years of school in the form of a "free and appropriate" education.

It's the "appropriate" part of this guarantee where things become questionable. Most, if not all, differently wired kids think differently, process information differently, and, as a result, learn differently. So it should be no surprise that securing a good education for differently wired kids is like panning for gold. It's rare and requires persistence, diligence, flexibility, and, in some cases, a plethora of resources not limited to time and money.

When we look at the traditional educational model, we're really talking about two primary options: public school (including charter schools) and private school, each with its own pros and cons. Here's a closer look at the various school options in relation to how they serve (or, in many cases, don't serve) atypical kids.

Public Schools and Charter Schools

By federal law, most notably the Individuals with Disabilities Education Act (IDEA), schools are required to meet the educational needs of students with disabilities, with the term "disabilities" legally extending beyond things such as blindness, deafness, and physical disabilities to include those children who, for example, have diagnoses of autism, specific learning disabilities such as dyslexia and dyscalculia, and ADHD. Children who qualify for support under IDEA work with the school to create an individualized education plan, which spells out specific accommodations and goals for a child's intellectual growth. Those who don't quality for an IEP or necessarily need specialized instruction but still have some sort of learning difference that needs to be supported can get what's called a 504 Plan. (Note: Understood.org provides a fantastic breakdown of the difference between these two plans if you're looking for more details.)

So that's the idea. Seems straightforward, right? Well, yes, but there's a catch. One of the more confusing aspects of IDEA is that for a child to receive services, their disability has to prevent them from making "effective progress" in school. And how exactly "effective progress" is defined is unclear, which creates challenges for parents trying to ensure that their kids realize their potential. For example, a student with ADHD might be progressing from grade to grade just fine (in other words, making "effective progress") while not actually coming close to working at capacity or getting the support they need for executive functioning deficits. A twice-exceptional student may be keeping up fine with her class but remain unchallenged and disengaged, her exceptional gifts never sparked, and, as a result, her future potentially dimmed.

When we moved Asher to public school for second grade, a therapist suggested accommodations to push for in his IEP, and even showed up at IEP meetings as an advocate, expert, and part of my "team." Because Asher tests extremely well and was excelling academically on paper, we worked to demonstrate how his behavior, executive functioning challenges, and social deficits were hurting his overall development and performance. After all, how could he learn anything when he was spending a good chunk of his day in the hallway or the principal's office?

Asher ultimately received what an educator friend described as a "decent" IEP that spelled out accommodations such as having a dedicated quiet space in the classroom, using a special chair cushion so he could wiggle his body, and a guarantee of several hours per week to work with the school's occupational therapist on emotional regulation and social skills. So, at the end of the school year, had Asher made "effective progress"? Well, I'll say this—he wasn't kicked out, so I considered *that* progress. But in truth? I can't say that he did. In fact, when I told his school therapist we were pulling him out to homeschool him, she surprised me by affirming our decision, adding, "We can't really meet Asher's needs here."

It was midway through third grade that Kerry knew her twice-exceptional son's schooling wasn't going to be smooth sailing. Her son was always well behaved and paid attention in class, so the teachers liked him, but no one could figure out what was getting in the way of his learning. Over time, he began to withdraw from his peers, lose self-confidence in everything, and have emotional meltdowns over homework; Kerry and her husband knew they had to make a change. She went outside the school system for private testing and finally got a diagnosis of dyslexia. But unfortunately, the diagnosis didn't equal a solution.

As Kerry explains, "Though the staff at his school was wonderful and truly wanted to help, they didn't have the tools or the time to give him what he needed." Kerry moved her son to a small, private Montessori school that allowed for a private learning specialist to come in and work with him a couple of times a week. She says it wasn't ideal, but it worked for a few years. He has since returned to the public school system, the adjustment to which she describes as rocky. "We're always looking for ways to make the system bend just a little so he can feel some level of comfort in his day-to-day learning experience, but it's a constant battle. Since the state we live in doesn't recognize dyslexia as a trigger for an IEP, no one in the system was able to tweak their approach to his education in a way that was helpful. We've pieced together a plan for our child, but that's only because we were able to educate ourselves, dedicate an incredible amount of time to his learning, and pay a lot of money to get him what he needed."

Even dedicated teachers often lack the tools and training to support differently wired kids.

I had gotten enough of a glimpse of Asher's school life and talked with enough parents to realize why so many atypical kids struggle in public schools. Because even a committed teacher dedicated to supporting unique learners can do only so much when trying to wrangle a classroom of twenty to thirty kids. Consider that out of the bunch, as many as six students may be neurodiverse, each with their own needs, triggers, and behavioral challenges. There's simply no way one teacher can adequately meet the criteria of each child's IEP or 504 Plan (if they even have one) in the long term and on the fly while simultaneously teaching a bevy of antsy elementary students how to apply the order of operations.

One of the biggest challenges regarding the education of neurodiverse students is that they typically require more support, resources, and effort to reach their potential. Simultaneously and consequently, they may detract from the learning happening for other kids in a classroom, since having a handful of children monopolize a teacher's attention because of disruptions or their falling behind affects every student's learning. On top of that, as dedicated, hardworking, and passionate as teachers may be, most don't have the tools, training, or knowledge for best supporting their neurodiverse students. As schools attempt to become even more inclusive, the challenges for teachers will only increase.

Despite the fact that alternative learning institutions are becoming increasingly common, the overwhelming majority of American schools are rooted in this traditional educational model—one that sees students as passive absorbers of information; uses teacher-centered methods; is based on external criteria such as test results; focuses on linear and rote learning, memorization, and skill mastery; delivers content through lectures, worksheets, and texts; and measures progress through grades. As long as this model is held up as the standard, or at the very least, is the primary option available, children with neurological differences will always be at a disadvantage, because these schools weren't conceived to support different ways of learning.

Charter schools offer a twist on the traditional public school model in the United States, but they have become an especially controversial topic among the special education community. The problem identified by many special education advocates is that, though government funded, charter schools aren't required to follow the guidelines laid out in IDEA; as a result, some choose not to support the needs of differently wired students if they have them (some refuse to enroll them in the first place).

What does all of this mean? It means that the most affordable (read: free or mostly free), most accessible, and most protected form of education for differently wired kids comes with a lot of potential stumbling blocks. Of course, there are differently wired kids who do just fine in public education—their success depends on multiple factors such as their specific neurodifferences, a school district's flexibility and willingness to accommodate, teachers' ability to meet their needs, and the parents' level of engagement. But the fact remains that many of our kids struggle to navigate a system that was initially designed to teach compliant, neurotypical students who learn in a very specific way. Kids who don't fit into that narrow mold, even if they manage to push through it, will often compromise some aspect of their emotional, mental, or academic well-being.

Private Schools

Many differently wired kids spend at least some of their school years attending a private learning institution, which could be anything from a religious school to a private school subscribing to a particular educational philosophy or catering to a specific type of student. But I can't write about private schools without addressing the obvious barrier to entry—*money*. Although Catholic and other religious schools tend to be substantially less expensive than secular private schools—an average cost of around $9,000 per year versus an average of $23,000 per year respectively—schools specifically serving neurologically diverse learners may cost upward of twice as much or more as a school designed for neurotypical kids.

In those circumstances where money isn't a factor, there is the question of access. Not every city has a school specializing in learning problems such as dyslexia and dysgraphia. Even fewer accommodate kids on the spectrum or students with attention challenges. And if you've got a twice-exceptional learner, the options are fewer still. In fact, as this book was being written, only eleven schools in the United States were specifically designed to support 2e learners, and most were full and with deep waiting lists.

Landing a coveted spot at a private school designed for neuro-diverse kids is no guarantee of a happily ever after, either. For instance, Giselle Marzo Segura, the founder of an organization aiming to shift the conversation about neurodiversity toward a focus on character assets called Strength Clusters, was speechless when the special-needs private school she'd been sending her daughter to in Miami announced that her daughter wasn't performing as well as they would like. Their recommendation? *Homeschooling.*

When parents do have access to a private school ideally suited to their child's wiring, have the money to afford it, and are able to get their child admitted, it's possible for atypical kids to thrive. And I've known of families who've sold the house and picked up and moved to other cities, states, and even countries so their child could attend a school designed to support them. But of course, such drastic measures are simply not possible for most families.

Homeschooling

When the traditional educational model isn't working for our kids and we have the resources and ability to consciously opt out (or we get there by default because we've burned through the school options available to us), many families raising differently wired kids ultimately homeschool. According to the National Center for Educational Statistics, about 5 percent of homeschooled children are home educated because their parents or caregivers have deemed it the best option for meeting their child's special needs.

Homeschooling can vary greatly from family to family. Online education can be a good option for children who struggle with panic attacks at school, are being bullied, or are quickly losing their love of learning, not to mention their confidence and sense of self. "Unschooling" allows for wholly child-led learning and aims to ensure that kids retain their sense of curiosity and love of learning throughout their lives. Many families, including mine, end up cobbling together an education from a variety of curricular sources, such as online classes and homeschool co-ops, which allows them to go with the flow and follow a child's lead in some areas while also making sure a child hits certain age- or grade-based milestones.

Because there is no one way it needs to look, and because many of the challenging aspects of educating a child in a traditional setting aren't a factor at home, homeschooling often turns out to be the best solution for families with differently wired kids. Think about it—classroom management isn't a problem when the student body consists of one to a handful of kids. Rigid routines can be strictly enforced if a child needs that kind of structure, and the freedom to toss schedules out the window and allow a child to dive deeply into an area of interest is perfect for others. In a typical school setting, triggers are everywhere: the unpredictability of other children and the classroom dynamic, being forced to work in ways that highlight a child's challenges (such as group projects), stimulation overload from a sensory perspective, and much more. At homeschool, a child can progress at their own pace and take sensory breaks when necessary. A homeschooled child doesn't have to worry about a fire drill in the middle of PE or another student giving them a hard time on the playground.

But, like any solution, homeschooling isn't always perfect, nor is it an option for every family. Many families can't afford to have a parent stay home from work to teach their child, and in single-parent households, the chances of homeschooling as a viable option are even slimmer. Though an increasing number of parents are working from home and managing to juggle a job and homeschooling, I can personally attest that it can be a tricky balance.

Of course, differently wired kids don't corner the market when it comes to the stresses involved in identifying the right school solution. Struggles surrounding education exist in every city across the country. But that doesn't change the fact that the current educational model is in dire need of an update. How exactly to do that is being debated among scholars and educators around the world, and likely will be for many years to come. And how to enact the necessary changes in a system weighed down by bureaucracy and scarce resources is an even bigger problem. Regardless, *something needs to give*. And until it does, our differently wired kids, especially those living in families lacking the resources to seek out alternative educational solutions, are going to continue to be stuck.

The Broken System

In negotiating both the school system and the mental health system, Maratea, mother of a twice-exceptional teenager with more than a dozen diagnoses, experienced a huge amount of frustration, in part because it took her several years, several schools, and multiple assessments to finally get the right diagnoses and the right learning environment for her son. Ever since their son was a young boy, Maratea and her husband suspected he was on the spectrum because of his lack of eye contact and sensory problems, yet no one, including the speech pathologist and occupational therapist he worked with, as well as trusted educators and consultants, agreed with their thinking. It wasn't until years later, when he finally received a diagnosis of autism, that the pieces, and the appropriate support, finally came together. "There was a lot of frustration in terms of finding behavioral therapists, psychiatrists, and other providers who could help us create a path," Maratea said.

Unfortunately, Maratea's story isn't unusual. It's representative of one of the more frustrating obstacles keeping parents raising unique kids stuck—what I refer to as "the system," aka the formal structures and procedures in place to provide children with the support they need, be it occupational therapy, tutoring, enrichment opportunities, coaching, medication, or something else. There is no step-by-step handbook to tell parents like us where to start, how to find resources, how to navigate insurance companies' coverage plans, or even what kind of help we should be looking for in the first place. We need our own version of *What to Expect When You're Expecting*, but applied to what we can anticipate along our off-road journey.

It is this "system," and the difficulty in cobbling together a plan for moving through it, that leaves many parents at their most hopeless and confused. Because once a parent has realized they need more information or services for their child—often after months or even years of questioning, wondering, and uncertainty—they usually want that information and support ASAP. They are eager for someone to point them in a clear direction with the knowledge that when they make the right appointments with the right people, they'll get the right instructions to be on the road to an easier, more supported reality. In cases where they've already discovered which interventions or accommodations their child needs to thrive, they want to be able to secure and pay for them without delay or having to jump through confusing hoops. Unfortunately, for most parents, this wished-for experience is far from a reality.

Ask any of my close friends and they'll tell you I'm one of the most organized and productive people they know. I'm a research junkie and a lover of color-coded charts, and I know how to get things done quickly and efficiently. It's because of all these traits that I feel confident in saying that if I struggle as much as I do to know where to go, how to get help, and what to do next, *something is seriously wrong here.*

When we first realize something different is going on with our child, most if not all of us feel overwhelmed with one big question: What now? Many of us are relying on word-of-mouth referrals and hours-long Internet searches for things we don't even have the language for. We're pioneers without a map, let alone a destination. And this lack of clarity about how to move forward adds an incredibly stressful layer to our already tapped-out lives.

And then there's the matter of time lines. There is an enormous disconnect between the sense of urgency we're experiencing and the response time from the people and organizations we're turning to for help. When we had Asher assessed for sensory processing disorder, we had to sit out a three-month-long waiting list. The same went for his diagnostic assessment at a clinic two years later. Three years after that, getting him in at the University of Washington Autism Center involved a five-month wait, and I had chosen that clinic in part because the waiting list was shorter than at some other places in the city. When it was suggested that we find a more traditional "talk therapist," I called practitioner after practitioner only to be told repeatedly that they weren't taking new clients. I have a feeling Asher's therapist Dr. John took Asher on despite a full slate because he sensed the desperation in my voice when I told him how disastrous school was for Asher and that I didn't know what else to do.

This probably goes without saying, but when your child isn't thriving and things at home and at school are rapidly deteriorating, sitting around twiddling your thumbs for months waiting to even *begin* the process of getting help is pretty rough. That the waiting lists at clinics and therapy centers are so long suggests there's a dearth of psychologists qualified to assess children. I can only imagine that in smaller towns the lack of resources is even more profound.

Even in cases where a child is able to secure some extra support, either in school or through therapy, finding the right kind of help—such as critical life skills or social skills that many of these kids need help fostering if they're to reach their potential—isn't easy. As one mother of an eight-year-old autistic daughter with motor coordination delays explained to me, "It ends up putting a lot back on us. My husband and I are trying to make stuff up to try to help her move forward in the way she needs to move forward in order to eventually be independent."

Us–Parents of Atypically Developing Children

Because I earlier spelled out the ways in which parents with *typically* developing children play a paramount role in keeping differently wired kids stuck, it's time for the rest of us to take a good hard look in the mirror. Because like it or not, and consciously or not, we—you, me, and everyone else raising atypical kids—are contributing to this very same outdated paradigm every day through our actions, words, and thoughts.

In my early twenties, I went through a traumatic breakup with my college boyfriend after he cheated on me. (I know, *right?*) I was heartbroken, hurt, furious, and shell-shocked. Plainly put, I felt *wronged*. My close friend Loch, seeing I was in need of a deep conversation, not to mention a few calories, took me to lunch to talk things through. As I explained through tears and outrage what had happened, Loch did something I wasn't prepared for—he suggested that I bore some of the responsibility. He told me I either had or hadn't done certain things that contributed to a dynamic that obviously wasn't healthy in the first place. He went so far as to say that if I didn't consider the way in which I had participated in said relationship's going down in flames, I would be doing a huge disservice to myself, not to mention to my ex.

At the time, I was taken aback. But today, twenty years later, that moment over Thai food in midtown Manhattan is one I'll never forget. And it's one I often look back on as the parent of a differently wired kid. Because I've come to realize that if we really want a parenting paradigm that embraces and appreciates who our children are, we have to first own up to the ways in which we are contributing to keeping the outdated one in place.

Many of us legitimize the current paradigm by trying to fit into it with every fiber of our being. We keep information about possible diagnoses close to the chest and focus our energies on tamping down behaviors that, although normal and fine in the context of who our child is, might make them stand out among their peers. We desperately hire help, bring in specialists, medicate, and try to will our kids into assimilating. We lament our membership in a club made up of emotionally tapped out parents and the kids that schools refer to as "challenging" and do what we can to switch into the *other* club.

I'm not suggesting we shouldn't support our kids in developing in areas where they have deficits. I'm all for therapy, social skills clubs, enhanced learning opportunities, special camps, accommodations, and everything else that helps our child foster skills and habits that will benefit their future growth. Rather, I'm referring to the *intention* behind our actions. Are we doing these things because we want to get into the "normal" club? Are we hoping that with enough therapy and support, our kids will outgrow who they inherently are and develop in a way that renders their differences not only invisible but undetectable to anyone but them? Because what I know about autism and ADHD and learning and processing differences is that these things do not go away. Our children can certainly learn skills and strategies and work-arounds so they can thrive, but for the most part, no one outgrows their wiring.

I remember talking with Dr. John a few years ago about some of Ash's tricky behavior in school. "I'm having a hard time differentiating between which behavior is related to his autism and what is just 'behavior' or something he's making a choice about," I said.

Dr. John replied, "Well, Asher is always autistic. So his behavior is *always* connected to that in some way."

So simple, but it took Dr. John spelling it out for me to realize I was still trying to separate out parts of who Asher was that were "normal" and those that needed "fixing." I was still clinging to the hope that certain behaviors and characteristics would eventually fade away so his childhood could be more typical... and easier (and more of what I envisioned when I first became a parent). I was still caught up in trying to fit into the current paradigm, because even though it wasn't necessarily working for us, it felt somehow safe and known.

> No one outgrows his wiring. An autistic child is always autistic.

It makes sense though. Many of us on the outside looking in crave a sense of fitting in for once. We imagine that if we could just find a way to squeeze our child into the system, we might have some control over their life and, more than that, ensure for them a bright and successful future. In their quest to try to force this outcome, some families plow ahead, trying to fit into the "normal" construct for years, fighting schools, fighting labels, and ultimately fighting themselves.

For instance, Emily and her husband insisted on staying the course despite the fact that their daughter's needs clearly weren't being met in her elementary school, as was evidenced by her increasingly extreme behavior both at school and at home. They became upset with anyone who suggested they have their daughter assessed, continued to use admittedly ineffective discipline strategies at home, and focused all their frustration on the school, blaming their daughter's problems on her teachers' failure to see that she wasn't a "typical compliant girl." Finally, when their daughter was in fourth grade, Emily and her husband realized that by continuing to try to force her to fit in, they were denying who she actually is. As Emily said of her aha moment, "From now on, I'm going to celebrate her uniqueness. My daughter isn't typical and never will be."

Many parents with atypical kids—especially those with younger kids whose neurodifferences aren't so apparent or whose atypical wiring is becoming apparent only over time—exist in a liminal space between stark denial, CIA-level secrecy, and aggressive fix-it mode. Many of us have exhausted every resource in an attempt to fit into the current paradigm before finally crying uncle and acknowledging there's a vast disconnect. At that point, we often quietly struggle, suffer, or experience shame when it doesn't work out. Still, we soldier on.

Other times it's the way we experience our lives with our differently wired children that contributes to our keeping the status quo in place. We compromise too much, we don't think outside the box . . . we play small. We neglect our self-care, which leaves us exhausted and unable to meet our child where they are. We buy into the stigmas that surround our child's differences by staying silent and hiding what's real in our lives. Like I used to do, we consider conformity and fitting in to be a desirable goal rather than fully leaning in to all of who our child is. Just as I spent years looking for a school fit for Asher, it can take parents a while to realize that what exists is inadequate and they've got to get creative in forging their own path. But until we get to that point, we're unwittingly playing into the broken paradigm.

．　．　．　．　．　．

The factors keeping the status quo in place, which must include inertia, are formidable. It's no wonder things are the way they are—we're essentially being set up to fail, because there is nothing in place, systemically or culturally, to support us. But that's okay. Because now we know what we're up against, and that means we have what it takes to figure out exactly what needs to change. And because we have the most at stake and the most to lose, the change has to start with us.

//

CHAPTER 5

It's Time for Something New

//

Imagine, if you will, what your life would be like if fear, worry, or guilt were no longer part of your day-to-day parenting experience. If you could talk openly about your kid's wiring without concern that they'd be ostracized or perceived as "less than." Imagine sending your child to any school or camp or club and knowing they would be treated with respect and understanding instead of punished for who they are. Imagine feeling secure in the knowledge that you could handle whatever comes down the road because you have confidence in yourself as a parent and the awareness that you're not alone.

Not only do I believe everything would change, but I believe this vision is possible. And I believe it has to start with us.

It starts when parents of atypical kids—parents like you and me—commit to staying open, paying attention, and questioning our preconceived notions. Because when we do that, we create the possibility for transformation and deeper connection. We *all* have what it takes to become fluent in our children's unique language. When we are willing to work on ourselves, on our relationships, and in our communities, our children can be seen and celebrated for who they truly are.

So my question to you is, Are you in?

Good. Because that's what the rest of this book is about. In the pages to come, I share my ideas for how I believe we can begin shifting this paradigm right here, right now, one thought, belief, feeling, and action at a time. The ideas to come don't involve us sitting around and waiting for things to change. They don't require anyone else's sign-off or approval. In fact, the only thing they require is a willingness on your part to be curious, look inward, go outside your comfort zone, and show up with as much presence as possible every single day.

Each of the following chapters centers on one big idea for a tangible, doable shift we can make in our lives. When embraced, these shifts—or, as I call them, "Tilts"—will positively alter your day-to-day reality. You will feel better. Your child will feel better. Your family will work better. And as a result, you'll be helping the world move closer to a place where difference is genuinely seen, supported, and accepted.

Though I've presented these Tilts in an order that makes the most sense to me, this doesn't have to be a linear process. You don't have to tackle all the Tilts at once—feel free to jump around and work on things that resonate with what you're experiencing in your world right now. You'll also discover that some concepts show up in more than one Tilt, and that's okay. What we're experiencing, thinking, and feeling as we walk this path overlaps with other aspects of our lives.

In case you're worried about not having time or energy to do one more thing, know that for the most part, these Tilts won't add more to your plate. I promise that what I'm proposing aren't big, overwhelming changes, but rather small tweaks or adjustments with exponentially powerful effects. To make them as practical as possible, I've included several strategies for incorporating each Tilt into your world. I also end each chapter with a *Start Now* challenge—a suggestion for something you can commit to doing immediately.

We are in the best possible position to make this paradigm shift happen—we have the context, the experience, and the most compelling motivation around. All we need to do now is begin and move forward as best we can.

Let's get started.

PART TWO

How Everything Can Change

Tilt 1

Question Everything You Thought You Knew About Parenting

"Everything is an experiment."
—Tibor Kalman

Depending on how you were raised, your personality type, or your relationship with authority, the whole idea of questioning everything might be a big ask. I've been doing it pretty much since I knew how to talk (just ask my parents); with the exception of a few years in college when I got swept up in some peer-pressured shenanigans, I've never done something because "that's what everyone else was doing." But I acknowledge that bucking the norm when it comes to parenting choices makes an awful lot of people very uncomfortable.

To that end, I share with you a favorite quote by author Neale Donald Walsch: "Life begins at the end of your comfort zone." That's a good thing, because parenting a differently wired kid is not about being comfortable. As it turns out, comfortable isn't even an option for most of us. So rather than spin our wheels, we're better off learning how to get comfortable being uncomfortable. And step one of that process? *Question everything.* And when I say "everything," I'm being literal. *Every single aspect* of what we thought we knew about raising kids has to be up for consideration, including all of these:

- **Education:** Most of us have strong ideas about what we want our child's educational path to look like long before we pack their first lunchbox. These ideas are based on things such as our personal values, what we know from our own childhood, and the choices we see friends and family make with their own children, as well as what's available to us in our community. Yet for most differently wired children, some aspect of school is going to look different from what we expected and will need to be rethought, maybe from the ground up.

- **Parenting styles:** Most parents enter into their new role already subscribing to a specific parenting philosophy. We're largely influenced by the way we were raised—some of us looking to emulate our parents' approach and others using that as an example of what *not* to do. Needless to say, not every approach works for every child, especially for one who's wired differently, yet it can be difficult to know when and how to change course.

- **Nutrition:** As a new mom I got caught up in the homemade baby food frenzy, producing tens of batches of mashed broccoli, zucchini, and squash. Six years later, I was sending Asher to school with Lunchables, certain the lunchroom parents were judging my poor nutritional choices. Packaged, preservative-laden food wasn't what I'd hoped for, but the kid needed calories, and back then, Lunchables were the only thing he'd eat. Because of factors such as sensory challenges, inflexibility, intolerances, and allergies, we need to be flexible about our ideals when it comes to our child's diet.

- **Our child's social life:** We all come to parenthood with a host of expectations for what our child's social life will look like, many of which stem from our own emotional baggage we've been collecting since childhood. Add to that societal expectations about rites of youth such as birthday parties, playdates, sleepovers, and proms, and we're constantly getting the message from media, friends, and family about what a child needs to be "normal" and progress. Yet expecting the social life of atypical kids to mirror a typical experience can set ourselves and our children up for disappointment.

- **Personal characteristics and traits:** When Susan Cain published *Quiet: The Power of Introverts in a World That Can't Stop Talking* in 2012, she sparked a movement in which people everywhere, perhaps for the first time, questioned why extroversion as a personality trait is more highly valued than introversion. Her book reminded us of the way parents may inadvertently value certain qualities they believe are important for their child's success without considering whether those characteristics connect with who their child inherently is.

When We Don't Question, We Stay Stuck

Those are just five examples of areas we'll want to get curious about, but in truth, questioning everything is best applied across the board. Because unless and until we honestly examine how we think and feel about *every* aspect of raising our differently wired kids, we'll be subconsciously seeing everything through the default lens of the old, outdated paradigm. That model will become our benchmark for how things *should* look and feel. (And I think we're all in agreement about how *that's* working for us and our kids, right?)

We want to shift our mindset to a questioning one because, unfortunately, the insecurity and fear that accompany our journey aren't going anywhere. As our kids get older, we'll continue to face doubts (from ourselves and others) about the way things "need" to look versus the way things actually are. It's critical that we channel our inner toddler and keep asking those *why* questions about everything, cut out the noise, and get clear on how we actually think about and experience our lives as parents.

What Questioning Everything Brings Us

In his 1992 song "Anthem," musician Leonard Cohen sings the beautiful line "There is a crack, a crack in everything. That's how the light gets in." I adore this line because it's teeming with this sense of *What if?* I mean, just imagine what could happen for our children and our own lives when we let this light... this *possibility*... shine in through the cracks, when we release ourselves from the pressure of fitting our kids into some predefined mold that doesn't reflect who they are. In doing this, we give ourselves permission to be empowered and inspired. We can experience a new kind of freedom and choice, and see our children as people who are creative, resourceful, and whole. We can realize that we're more than capable of meeting our child's needs, no matter what that looks like.

Bottom line: There is no one way this parenting journey has to look for *anyone*, especially for those of us raising children with neurological differences. Start questioning! Embodying a questioning mindset doesn't happen overnight, but it does get easier with practice. Once we begin to unlock our thinking and recognize that true choice exists in every aspect our lives, the shift has already begun.

//////////////////////////// **Embracing the Tilt** ////////////////////////////

Get Out of Limited Thinking

Questioning everything we thought we knew about parenting means coming clean with our beliefs about what our child's life "should" look like. In fact, by the time you're finished reading this, I hope you'll consider eliminating the word "should" from your vocabulary altogether. Because when we start throwing around words such as "should," "has to" ("He has to get into that school"), or "needs to" ("She needs to be able to handle working with a group"), that's a clue that we're operating from a rigid belief system rather than questioning a set of circumstances.

Reflect

How willing am I to question my ideas of what I expected my child's life to look like?

. . .

Where am I regularly coming up against my own parenting expectations not meshing with our current reality?

. . .

How might my beliefs about the way things "should look" be keeping me stuck?

Plainly put, words like those don't jibe with the business of raising differently wired kids. Words like those get us into trouble. They reinforce the idea that things *should* be easier or that our child *should* be able to control himself or that she *shouldn't* get so upset over the littlest of things.

But to eliminate those words, we've got to first consider where and why they might be showing up. I encourage you to take a few moments to reflect and write down any thoughts that come up when you ask the following "should" questions:

- Do I have expectations about how my child should respond when I ask them to do something?
- Do I have expectations about the way my child should behave in certain public situations or environments?
- Do I believe my child should be able to handle challenging situations differently from how they do?
- Do I believe my child must participate in certain activities to become a well-rounded or successful adult?

You can do the same with "needs to," "must," and "has to." Make a list of the things you believe you "have to do" when it comes to raising your child, paying special attention to school, activities, friendships, summer camps, vacations, and birthdays. For example, here are a few of my limiting beliefs about raising Asher (some I've already dealt with, and others keep rearing their ugly heads during stressful moments):

- Before going to college, Asher will need to attend a traditional school again.
- He needs a bigger circle of friends.
- He must handle unmet expectations better, because life is full of them.
- He needs to care about school more.
- He has to do some sort of organized sport.

Do you have *your* list? Great. Now question each assumption one by one by asking yourself, *Is this really true?* To take it one step further, come up with at least one piece of evidence for how each assumption might actually *not* be true. This is a spin on a process developed by author and speaker Byron Katie called The Work, which encourages people to get familiar with and poke holes in their limited thinking.

For instance, take my belief *Before going to college, Asher will need to attend a traditional school again.* This is a thought I wrestle with a lot, because with each passing year of homeschooling I feel like we're getting further away from a "typical" experience. The constant questions I get from friends about what our plans are, how Asher will learn to work in groups, how he'll develop the skills necessary to balance a heavy workload don't help. In fact, this particular belief sometimes keeps me up at night.

But when I step back and ask myself if I'm *certain* he'll need to spend time attending a traditional school before college, I always come up with the same answer: *no way.* In fact, a growing number of students entering college each year haven't spent one day in a traditional education system, and they do just fine. What's more, many colleges, including Asher's dream school, MIT, have a long history of admitting and even embracing homeschooled students. I also know that the experience of college students is very different from that of kids in kindergarten through twelfth grade. And there's no evidence to suggest that traditional schools are the only place for a student to learn how to study, take notes, write papers, and pass exams. I could go on, but you get the point.

My thoughts about Asher needing to return to traditional school keep cropping up because part of me is still stuck in the belief that his education needs to look a certain way. But when I *question* that assumption, along with my outdated beliefs about school, I can experience the freedom of imagining what could be rather than what isn't.

Imagine What Could Be

As someone who describes herself as hating "to be expected to color inside the lines," storyteller Jill Emmelhainz is used to questioning everything. But in trying to figure out how to best support her teen daughter Anna, who struggles with severe anxiety, Jill and her husband took their "what-if" perspective *way* outside the box. Or perhaps more accurately, outside the home. Recognizing that Anna, who was already being homeschooled, thrived when outdoors and in nature, they wondered what might happen if she were fully immersed in nature for an extended period of time. The result was a five-week mother-daughter backpacking trip along the Appalachian Trail, an adventure Jill and Anna have since repeated three times. In the clean air, peace, and stillness of nature, the two hike for miles every day, brave the elements, write poetry, read, and study. But even better, during the weeks that they're immersed in their mountain life, Anna's anxiety symptoms all but disappear.

Thinking outside the box like Jill and imagining *what could be* requires intention. It means consciously setting aside time to explore what an ideal day (or life) in a perfect world would look like for your child. It means meditating on the question *What would I create or do for my child if I knew it would be successful?* When we honestly explore and question every aspect of our child's life—each decision we make as well as what we're telling ourselves about why we're making it—we discover that what's possible is limited only by our own (limited) imagination.

Fill Your Inspiration Bucket

Questioning everything requires bravery, because we're essentially admitting that something in our lives isn't working and accepting that change is necessary. Even when things may not be going well to begin with, shaking things up can be a scary prospect (and we'll talk more about this in "Tilt 5," when we look at parenting from a place of possibility rather than fear).

> **Pro Tip** Do an "Ideal Day" exercise to explore *what could be* by closing your eyes and visualizing your way through an ideal day in the life of both you and your child, from first waking up through bedtime. The more detailed, the better. Then, explore ways to bring even one piece of that vision into your current reality. For instance, if part of your ideal day involves afternoons free of homework battles, get creative and think about ways you could break out of the rut of your routine, change the dynamic with the help of an engaging tutor, or even tell the school your child will be opting out of the kinds of rote assignments that tend to result in meltdowns.

One way to build up those bravery muscles is by taking in inspirational stories of people who are "breaking the rules" and forging their own paths. Watch Sir Ken Robinson's TED Talk "Do Schools Kill Creativity?," in which he shares the story of world-renowned choreographer Gillian Lynne, who discovered her passion for dance after her mother questioned the school's assumption that there was "something wrong with her" and realized her daughter needed to "move to think." Watch the documentary *Life, Animated* and get inspired by the way Ron Suskind and his wife questioned what was possible for their autistic son, Owen, and immersed themselves in Disney animated films to help him reconnect with the world.

When we actively engage in stories that inspire us and commit to regularly asking (and honestly answering) the question *How am I willing to forge my own path in support of my differently wired child?*, we begin to see that what's possible is much greater than we may ever have imagined.

Start Now Make a list of the things you want to question in relation to your child's life, and start getting curious today.

Get Out of Isolation and Connect

"Vulnerability is about showing up and being seen. It's tough to do that when we're terrified about what people might see or think."
—Brené Brown

I'd never worked with a life coach before, but when a professional acquaintance offered to coach me pro bono as part of her certification process, I jumped at the chance. The timing couldn't have been better. I was feeling a bit lost—I'd just finished a big writing project, and my freelance gigs were fizzling out. I excitedly rolled up my sleeves, ready to get clarity about what was next for my career. What I didn't know was that "life coaching" meant that *all* aspects of my life would get some love, including the area where I was most definitely getting the least amount of satisfaction—*my life as a mother*. Focusing only on my career would have been like fretting over what color to paint the walls when the whole house was burning down. But Courtney detected a note of sadness in my voice during a session, so I shared with her how I was feeling. By the end of the call, I had only one homework assignment: *Reach out and get help.* Not for Asher, *but for me.*

Looking back, it's hard to believe I was so clueless about the fact that I needed assistance, but I honestly don't think the idea had even crossed my mind. Perhaps I was so focused on Asher that I'd forgotten I was part of the equation. Or maybe, accustomed to overcoming obstacles with a little determination and moxie, I had subconsciously concluded that asking for help was admitting defeat. Maybe I'd decided I didn't have the time to focus on myself. Whatever the reason, I hung up from that call crystal clear on one thing: I felt deeply alone.

The Cost of Isolation

In email after email I receive from parents, the sense of isolation comes up, perhaps second only to the feeling of being overwhelmed. Intellectually, we know we're not alone, but when we're in the thick of the really hard stuff, not seeing our reality reflected around us, no one genuinely *knowing* our experience, it sure can feel that way. Danielle Myers summed it up perfectly in a piece she wrote for The Mighty website in 2015: "As a special needs parent, I'm in a unique situation. I know others will not intimately know the details of our child's diagnosis or abilities, and this can lead to feelings of isolation. This is only exaggerated by other people's unwillingness to learn."

Perhaps one of the most common reasons why isolation is so pervasive among parents like us is that many people simply don't know how to "be" around difference, a fact we're reminded of anytime someone with a neurotypical child says inappropriate or unhelpful things without realizing the effect of their words. *I bet he'll grow out of it* or *I can't even tell anything's wrong with her* or *He seems normal to me!* Other times they'll mention that they know another child with ADHD or autism or a learning disorder, as if by some special-needs transitive property, they know exactly what our everyday life is like. *My cousin's youngest daughter has autism, and she's doing really well now. My boss has dyslexia, and he's very successful!* Sometimes it's not their words at all but rather their inaction—ignoring obviously difficult moments or not reciprocating offers of childcare or playdates—that sends an equally clear message.

These regular interactions put us in tricky situations, because connecting with others is part of what humans inherently need to do. Even people with fierce streaks of independence long to connect with others on some level. This innate need is something author and vulnerability researcher Brené Brown has explored extensively in her work, noting the harmful consequences for people lacking connection in their lives. In her book *The Gifts of Imperfection* she writes, "A deep sense of love and belonging is an irreducible need of all women, men, and children. We are biologically, cognitively, physically, and spiritually wired to love, to be loved, and to belong. When those needs are not met, we don't function as we were meant to. We break. We fall apart. We numb. We ache. We hurt others. We get sick."

When the people in our world—our friends, our parenting peers, our own parents, our extended family—don't understand or relate to what we're dealing with, many of us simply withdraw. We censor ourselves, choosing not to talk about how hard it is avoid feeling disconnected when others don't get it. Many of us would rather give the appearance of being in the "club," even if on the inside we're slipping into self-imposed solitary confinement.

Despite feeling that we're alone in what we're experiencing, in reality, we are far from it. Parents like us exist in every community on the planet. We're not outliers, just as our kids aren't aberrations. And though our children's unique wiring may present differently, as a community we're more alike than we are different.

In his powerful book about living with exceptional children, *Far from the Tree*, Andrew Solomon writes about the ties that bind us all: "Having always imagined myself in a fairly slim minority, I suddenly saw that I was in a vast company. Difference unites us. While each of these experiences can isolate those who are affected, together they compose an aggregate of millions whose struggles connect them profoundly."

The Gifts of Connection

During Asher's last year of preschool, my husband and I regularly found ourselves feeling beaten up and broken. Asher's rages were exhausting, and our emotional reserves were depleted. Once, after

Reflect

How open am I about what's hard in my life right now?

. . .

Where do I find myself censoring, keeping mum, or dropping out of conversations or opportunities because it feels too hard to be in community with others?

. . .

How might our family's life improve as a result of my becoming more engaged and connected?

an especially hairy transition from dinner to bedtime, I numbly called my girlfriend Mardi across the street. When she picked up, I wanted to hear only one thing. "*Please* tell me it's not always going to be this hard." Sensing my despair, she rounded up my friend Alison; within fifteen minutes, they were ringing the doorbell with brownies and a bottle of wine in hand, and enough compassion to lift me out of the hopelessness I was sinking into. By the time they left two hours later, I felt more peaceful, heard, and supported than I had in weeks. I was no longer alone. And I had learned that if I was willing to receive it, I could ask for help.

When it comes to parenting atypical kids, isolation and disconnect won't work in the long run. Not for us, and certainly not for our children. On a micro level, isolation keeps us stranded on our own desert islands of pain and confusion. It can lead us down the path of "parental burnout," a phenomenon family therapist and author Neil Brown says is not uncommon among parents of atypical kids, and one that, if not addressed, can ultimately lead to clinical depression. On a macro level, isolation prevents us from joining with others like us to create a collective voice that can't be ignored.

If things are going to change for us and our children, we are *all* going to have to be a part of it.

Or put another way: Getting out of isolation and genuinely connecting is our only option.

Consider Where You Might Be Isolating Yourself

The first step when making change from within is almost always going to be this right here: reflecting on our personal patterns and experiences. This is a critical step, because meaningful and lasting change can happen only when we're honest with ourselves. Therefore, to get out of seclusion and connect, we've got to first recognize where we may be isolating ourselves, consciously or not. Take a good, hard look at your relationships with friends, family, neighbors, and other parents in your child's orbit and consider the following questions:

- Am I avoiding certain situations or conversations because of who my child is or concerns about how they might behave?
- Am I being inauthentic in the way I show up in my daily life?
- Have I become less engaged in outside interests or more secluded in general as challenges with my differently wired child have increased?
- Do I feel as though most everyone else doesn't (or can't) understand what I'm experiencing and what's hard in my world?

If you answered yes to any of these questions, it's important to recognize that this kind of isolation is a choice, and a harmful one at that, since it feeds our insecurities. Like any self-fulfilling prophecy, isolation begets isolation. Rather than keeping us emotionally "safer," a lack of connection invariably leads to increased anxieties in ourselves and our children, which is the exact opposite of what we need.

Find Your People

When I suggest reaching out and connecting, I don't mean with *every-one*. There are "safe" people to align with and there are "not-so-safe" people. I'll talk about this more in "Tilt 14," where we'll look at letting go of relationships that don't serve your child or your family, but for now, I encourage you to identify the people in your life to whom you've been able to turn in the middle of a crisis. Do you have at least one or two go-to people? People you can text or call with an SOS, whether you're in need of mental, emotional, moral, or physical support? What kind of support do you anticipate needing from these people, both now and in the future?

You don't need a whole team—a few good friends or family members who really get it are enough to keep you from withdrawing or spiraling into full-on isolation. Once you've identified your key people, tell them they're your "lifelines" and that you may reach out to them periodically when you need an empathetic ear, advice, distraction... *whatever.* You might even explicitly tell them what you'll need in those moments so they can be as supportive as possible when the time comes.

And if you're like Kristina, mother of two differently wired teenagers, you might even form your own group of parents who know exactly what you're going through. As Kristina's experienced, there's something incredibly comforting about openly sharing the hard stuff to perhaps the most understanding audience around. She says, "I started a support group by putting up posters and sharing some things online, because none of the moms on the playground are wearing T-shirts that say, 'My kid's having a really crappy time at school... How's yours?'" As a result of Kristina's efforts, she now has a small team of like-minded moms in the trenches with her, sharing resources and lending support to one another.

Before I move on, you may be wondering about the role of your spouse or partner in all of this. If you do have a parenting partner, it's worth noting that, *yes,* this person is part of your inner circle, but it's critical that your support network extend *beyond* this core relationship. Although your partner likely knows better than anyone else what you're experiencing, they've got their own personal stuff going on, too. It's possible they're too deeply enmeshed to be a voice of reason and a source of the kind of steady, nonjudgmental support you need. Instead, encourage your partner to find his or her own people, too.

Plug the Leaks

Back when my coach Courtney helped me realize I needed help, I immediately felt relief. Just knowing reinforcements were on the way was *everything*. In the end, that homework assignment led to my finding a parenting coach who ended up partnering with us for several years, not only helping Derin and me but being a trusted voice of clarity in meetings with school officials. But beyond that, having someone available for processing the really hard stuff reminded us that we weren't alone. I've since connected with and received compassionate help from a number of people, from parent coaches and acupuncturists to trusted confidants and curriculum advisers. The kind of support I need depends on what's happening at any given time, but I never forget that help is always available.

To tap into that help, we must figure out where we need it in the first place. Imagine our parenting journey as if we're floating in a life raft, smoothly drifting when seas are calm and holding on for dear life when the big waves hit. Whatever the weather, we've got to spot the leaks, even the small ones losing air so slowly we may not realize how dire things are until we're taking on serious water. Because once we find those breaches, we can patch them before they get any bigger.

Where are your leaks? Where would you benefit from specific support in your parenting life? Consider where and how you can get the help you need—a parenting coach, a therapist, a couples counselor,

> **Pro Tip** Make a list of the areas where you would love some extra support and make a commitment to identify help.

and/or online communities dedicated to supporting parents like you. Once you start looking, you'll find that help really is everywhere.

Be a Resource for Others

Long before I founded TiLT Parenting, I would regularly receive emails from friends and acquaintances that sounded something like this:

> My friend [brother/sister/cousin/colleague] has just discovered their child is [insert diagnosis here], and they are really struggling [with school/at home/with their siblings/all of the above]. They have no idea what to do, but they know they need help. Can I put them in touch with you? They are at their wits' end and don't know where to turn.

To emails like these, I would always respond, *Of course.* Because I know how it feels to not know where to turn, whom to call, or even where to begin. I know that a simple phone conversation or email exchange with a parent further down the road can mean the difference between despondence and hope. Even when the other person isn't ready to hear what we have to say—I've had long conversations with parents who brushed off much of what I shared because, in that moment, their need to stay in denial won out—our willingness to generously share our experience is an important thing. It's something I believe every parent navigating this path needs and deserves.

My friend Tia, a voracious researcher who's vetted every possible resource in supporting her daughter's dysgraphia, dyslexia, dyscalculia, and auditory processing disorder, has become known at her daughter's school as a resource for new families who are feeling overwhelmed, a role she embraces because she knows how important that connection is. In addition to sharing practical insights, Tia tries to instill confidence in other parents, encouraging them to trust their instincts as they begin this journey.

And being a resource to others truly matters, perhaps more than we'll ever know. As one mother of a nineteen-year-old 2e boy with ADHD and Asperger's shared with me, it was another parent who first recognized what a wreck she was when she was initially digesting her son's diagnosis. "This woman's older son had been diagnosed with ADHD, and she came up to me and told me about what she went through and said, 'You know, it's a grieving process, but you'll get through it.' And she was right. But it really helped to have one person reach out and say, 'I see you, I understand what you're going through, and it's going to be okay.'"

As important as it is that we reach out and connect when we're going through our own difficult periods, it's equally important for us to be willing to be a resource for other parents who are just beginning their own journeys (only when we're ready, of course). So make yourself available for virtual and live conversations with these parents when they're referred to you. Being that powerful point of contact at a pivotal time can make all the difference for them. The added bonus? You'll benefit from that connection, too.

Be Proactive About Connection

I'm a self-professed self-care junkie, and although I'll get into that more in "Tilt 10," for now, I want to encourage you to be proactive about connecting with people and staying engaged in the world around you for your social and emotional well-being. This might be as simple as picking up the phone on a rough night and calling a neighbor like I did. Or making a regular plan to meet up with a friend to walk the dogs or have a cup of coffee, or even have a weekly Skype check-in with a relative across the country. Again, your support circle doesn't need to be extensive—one to a handful of people you can safely share with and who know how to be there for you is all it takes.

> **Start Now** Consciously connect with one person, online community, or social media group for the purposes of getting out of isolation and building up your support network.

But don't leave this to chance or wait until you're in the depths of despair to reach out and connect. Get something in place now and make a regular "date" for connecting.

And a quick note about the value of virtual communities—for all the potential downsides of Facebook, the platform is awash with groups and communities of like-minded people facing the same challenges and questions as we are. Online communities have been a key part of Mary's support system. The mother of three differently wired children told me, "I have a fantastic Listserv that I found a few years ago with wonderful, smart, people—supportive people. So luckily I've been able to get support through them."

Seeking out supportive, generous, and safe groups for sharing, advice, and resources is something I recommend *all* parents of differently wired kids do. Find a tribe or two that feels like a match and lean in to the help and community that are available.

Let Go of What Others Think

"Care about what other people think and you will always be their prisoner."
—Lao-tzu

Asher and I recently read *To Kill a Mockingbird* for school, and the curriculum I used prompted an in-depth conversation about self-identity. When I asked Asher how his self-identity has been shaped by the way others perceive him, he matter-of-factly replied, "That's not a part of my self-identity at all." Self-confident perhaps to a fault, Asher explained that he didn't concern himself with what others thought, because he likes himself quite a lot, thank you very much.

Wow—to have that kind of sense of self. I can't imagine how different my teen years would have been had I not been concerned about what others thought of me, how I looked, what I did. *Who am I kidding?* If I didn't care about what others thought of me, my entire parenting journey with Asher would be a completely different experience. And by different, I mean *better*. Because worrying about what others are thinking—about who my child is, what he does, or how he behaves, and, consequently, what kind of parent I am—has taken up *a lot* of my time and energy.

And I know I'm not alone in this. In a culture of rampant parental judging about everything from a child's diet and amount of screen time to academic prowess or athletic or creative gifts, it's all too easy to get caught up in what others think. As one parent of a teen with learning disabilities confessed to me via email, "I was too hard on my child because I was embarrassed about things when he was young. I tried to hang out with parents with multiple kids and European parents, because both are so much more mellow than American moms, but I know I was still always too self-conscious about his behavior."

Of course there are always exceptions, but most of us look to others for validation and judge our success by measuring how we stack up against everyone else.

Why Do We Care?

Although the idea of Asher concerning himself with what other people think of him is a foreign one, for most people, it's not unusual at all. Just as people intuitively search for connection and community, most are also hardwired to crave *acceptance*. Being accepted helps us feel secure. Acceptance boosts our self-esteem. It provides a sense of belonging. At the same time, seeking acceptance and belonging has the potential to lead us down a path of bad decisions and unhelpful thinking. In fact, when we operate from this other-focused place, pretty much everyone loses. Because when we're considering the reaction and thoughts of others on how we parent, we

- don't advocate as loudly as we could,
- don't parent from a place of true authenticity,
- inadvertently tell our child they're not okay,
- parent with our ego instead of our heart, and
- make questionable parenting decisions.

In an article for *Psychology Today*, behavior expert Dr. Raj Raghunathan writes that most people overestimate how much (and how badly) others think about them. He notes that a small amount of concern can motivate people to behave more appropriately, but that when that concern takes up too big a space in our minds, the consequences can be much less beneficial. As Dr. Raghunathan writes, "Constantly wondering whether others like us enough can evoke anxiety, leading to neediness and insecurity, which in turn drive others away from us. This can propel a vicious cycle, resulting ultimately in loss of self-respect and social alienation."

Why Letting Go Is Hard

Many years ago, I was talking with an intuitive friend—the kind of person who nails exactly what you're thinking before you've even uttered a word. After spending very little time together, she zeroed in on my worry about the perceptions of others, suggesting that perhaps letting go was the big life lesson I was supposed to learn through Asher. I didn't disagree, and her words stayed with me as I reflected on the way my preoccupation with others was negatively affecting my relationship with my son. From that moment on, I committed to checking myself when talking with others about how challenging Asher was. While I firmly believe in being real and open about what's hard, I realized I was overexplaining out of a desire to convince people that Asher wasn't just normal challenging, but *challenging* challenging. It was like a compulsion, my need for other people to truly "get it." Because then I could control how they perceived me (or so I thought). In fact, maybe instead of thinking I was a lousy parent, they would conclude I was doing a stellar job, all things considered.

Caring too much about what other people think of my parenting has led me to do things I'm not proud of. Here are just a few examples of things I've done in the name of saving face:

- conspiratorially rolled my eyes about Asher's behavior while looking at another parent so they'd know I related to whatever they were thinking (aka I "sided" with them)
- went into too much detail about a parenting challenge to ensure another parent understood my plight and would therefore see

my parenting in context (aka thrown my child under the bus to make myself look better)

- reprimanded Asher in public because I knew that's what others would expect, even though it wasn't even remotely helpful to Asher in that moment (aka put other people's needs before my child's)

I could go on, but I'm sure you get the point. Rather than being the conscious parent I wanted to be, I had become a ridiculously *self-conscious* parent. And differently wired children deserve so much more. When we parent from a place of insecurity and distance ourselves from who our child is in an effort to make ourselves feel more comfortable, we're joining in a chorus of voices pointing out everything that's wrong with being atypical. We're placing acceptance of ourselves above fighting for acceptance of who our children are. So, caring about what people think? It needs to stop.

The Freedom to Be

I'll confess—this is still a hard one for me. Whenever someone I've just met asks me where Asher goes to school, I'm hyperaware of how my four-word reply—"I actually homeschool him"—is received. I can pick up on the smallest signs of disapproval—a flicker in their eye or a too-long pause before replying—and find hidden meanings in their questions as they try to determine what kind of radical parent I am. For me, not being triggered by others is a work in progress. But the way I see it, it's necessary work to take on.

The goal here is to stand in our truth. To show up authentically every day and parent with confidence and conviction. We want to be the same parent during a public meltdown at Cold Stone Creamery as we are in the privacy of our own home. Rather than apologizing for who our child is, we want there to be no doubt that we've got our child's back, knowing that that not only feels better for everyone involved, but models the kind of respect and acceptance that are necessary for us to shift the paradigm forward.

I don't know about you, but I'm committed to mastering this lesson . . . to really and truly letting it all go. If you are ever overly conscious of how others are perceiving you and/or your child, I invite you to join me in this mission. I guarantee that if you do, you will feel so much better.

/////////////////////////// **Embracing the Tilt** ///////////////////////////

Notice Where You're Caring

Parenting coach Margaret Webb and her husband regularly bring their fourteen-year-old autistic son with them when they go out to dinner—a sort of "adapted date night." They also bring their son's electronics along so he can be engaged while Margaret and her husband talk. Margaret admits she used to get upset about others' judgy looks, but she finally realized she was spending too much energy on strangers, and that it wasn't serving her or her family. Though the stares haven't stopped, Margaret's reaction to them has. "We get looks all the time from people, but we're so clear on why we're there and what we're doing that it doesn't matter. But if I give my time and energy to worrying about what those other people think of me as a parent or my child or of how we operate our family, it's such a waste. They don't know that that's an important part of my husband and I being a team to help our son. So it helps me to think, *Wait, am I giving this person or their comment or their judgment a lot of time and energy that could be better spent just taking care of myself [and] taking care of my child?*"

What kinds of judgments or comments or looks are a trigger for you? Begin noticing how sensitive you are to the thoughts and judgments of others (perceived or real) about the way you parent, the choices you make, the way you handle challenges, and the way your

Reflect

How concerned am I about what others think about my parenting style or choices?

. . .

How do I suffer when I prioritize others' thoughts and opinions over what I think, feel, or know to be true?

. . .

How is my child affected when I prioritize others' thoughts and opinions over what I think, feel, or know to be true?

child behaves, and explore how they affect you. A simple way to cut to the chase is by honestly answering this little question: How much meaning are you giving others' beliefs about your parenting?

Go ahead . . . Take a moment right now and answer that question. If I had answered this honestly five years ago, I could have filled up a page detailing all the different ways I was failing miserably as a mom. Until I got honest about that, I couldn't start changing the story in my head.

Make Sure Your Ego Isn't Running the Show

Do you ever feel compelled to overexplain in an attempt to control how another perceives you and your child? If so, make a commitment to navigate difficult or uncomfortable situations in new, more positive ways in the future. For example, when a parent once told me she didn't believe in Asher's diagnoses and implied I was overreacting by choosing to homeschool him, I made it my business to detail exactly what a train wreck school had been for him in an attempt to secure her "approval," when I wish I'd simply ignored her comment. That's what I do today when the same sort of thing comes up.

Come up with standard language for handling these scenarios moving forward. Now when people question our choice to homeschool, my default response is "Asher isn't a kid who thrives in traditional school. Homeschooling is working really well for our family." Full stop. No need for a lowdown on our whole educational journey. No explanation necessary. Boom.

One last thing before I move on. Perhaps you're wondering how to recognize when your behavior or emotions are being influenced by other people. Well, the answer is simple: We *feel* it. It's that uncomfortable niggle in our gut. Our inner voice may be telling us to stop talking already while the words keep pouring out. We might feel heavy after such an interaction, a pang of guilt, a flush of regret. Whatever the sensation, *we know it*. The key is to call ourselves out on it, give ourselves a pass (beating oneself up doesn't really help), and commit to doing better the next time. (And as we all know, there will always be a next time.)

Check Yourself

While we're noticing how our actions are influenced by others judging us, we have a great opportunity to consider where we might be doing the same thing ourselves. A recent survey by the *Today* show found that nearly 90 percent of moms judge other moms for a variety of parenting choices, from breastfeeding, a child's diet, and their weight to co-sleeping, screen time, and how "bratty" a child is.

First of all, we all do this. Moms, dads . . . all of us. But it's important to learn how to recognize when we're judging, and actively work to stop doing it by reminding ourselves that *we don't know the whole story*. Just as we don't want others to assume they know what's best for our family, we can't know why others make the choices they make. And really, it's none of our business. The added bonus? Once we put the brakes on our own judging nature, we'll find that others' judgments of us won't affect us the same way anymore. We'll know intuitively that it's not us—it's them.

Train Your Friends

Often a "judger" isn't even aware that they're judging. Another person may not realize that sharing their belief or something they're musing over might land in the wrong way with us. But rather than stew on another's insensitive words, consider it an opportunity for compassionate education. In other words, be willing to call people out, because they may not realize what they're saying. Let them know how and why their comment isn't helpful (as well as explaining what *would* be helpful).

For example, a friend used to regularly remark on Asher's behavior by saying things like *He seems totally fine to me* or *He's just being a boy* or *ALL boys are rambunctious!* Although I knew this friend was trying to normalize our experience, it still felt like a negative judgment—as though she was saying that I was overreacting, there wasn't anything different about Asher, and things would be fine and I should relax. I wanted to let the comments go, but because they had come from a close friend, I felt I had to address them. So I did, by letting my friend know how I interpreted his words and politely asking him to refrain from saying similar things in the future. He totally got it, and that was the end of that. Just like our kids, when people know better, they do better.

Proactively Plan for Public Challenges

The deer-in-the-headlights thing? It's *not* a good look. And when we're caught off guard when our kid is engaging in "inappropriate behavior" or having a massive meltdown in public, we may let others' perceptions influence us.

These are situations in which a little planning goes a long way. For instance, if I had planned properly, I would have handled it *much* better after Asher lost his cool at the MythBusters event when he wasn't called up onstage. (Two words: "lesson learned.")

To plan ahead, make a list of situations that have historically been challenging for your child (and likely will be again), and come up with a plan for how you'll respond when they happen. My plan when Asher was younger and had a public tantrum was always the same: Get him somewhere safe and keep myself calm by reading. (Yes, that *was* me standing outside a silver hatchback in the Bellevue Square mall parking lot in 2010 reading a magazine while an angry boy raged inside the car.)

Ever since her 2e son was young, Jill has recognized the importance of quick exits in tough moments, no matter where they are or what others might think. "There are many times I've had to take him out of McDonald's PlayPlace in a football hold with no shoes, socks, or coat on in the middle of winter. I had to put a bubble around us and say, 'I need to do what is best for my child in this moment regardless of what's going on around us. I cannot take in their judgment. I just have to do what's best for him.'"

The plan for Mary's two teen daughters is simple and straightforward. "It basically involves me saying, 'Here are the keys to the car. Go sit in the car and turn the air conditioner on and I'll be there in a few minutes.' Both of the girls know that they're always able to sit in the car no matter what we're doing. Everybody knows there's a plan.... They don't have to stay if they can't do it anymore."

Maybe for you, leaving playdates is a bear, or school drop-offs regularly bring anxious tears, or restaurant showdowns have become the norm. Or maybe it's not your child's actions at all but rather

> **Start Now** Commit to putting your child's emotional and physical needs above your own need to manage or protect your reputation, especially in challenging public situations, and develop language or a plan for one recurring situation so that the next time it happens, you'll know exactly how to respond.

obtrusive questions from strangers that cause you to stumble. If that's the case, make a list of those questions and figure out how you want to reply with boldness and integrity. Because when we have a plan, we can be confident. And when we're confident? Well, we just won't care so much about what other people think. It's a win-win.

Stop Fighting Who Your Child Is and Lean In

"When you argue with reality, you lose, but only 100 percent of the time."
—Byron Katie

During those first rocky months of homeschooling, I was getting schooled in a few subjects of my own. In fact, you could say I was enrolled in a full-immersion course about learning how to surrender to who Asher is, complete with pop quizzes and assignments in the form of daily meltdowns and unpredictable reactions to seemingly random things. It's fair to say that I flunked this course in the first semester. But eventually, the material began to make sense. I did all my homework and even hired a few tutors, and over time realized that when I trusted in my knowledge of the material, I could actually perform quite well in the class known as Asher 101: The Homeschool Years. I discovered that on rough days, sometimes it was worth pushing through—to stay calm, ooze patience and nonchalance, and hold steady in striving for the goals of the day. Other times it was better to throw all the "have-to"s and "should"s out the window. Learning to read the room and knowing when to pivot was my most valuable takeaway.

Some days just started off badly, like the day I made the mistake during our morning meeting of bringing up Asher's loss of screen time because of an incident the night before. Things fell apart immediately.

It was time to pivot: I left the room and told Asher we'd resume school when he was calm and respectful.

A few origamis later (including a stellar swordfish), Asher returned to school, but the tone of our meeting quickly deteriorated once again. Pivot 2: I asked him to take some more time to get calm, which he did, finally returning to the classroom another thirty minutes later. Pivot 3: I suggested we skip the "screen-time" conversation and begin school, since it was already noon and we had to leave for therapy by two. I made him lunch and we did what we could—some writing, a little math, and a little reading. But I had planned for him to accomplish more that day, so I told him we'd finish school after therapy. Well, *that* news didn't go over so well. (And judging from the expression on his therapist's face when I retrieved him, therapy didn't go so well, either.)

On the walk from the therapist's office to our bus stop, we got caught in what turned out to be a major storm—wind gusts of sixty miles an hour, hail, ice-cold rain, thunder, lightning . . . the works. Pivot 4: I gave up. We were *not* having a good day. And no amount of forcing my agenda was going to change that. So I announced we were finished with school for the day. The way I saw it, the only option at that point was warm drinks and pajamas.

As soon as I said the words "hot chocolate," Asher perked up. Twenty minutes later, we were running through a torrent of wind and rain from the bus stop to our apartment, laughing hysterically, united in our quest to get home despite the ridiculous weather. We peeled off our wet clothes when we walked in the door, and Asher changed into fleece PJs while I heated up milk for hot chocolate. For the rest of the day, Asher was happy and calm, enthusiastically sharing his *Minecraft* creations and thanking me for complimenting him on his structure. I let out a sigh—relieved the conflict was over and secure in knowing we could catch up on our schoolwork the next day (and accepting that maybe we wouldn't). If I had forged ahead with my own agenda and hadn't adapted to what Asher needed in the moment—if I hadn't pivoted—I would have remained in a losing battle with reality. It's only through leaning in to *what is* that the real learning can begin, for both child *and* parent.

Fighting What Is

Whitney, mother of a differently wired daughter, remembers the moment she made the leap from fighting who her daughter is to leaning in. It happened during the first meeting about her daughter's IEP. "After hearing the summaries from my husband and me, my daughter's teacher, and each of the evaluators, the director of the meeting turned to us and said in the kindest, most supportive voice possible, 'You know, she's not a normal kid.' And I realized she was right. It was genuinely life-changing to embrace the idea that yes, my daughter *isn't* 'normal,' and that doesn't mean she's bad; it just means she's different and that she's going to need different things from us. I had been beating myself up for years about how difficult parenting my daughter felt to me, and to have someone else validate that just cracked me open in the best way."

Fighting with reality about who our children are is undeniably one of the biggest hurdles parents raising atypical kids face. Sometimes we're doing this even as we're convinced we've come to a place of acceptance, like when I get frustrated if Asher interrupts me because he just thought of something he *has* to share that instant. I know this is his ADHD. It's not a choice. Yet my response is often to not-so-gently cut him off and tell him to wait until I'm finished. I'm arguing with *what is* instead of leaning in to *who he is*. Do I have to love being interrupted? Um, no. But Asher deserves to be reminded *with patience* about how to work toward "holding that thought" and managing the urge to blurt.

When we're fighting who our child is, we can't implicitly support them. We ignore their needs, neglecting to buy them that weighted blanket for their bed or bring earphones for them to the movie theater. We may regularly become frustrated with their perfectionism. We reprimand them for being who they are.

Some of us are dealing with feelings of self-blame or the belief that our child's wiring is "our fault." True story: I used to believe that if I'd done a better job of mothering Asher when he was a baby, then maybe he would be neurotypical. I also wondered if all the Pitocin I had in my system during labor triggered his ADHD. Thoughts like these are thinly veiled regret, which is just another way of not accepting who our child is. Anytime we wish our child were "normal," we are not only fighting reality, but contributing to that outdated paradigm by making difference a "bad thing." As autism activist Jim Sinclair once said, "When parents say, 'I wish my child did not have autism,' what they're really saying is, 'I wish the autistic child I have did not exist and I had a different (nonautistic) child instead.' Read that again. This is what we hear when you mourn over our existence. This is what we hear when you pray for a cure."

When We Lean In

Leaning in looks different for each of us, but at its core it's about surrender. That's what one mother of a boy on the spectrum did the summer between second and third grade. As she explained to me, "I decided I was going to accept him one hundred percent for who he was and extend myself as far as I had to in order to adjust for what he needed. It was hard because I had another child to take into account, but as much as was possible, we cleared the schedule that summer and I just focused on leaning in to his interests. And I do think it helped."

My friend Cami used to think she could make things happen for her kids—that she could make them be who they needed to be—until her atypical son came into the world and set her straight. "Because my daughter was such a well-behaved, thoughtful child, I kind of thought I was rocking it," Cami said. "And then my son came along and made it abundantly clear to me that I was a fool and I couldn't control anything. That was probably one of the hardest things—kind of having to regroup and really think through strategies for helping him and then also allowing him to be different than maybe I expected him to be."

When we stop fighting and surrender to who our child is, everything suddenly begins to get easier. Our child gets to be who they are without receiving the message that they're doing it wrong or that they're annoying or frustrating. Over time, they feel more confident in who they are and may begin recognizing their personal strengths while feeling inspired to work on areas of weakness as they grow.

Dr. Ellen Braaten, coauthor of *Bright Kids Who Can't Keep Up*, is an expert in processing speed disorder, a neurodifference that has no "cure," because slow processing speed can't actually be sped up. When I asked her how parents can support their kids with slow processing speed, she walked me through her "three A's of processing speed": Accept, Accommodate, and Advocate. See that first one? *Accept*. Lean in. Ellen says that embracing that one piece alone can change everything for a child. For instance, when we accept that our child needs a full ten minutes to put on their shoes and get out the door, not only do *we* feel calmer during those transitions, but our children don't feel our frustrated energy. And our parent-child dynamic can remain positive and respectful.

////////////////////////// **Embracing the Tilt** //////////////////////////

Let Yourself Mourn

Even the most pragmatic of us likely have a vision of what our child's life will look like—soccer tournaments, piano or dance recitals, debate team, family volunteer vacations, honor roll, homecoming dances. I've no doubt *all* parents do this, and my hunch is that a majority realize at some point that things are actually going to look quite different from

Reflect

What aspects of who my child is am I not fully accepting?

· · ·

What implicit biases might I have with regard to neurodiversity?

· · ·

In what ways, if any, am I secretly hoping an issue/trait/aspect of who my child is will eventually "go away" or that he or she will ultimately become "normal"?

what they thought. Those of us with atypical kids often feel as if some options are simply closed off to us because of who our children are.

Some might say "mourn" is too strong a word when referring to letting go of this vision, but I think it fits. It's important that we allow ourselves time and space for some guilt-free grieving for the image we had of what our life would be like in contrast with how it actually is; we need to be prepared for associated sadness to pop up as new situations arise. Just last week, I sat in a café working and caught myself staring out the window at a group of kids Ash's age running around a square playing tag after school. It reminded me of my own childhood playing kick the can, climbing trees, and skateboarding up and down the neighbors' driveways. And then I felt that familiar pang of sadness as I (once again) remembered that this isn't what Asher's childhood looks like, and it never will. But rather than push that sadness away, I acknowledged it, let myself feel it, and moved on.

Michelle, mother of a differently wired eight-year-old, has allowed herself to mourn who her child isn't even as she grows to appreciate who he is. She described to me one painful situation where her son asked to leave a party early because he wasn't connecting with the other kids, but when he saw a fountain across the street (fountains were his area of interest at the time), he lit up and was happy. "I'm all about people and connections. . . . I mean, for me that's the most important thing in life. And I just felt so sad that an inanimate object could mean that much to him. But I had to realize that that's me and that's not everybody. We had a long drive home, and I cried the whole way. For some reason it just really hit me that day."

Where do you experience sadness about the way your child is wired? What vision did you have about what life for your son or daughter would look like that now feels off course? What dreams for the way their life would unfold do you want to acknowledge and ultimately release? There's no shame in feeling sadness or mourning what isn't. In fact, by giving it a voice and letting it know we see it, our sadness loses its hold over us and we're freer to lean in.

Recognize When You're Fighting Reality

Angela Pruess, a parenting coach and mother of an atypical daughter, learned early that going the "controlling route" wasn't going to fly, because her daughter had strong convictions, determination, and a powerful sense of personal integrity. "When I was able to separate my 'vision' for who I thought my child would be from who she actually was at her core, I began to not only recognize these traits but also to nurture and appreciate them. I started to view her as her own unique individual, on her own separate journey, as opposed to an extension of myself, which opened the door to all sorts of new possibilities, including working together instead of against each other."

To argue against reality is normal and human, so we want to recognize the areas where we consistently do that. Where are your blinders? Where are you in a place of nonacceptance? One way to identify these areas is to keep an ear out for those universal fighting-reality cues—beginning any sentence with the two words "She [or he] shouldn't," followed by a behavior, trait, or characteristic. The opposite works, too: "She [or he] should be," followed by a behavior, trait, or characteristic.

For instance, Derin used to say things such as "He shouldn't get so angry when it's time to stop playing that game" or "If I tell him to stop doing something, he should stop doing it." To which my response was always the same. "Yes, but he *is* getting angry" or "But he's *not* stopping it." All the evidence pointed to the fact that the opposite of Derin's "should" was actually true; hence the arguing-with-reality thing. Here's another example: I used to hate using point systems as part of Asher's positive behavior reinforcement plan, because I was concerned they would result in his becoming extrinsically rather than intrinsically motivated. Asher's therapist said, "I completely understand, but this is what we know works for kids like Asher. This is the way to get negative behavior to stop." Once again, I was arguing with reality.

Get to know your hot-button issues—those things we'd see trending on your Twitter feed with the hashtag #arguingwithreality. We need to name it to tame it. Or in this case, reframe it.

Reframe What Is

In his pioneering book *Unconditional Parenting*, author and child development expert Alfie Kohn presses us to consider the value many parents place on compliance rather than allowing children to express who they are. He writes, "I realized that this is what many people in our society seem to want most from children: not that they are caring or creative or curious, but simply that they are well behaved."

Kohn's book isn't explicitly for parents raising neurologically diverse kids, but when I first read it, something deep within me switched, and I began to question the behaviors Derin and I were routinely "correcting." I realized we were trying to get Asher to behave in a way we deemed appropriate rather than one that respected him as a person. For instance, *Can you please look at me so I know you're listening?* Derin and I were stuck in our thinking. We were parenting the child we thought we had rather than the child we did have. Forcing Asher to look someone in the eye to "show he's listening" actually requires so much focus that he can't actually pay attention to anything else, least of all what we're saying.

We want to take note of the things our child does that regularly get under our skin (interrupting, fidgeting, perpetually dillydallying, overreacting, talking too loudly) and reframe them not as conscious choices, but rather the manifestation of who our child inherently is. When we can reframe in this way, we can grow to accept who they are. We stop expecting them to conform to arbitrary societal norms that don't matter in the big scheme of things. After all, in some cultures, looking someone in the eye when they're speaking is considered disrespectful.

When we reframe what is, our child can spend less time in "defense mode" and more time feeling secure about who they are. As Alfie Kohn wrote, "What counts is not just that we believe we love them unconditionally, but that *they feel* loved in that way." Reframing what we expected to *what is* promotes this experience.

Actively Appreciate

When I interviewed child development expert Dr. Robyn Silverman for my podcast, we talked about the way we parents often dwell on what's hard or not working when telling another person about our child for the first time. Many of us begin by talking about our child's diagnosis, as if that label defines who they are as a person. *My child has an anxiety disorder. My child has some pretty severe visual processing issues. My child can be incredibly explosive.*

The problem is that when we do this, we're burying the lede. Imagine a news story about Scott Kelly that focused on what a bad student he was, how he was highly inattentive and easily distracted, and that he graduated in the bottom half of his high school class, getting

> **Pro Tip** Develop a sound bite that reframes the way you introduce your child, emphasizing his or her strengths.

to the good stuff—*Oh, and he's also an astronaut who holds the American record for the longest space mission*—only in the last paragraph, when everyone has already skipped ahead to the next story.

This is what we do when we talk about deficits first. We're emphasizing a deficits-based way of seeing the world, which not only affects how others perceive our child, but also prevents us from truly seeing, appreciating, and nurturing our child's strengths. Says Dr. Robyn, "You want to first talk about your child in terms of their strengths, even as they're working on their challenges. We want to start with the positive. *My child, he is so incredibly curious. He has an explorer's brain, and when he is out and about in the world, he is the first to find things—the first to help you find something. He just has an eye for it. It is amazing.*"

> **Start Now** Identify one habit or behavior tied to your child's wiring that you find particularly grating or annoying, and commit to authentically accepting it and reacting accordingly (which may mean not reacting at all).

Our goal? To actively recognize and appreciate our child's unique wiring, and to commit to seeing the extraordinary gifts that make them who they're meant to be in the world.

Parent from a Place of Possibility Instead of Fear

"Love is what we were born with. Fear is what we learned here."
—Marianne Williamson

I think it's time we talk about fear, don't you? We've touched upon it here and there, but let's go all in. Because parenting children from a place of fear—with fear as our default even when we may not realize it—is a surefire way to ensure sameness and stuckness. And to truly tilt things—for our kids, for our families, and for society—letting fear run the show just isn't going to cut it.

In his bestselling book *Conversations with God*, Neale Donald Walsch writes, "All human actions are motivated at their deepest level by one of two emotions—fear or love. In truth there are only two emotions—only two words in the language of the soul. . . . Fear wraps our bodies in clothing, love allows us to stand naked. Fear clings to and clutches all that we have, love gives all that we have away. Fear holds close, love holds dear. Fear grasps, love lets go. Fear rankles, love soothes. Fear attacks, love amends."

I read those words more than twenty years ago, and I've never forgotten them. Back then, I felt compelled to test Walsch's theory, to pick apart every big and little choice to see if his statement held up. And it absolutely did. Fear-based decisions never quite gave me the result I was looking for, whereas choosing love and possibility, scary as it may have been, always benefited me in some meaningful way.

Since then, I've felt a personal responsibility to question my motivation anytime I've faced a decision, from the biggies such as getting married, quitting a job, moving across the country, and having a child, to the smaller ones, like accepting a coffee invite or taking on a freelance project. Over the years, I've learned how to listen to my gut and tune in to the messages coming from my body and brain. And Neale Donald Walsch's sentiment continues to hold true.

Yet, raising a differently wired child brought my habit of choosing from a place of love to a screeching halt. With each passing year, I felt increasingly limited by our options and by the power of fear—of what would happen if we chose the wrong school or got the wrong diagnosis, of the million "what-ifs" that plagued me each night. I learned what many parents raising unique kids know so well—living a life driven by fear is cumbersome and painful. Yet it's the modus operandi for plenty of us. Fear is a recurring theme in the hundreds of emails I get from parents who are feeling stuck and overwhelmed.

- "We're worried she won't be able to function independently. She has a really hard time following through on just about everything."
- "I know that I'm worrying about a future that doesn't exist yet, but I can't help it."
- "I am very concerned about the new school year and how to talk to him about the school day."
- "I love my daughter more than is humanly possible, and I'm just so scared of the unknown."

I totally get it. Because when it comes to fear and our children, the struggle is real. I mean, there is *so much* to be afraid of:

- Am I screwing up my child?
- Will he ever be able to [insert verb here]?
- Am I doing enough to help him/her?

- How will I afford to pay for the tutor/therapist/services?
- What happens if I lose my job and can't afford private school?
- What will happen if my partner and I don't make it?
- Will my child ever graduate high school? Attend college? Get and hold down a job?
- What will happen when our child becomes an adult?
- Will my child ever fit in?
- Will things always be hard?

We can find ourselves worrying about just about anything, most often some form of future unknowns. As one parent wrote to me, "The worries I have about his future and what kind of an adult he's going to be are really interfering with the *now*, and causing a lot of anxiety. Actually, his anxiety seems to be improving, but mine isn't. Things are good right now, but I'm walking on eggshells for it to be bad again, because it seems the roller coaster always goes back down the hill."

Parents who don't know where to turn or what comes next can be especially plagued by worry over how their child's story will unfold. Yet such worry does zero good. Choosing fear equates our child with their diagnosis, rather than seeing them as creative beings who are here to shake up the world in their own magnificent way. Choosing fear is the very thing that keeps us stuck. Choosing fear creates a culture of apprehension and anxiety in our families, and affects the way our children, many of whom are already highly sensitive and anxious, feel about themselves. Operating from fear leads to more limited thinking and fearful energy, which both we and our child will feel, and less chance of our child's uncovering and experiencing their extraordinary possibilities. It's the epitome of a self-fulfilling prophecy.

The Power of Possibility

While Neale Donald Walsch talks about love being on the other side of fear, I'd like to introduce an alternative to fear, a word I believe is transformational for parents who feel limited in their ability to help their children thrive. And that word is "possibility."

Emily Dickinson wrote about the limitless nature of being a poet in her sweet, lovely poem "I Dwell in Possibility," but those four words—"I dwell in possibility"—can also be incredibly powerful anytime we say them, own them, and meditate on the meaning behind them. Because when we dwell in possibility, there are no limits. When we dwell in possibility instead of fear, we aren't stuck . . . we're curious about what could be.

Author and life coach Allison Carmen shares a similar sentiment in her book *The Gift of Maybe: Finding Hope and Possibility in Uncertain Times*. In it, she writes about how weaving the word "maybe" into her everyday vernacular helped her see the infinite ways in which every situation *could* unfold. As she explained to me when I interviewed her for my podcast, "Whatever I was thinking, whatever I was projecting, whatever I was worried about, it might unfold differently. It sounds so simple, but this idea of *maybe* takes you from a place where you're so positive life's *not* going to work out to a place where you realize *maybe* things could get better. *Maybe* there's more. *Maybe* I don't know the answer. *Maybe* everything is still okay."

Shortly after we moved to the Netherlands, Asher began working with Kate Berger, an American psychologist living in Amsterdam who helps expat kids adapt to their new lives. I met with Kate a few times before Asher started, to bring her up to speed, and in one such conversation, I asked her how other expat parents with atypical kids handled the transition. "Where do they go to school? Where do they hang out? You know"—I paused—"*where are other parents like me?*" Her reply surprised me, although looking back, I'm not sure why. Kate told me most parents with atypical kids don't move abroad in the first place—they're too afraid of the uncertainties that come with a big change. They're operating from a place of fear instead of *maybe*.

I won't mince words: For us to do what's best for our kids, we need to *stop* making decisions out of fear. The tough part, unfortunately,

Reflect

Do I make decisions from a place of fear or from possibility, both in my life at large and in my life with my child?

• • •

How might fear be holding me back from making decisions that could benefit or better support my child?

• • •

How might my concerns about the future be unhelpful in the way I'm parenting my child and the choices I make?

is that moving forward in love and possibility can feel incredibly scary. (Ironic, right?) That's because in many ways, fear is the safe option. Fear fits within the parameters of what we already know. Choosing from fear makes us feel as though we're in control, when that couldn't be further from the truth. In fact, using fear as a guidepost results in our feeling as if we don't have a choice about anything. We must do x if we want y. *She must learn how to pay attention or she's going to fail. I must stay in this miserable job or we won't be able to afford his therapy. I can't advocate for her too loudly or they might kick us out of the program.* By recognizing the fear and choosing love and possibility instead, parents can discover just how much choice they have in their lives.

///////////////////////////// **Embracing the Tilt** /////////////////////////////

Get It All Out on the Table

Kaitlyn's daughter had always hated brushing her teeth, and no amount of treats, stickers, or different types of toothbrushes and toothpaste would make a difference. One day when it was time for the teeth-brushing tango, her nearly four-year-old daughter said, as usual, "No brushing." And per usual, Kaitlyn calmly began squeezing toothpaste onto the brush, until she felt the stinging smack of the toothbrush on her arm and found herself looking into her daughter's furious eyes. Though her ego was hurt and she was once again feeling helpless, Kaitlyn realized that much of her urge to respond with anger was rooted in fears: One was that her daughter would never brush her teeth without being forced and she'd have a ton of cavities, and the other was that her daughter would grow up to be a violent person. But when she recognized those fears, Kaitlyn was able to stop the spiral and realize this was just a situation of her daughter not liking to brush her teeth. She didn't have the skills yet to appropriately express her anger and frustration, and she was likely feeling helpless because her mother didn't seem to understand why she was upset.

Just as Kaitlyn did, the more we can get clear on our fears, the more we can figure out how to respond differently in the moment. So, let's get it all out on the table, shall we? What are your greatest fears involving your child? I'm talking super-irrational, nightmare-inducing, worst-case-scenario fears. It might seem like avoiding thinking about them is the way to go, but I suggest the opposite—*give them a voice*. Get super-familiar with them by saying them aloud or writing them out. Because to find a way to live with fear, we need to create an uneasy alliance with it. Think of fear as that pesky ex who just won't go away, a pimple that reemerges just when we're sure it's gone for good. After all, just because fear keeps showing up, that doesn't mean we have to roll out the red carpet and pour it a drink. We can recognize it, look it straight in the eyes, and say, "I see you," and then ask it to please move along.

I asked my friend Kate Swoboda, who is a coach and author, if she had any words of wisdom to share with us about facing and dealing with our fear. Since she wrote a book on it—*The Courage Habit: How to Accept Your Fears, Release the Past, and Live Your Courageous Life*—I knew she'd have a powerful perspective. Here's what she had to say: "Many people avoid, placate, or attack their fear—they're numbing out, trying to reason past feeling afraid, or telling their fears to shut up and go away. But fear isn't logical; it's primal. We feel it in the body, so we need to first deal with it in the body, and then start pulling apart what fear says. First, I suggest some kind of short pause to just take a breath, without even trying to do anything to change feelings of fear. Next, listen to what fear has to say—but listen without attachment, without thinking that the voice of fear is the voice of truth. As your fear tells you all of the things that could go wrong, it's time to reframe any limiting, fear-based stories that come up. Just a simple reframe from 'If my child doesn't listen to me, it'll all be out of control' to 'It's frustrating, but I'm going to keep working on this until we figure it out' can be helpful to remind yourself that you're doing your best and that no one

> **Pro Tip** Make a "fear's greatest hits" list by writing down the parenting fears that regularly get you spinning. Calling them out lessens their impact almost immediately.

changes overnight. Finally, I can't say enough how important it is to reach out and create community. Fear thrives when we are isolated, thinking we're the only parents who have encountered a particularly difficult situation or fearing that if others know that we struggle, they'll judge us. In truth, absolutely every parent encounters bad parenting days and makes mistakes. Connecting with other parents who are willing to be open about that will leave you more likely to reach out than to keep repeating the same frustrating cycles."

Turn "Oh No!" Moments Around

My biggest fear moments these days are usually triggered by a particularly bad day of homeschooling, at which point I'll invariably begin Googling "homeschooling twice-exceptional children" and "homeschooling gifted children with Asperger's" only to find more articles speaking to the cons than to the pros. Then the fear spiral begins in earnest as I sink into beliefs that I'm screwing Asher up on a daily basis. But then I remember that's just the fear talking. So I reframe my thinking and consider the possibility that bad days give Asher the chance to learn more about himself, push through adversity, and learn how to collaboratively problem solve. Maybe, just maybe, a bad day is actually a good day in disguise.

A simple way to spark this reframing in the moment is to first employ the two little words "Oh no," followed by an exclamation point. Try sticking these to the beginning of a thought, and if the complete sentence captures what you're feeling, then you're rooted in fear. For instance, *Oh no! He might not be able to ever attend a traditional school again!* or *Oh no! She doesn't have a best friend yet!* or *Oh no! He still can't read a book from start to finish!* To turn it around, incorporate words such as "maybe" or "perhaps" or "I'm curious" to come up with a new way of looking at the situation—one rooted in possibility. *Maybe homeschooling is going to be the best option for him all the way through,* or *Perhaps she'll find a special friend next year,* or *I'm curious to know when he'll be able to read a book from start to finish.*

Learn to Tune In

Despite the fact that their local, family-centered elementary school had a fabulous reputation, Jessica's six-year-old, differently wired son's first year was nothing short of disastrous. Over the course of their rocky year, it became clear that the school staff not only didn't understand or respect their son's unique wiring, but actually blamed and shamed Jessica and her husband for not "fixing" him already. They were terrified to uproot him and try a different path full of unknowns, but ultimately they couldn't ignore the message their gut was sending loud and clear.

They reached out to another school, and after they'd spoken with the school psychologist about their son's challenges, the principal handpicked a teacher for him: a new, young teacher with no children of her own. Jessica was doubtful, but they took a leap of faith and made the move. And it turned out to be the best decision they could have made. As Jessica describes it, "This teacher not only accepted him and his fidgeting and inattentiveness and emotional outbursts... she loved him through it. She communicated to his classmates that they should have empathy for him, and it worked. But the most surprising thing was that she helped my husband and me be more accepting. She was so patient with him, we couldn't help but join her. It was a real learning experience."

Just as Jessica knew she needed to take the leap, get out of her comfort zone, and choose possibility in trying the new school, we all have the ability to tune in to the voice within, the one that inherently knows what's best for us and our family. We all have gut responses that tell us when something is wrong and, conversely, when something is right. In fact, the information we get from our intuition is worth more than anything we could learn from reading a book or blog or listening to a podcast. We have to filter out the unhelpful voices and learn to trust our inner voice. No one—not a therapist, not a psychologist assessing your child, not a teacher, not another parent with a child "just like yours"—knows what's possible. Practice the art of tuning in to your intuition, of trusting it, by recognizing the ways your body responds to both fear and love.

> **Pro Tip** Channel your inner Oprah and reflect on the following question about why your child's potential is limitless: *What do I know for sure about my child in every fiber of my being?*

Get Your Brave On

The bravest thing I've done so far in my parenting journey with Asher is relocate halfway around the world and take responsibility for his education. At the time, it felt terrifying and nothing like bravery at all. In fact, back then the words I would have used to describe our life change would probably have included "risky," "irresponsible," "scary," and "stupid." After arriving in Amsterdam, I wanted to take our decision back a thousand times. But I knew in my heart it was the right thing. I trusted in what was possible. And I got my brave on.

The best thing about bravery, scary and uncomfortable as it may be, is that it becomes the impetus for even more bravery and, more important, more possibility. Bravery is a muscle, but instead of building it through exercise, we strengthen it with each brave act we do, big or small, parent related or not. Bravery isn't a limited resource, and it's also something we *all* have within us. I encourage you to reacquaint yourself with your personal bravery by recalling times in your life when you made a tough choice—one viewed skeptically by others—and pushed ahead, fueled only by your own faith, courage, and strength.

> **Start Now** Tackle a major or minor child-related decision by tuning in, determining the best choice from the perspective of love and possibility, and trusting in what could be by embracing that choice.

I asked my friend, the entrepreneur, author, and cultural change-maker Jess Weiner, how she's developed the bravery she demonstrates every day in her work, and she replied, "I define bravery, much like I would courage, as feeling fear and doing it anyway. I have really developed and cultivated the bravery muscle for myself in that I'm connected to my fear. My fear voice has her own name and I get to really get connected to that because my fears become my greatest teacher, and through that, I've learned bravery."

Let Your Child Be on Their Own Time Line

"Optimist: Someone who figures that taking a step backward after taking a step forward is not a disaster, it's a cha-cha."
—Robert Brault

Despite being in an inclusion class in a progressive public school with an IEP, twice-exceptional Sadie began struggling in fourth grade. As her mom, Jennifer, explains, "She hated school so much that almost every morning, she'd beg not to go. The school nurse told us she was appearing in her office daily with stomach pain and headaches. She went to bed every night saying, 'I'm the dumbest kid in the class' and was so wracked with anxiety, she had sleep problems and acted out to family and friends."

Luckily, another school in the community—a small, progressive arts-based school—seemed like a perfect fit for Jennifer's daughter, and they were fortunate enough to land a spot, but only in the fourth grade, meaning that Sadie would repeat the same grade. The thought of holding her back worried Jennifer. How would her daughter feel about it? What would being a year behind her friends mean when Sadie returned to public school for high school? But then Jennifer had a revelation.

"I pictured Sadie's life up until now as a conveyor belt that was moving too fast for her. Then I pictured us lifting her off of it and placing her on the ground, where she needed to be at that moment, and where she could walk on her own from there. There was something beautiful, and brand-new, about looking at who she was at that moment and being able to give her exactly what she needed and wanted—a choice from within instead of from an exterior force moving her along at an artificial rate."

They decided to go for it, and Sadie ended up having a life-changing year at a place where she could catch her breath and feel supported. Since then, her confidence has skyrocketed, as have her maturity and independence. Jennifer admits to still sometimes questioning whether they made the right decision, but "once again, I come back to that image of Sadie's path. How it was never mine to plan out in advance. How wonderful it is to be able to have the freedom to take a few steps, then reexamine whether we're going where we want to go."

The Importance of Measuring Up

From the moment a child is born, *the measuring begins*. Apgar scales, growth and development charts, key developmental milestones. Once kids hit the school years, the measuring never really ends. There are IQ tests, standardized tests, teacher assessments, grades . . . even the Presidential Physical Fitness Test. Then there are countless academic, cognitive, and social markers, everything from learning to read or mastering riding a two-wheeler to being mature enough to stay home alone or knowing how to cook breakfast by themselves. These all have the potential to be points of pride for parents, an opportunity for them to tick off the box—*Yes: My child is on track*—and feel secure that they're doing a good job. And even though the information gleaned from assessments and milestones can be useful, there is a downside to all of this measuring—namely, getting caught up in worry and concern when our child *isn't* measuring up.

As parents, we like to know where our child fits in. We want to know our child is progressing nicely, that there are no barriers to their developing into capable, successful adults. Formal metrics are an easy way to get information quickly. But when a child is developing differently, the urge to compare (and despair) can be overpowering. It's critical that those of us raising atypical kids honor our child's unique time line so they can become secure in who they are.

We live in a society preoccupied with deficits as opposed to strengths, a tendency on display in schools that typically identify areas of weakness and teach to those. *Your child is an incredible writer, but she struggles in math, so we're going to give her more math.* In a traditional educational model, once a child's deficits are identified, school becomes about "fixing" those, their strengths all but ignored. Parent Giselle was shocked to discover her daughter's special-needs school had made no effort to identify her daughter's strengths, let alone tap into them to help her daughter thrive. "I asked them, 'Where are the strengths in this report?' And the psychologist looked at me and said, 'Strengths? We don't look at strengths.' I assumed a psychologist would be looking at the whole person to make recommendations, but what I experienced was that they are only looking at one part of the child, not the child as a whole."

Giselle's experience is indicative of a systemic problem. Historically it's *always* been about "fixing what's wrong" rather than leaning in to what's right and using that as a foundation for engaging a child's gifts. But when we focus on weaknesses, we miss out on so much. And our kids pay the price.

The Problem with Arbitrary Time Lines

One of the things I hear all the time is that kids need to know how to work collaboratively, that being able to navigate small-group situations is a key predictor of future success. In fact, although the most common question I get from non-homeschooling parents is the classic *But how will he learn social skills?*, I know inquiries about how Asher will master working in a group aren't far behind.

I admit to having pangs of insecurity when that question comes up. After such an exchange I might even frantically research summer programs where Asher can work on developing those skills, and pronto. This despite the fact that group situations are a recipe for disaster for Ash and have always presented the biggest challenges for him.

A few years ago, I enrolled Asher in an after-school technology class. I knew he was in good hands, as one of the instructors had experience with kids on the spectrum and they were genuinely committed to Asher's success.

It went well for the first few weeks, but Asher's behavior began to negatively spiral with each passing class, despite his instructors' noble attempts to figure out a solution.

I knew it was time to call it quits but let the instructors convince me otherwise. In a thoughtful email, one of the instructors wrote, "Asher's programming skills are advanced, but he needs to work on his teamwork and communication skills. We don't recommend that you give him private lessons, as this does not solve the issue or prepare him for the future, where any technology education or career will require teamwork and collaboration skills." Once again I panicked. *If he doesn't learn how to do this, he will fail!* So against my better judgment, I kept him enrolled for another two weeks before realizing it was okay for me to pull him out. *Yes, he may need to know how to do that someday, but he doesn't need to learn this particular lesson right now.* And just like that, the anxiety was gone, for Asher and for me.

It's not easy to know what's best in situations like these, but I do know that when we push our children to do things they're truly not ready for, it never ends well. There's plenty of research showing that pushing kids to master cognitive skills at young ages can actually hurt their later academic performance, not to mention their love of learning.

Pushing children to do more than they're ready for has the potential to crush their self-worth, result in lost confidence, cripple them with pressure to succeed, and even turn them against whatever we're trying to get them to learn.

Respecting Unique Time Lines Benefits Kids

In the case of Asher's tech class, I realized that pushing him wasn't worth the emotional toll. I know that the more time Asher can spend feeling calm and regulated, the more room he has to become self-aware, confident, and secure, which will ultimately help him learn how to behave in a group.

As my friend Jennifer learned in recognizing her daughter Sadie's need to slow down, every child learns differently and follows their own perfect time line. A recent study by the Bill & Melinda Gates Foundation found that when students are given the opportunity to learn at their own pace and in their own way, "these methods drove students' math and reading scores up significantly. In fact, their impact was larger than those found in 95% of other educational intervention studies."

Why? Because children learn best when they feel secure. They feel confident in their abilities. They feel safer taking risks and they are more resilient when they have setbacks. Respecting our child's unique time lines gives them a chance to strengthen their wings and trust in themselves before they have to fly. And because they're growing up in a world where their neurodivergence may not always be appreciated, keeping their self-worth intact by reinforcing the idea that they're right where they should be will pay off.

//////////////////////////// **Embracing the Tilt** ////////////////////////////

Notice the Compare-and-Despair Cycle

If we want to respect where our children *are*, we have to first recognize when we're being triggered by where they *aren't*. One hotbed of fodder for unhelpful comparisons is, of course, Facebook, where time lines tell picture-perfect tales of sporting victories, enviable achievements,

Reflect

How concerned am I about areas where my child may be on a "delayed" time line?

. . .

What am I afraid will happen if my child develops at his or her own unique pace instead of what's typical?

. . .

What aspect of his or her developmental time line is most concerning to me and why? What is at the root of my concerns? Are they based in reality?

and ideal lives. But comparing (and inevitably despairing) can happen in *any* environment.

Here in the Netherlands, I have to confront my own compare-and-despair tendencies the moment I step outside my front door, because kids Asher's age are biking solo to and from school and friends' houses, having full run of the city, and living incredibly independent lives. I love this about the Netherlands *and* that's totally not where we are right now, at this moment.

Asher may be able to explain the theory of relativity, but safely cross the street on his own? Not so much. Will Asher ever learn to do that? Of course. Will he eventually be able to bike around the city on his own? I'm certain of it. Does he need to know how to do those things right now? Definitely not. He's working on his own things in his own time. For now, we'll continue to help him develop his confidence and awareness. And eventually he'll get there.

So—what are the things that trigger *you*? Where do you think your child "should" be that he or she is not? What specific actions or activities do you think your child should have mastered by now? I encourage you to reflect on this question and make a list. Because chances are, even if you're not actively pushing your child to master said ability, that child may sense that he or she isn't living up to your expectations.

Here are a few examples of things I commonly hear from parents when considering time line disconnects. Have any of these made it onto your list?

- tying shoes
- brushing teeth independently
- riding a bike
- expressing empathy and compassion toward others
- being a good sport
- packing their own lunch or making their own meals
- buying something from a store by themselves
- reading a novel from start to finish
- writing an essay
- doing their homework without reminders
- staying home by themselves
- doing their own laundry
- safely crossing the street
- getting themselves to school or to a friend's house by themselves
- memorizing their address and phone number
- finding their way home from a regularly visited location
- taking care of a younger sibling

Challenge Those Time Line Beliefs

Once you've identified areas where you believe your child is behind, challenge those assumptions and, even more important, consider ways you may be "awfulizing" or having a doom-and-gloom perspective about any delayed time line. Are you, like I was, making your child's straying from the "expected" time line mean that their future dreams are shot? Or are you convinced that if they don't learn how to do something now, they'll *never* learn it? Consider some of the areas where you're concerned and explore these two questions:

- Why does my child need to know how to do this now?
- What "negative thing" would happen if he [she] learned this later?

When we noodle on these questions, we typically find that the answer to that last one is *Not much*. Who cares if our child wears Velcro sneakers until they're sixteen? Will his quality of life suffer for it? What's the big deal if our kid can't bike independently to a friend's house or run to the store by the age of thirteen? She'll be able to do it in her own time. When children are ready, they can not only learn something much more quickly, but feel proud of their new skill or ability.

To truly challenge those time line beliefs, go back through every area of concern you listed and come up with at least one example or thought for each about why your child mastering that skill in their own time is actually *perfectly* okay. You may have to dig deep, but if you stay with it, I know you'll come up with a great reframe.

Here's my example from above:

- **My concern:** Asher doesn't bike independently around the city.
- **Why this is perfect:** Many of my friends spend a lot of time worrying about their kids' safety while they're biking, and I get to skip that for now! Also, rather than sitting on the back of my bike, lately Asher has been choosing to bicycle side by side, showing me that letting him progress at his own pace has resulted in increased confidence.

Before I move on, I want to acknowledge that some developmental time line concerns, especially ones relating to that scary concept otherwise known as *the future*, can feel too important to let go of. If that's the case for you, consider how you might be enmeshed in the expectations you have for your child rather than honoring and respecting that they are on their own unique journey. I like the way

Julie Neale, founder of Mother's Quest and host of the *Mother's Quest* podcast, summed it up in a recent interview. I asked Julie how she and her husband reframed things when they realized their son was on a different time line: "My husband was able to say, 'We don't know what the future holds, but what we do know and what we can focus on is *How can we help Ryan just become the best Ryan he can be?*' And it really is true. Once I was able to let to go of all my expectations and focus on *Oh yeah, that's right. What do I need to do to just help him live to his fullest potential?*, then I could get out of focusing on the future and become more present and enjoy all of the great qualities he had already. And *then* working on *Okay, where do we need to get support to help him grow?*"

Talk Openly About Time Lines

Because differently wired kids are often highly in tune with not only us, but the world around them (even when it may seem as though they're not paying attention at all), many are hyperaware of where they net out in comparison with their peers. This is especially true for gifted children, many of whom are extraordinarily tough on, and have extremely high expectations of, themselves. It's important to talk with children about personal time lines as a way to celebrate their strengths, as well as bring up areas where they may want to work on developing their skills.

Start by pointing out areas where they're excelling and doing really well, or perhaps are even ahead of their peers, and not just in academics or cognitive areas, but also in character strengths: *You have a neat ability to design imaginative spacecraft with Legos*, or *You are someone who cares a lot about the little details, which is a really cool and important quality*, or *You are really good at noticing when someone is feeling upset*. Often, such strengths are overlooked when, really, they are the foundation on which all growth can occur. Dr. Robyn Silverman suggests, "I would challenge people to relabel their children in their own heads based on strengths. How do you talk about your child? You want to surround your kids and yourself with the type of people who see your kids for their strengths. And you want to talk about your own shortcomings and what you did to work on them, too."

Be Prepared to Deflect the Doubters

As our children grow, we will unquestionably be confronted by many people along the way who may have, shall we say, *strong opinions* about our child's progress in certain areas. It's gonna happen. And as we talked about in the chapter on letting go of what others think, we can help ourselves by proactively formulating language to use when these "muggles" imply that our child is "behind" in some way. Here are simple, clear, and kind responses to have at the ready:

- He's focusing on developing other skills right now.
- We're working with someone to help him grow in that area.
- Thanks for your concern—we've got it covered!
- She's someone who is passionate about *x*, so we're supporting her in developing that talent/skill/ability right now.

Being prepared for the questions or comments we all know will come from doubters helps us respond with confidence instead of defensiveness, hurt, or embarrassment. In turn, that confidence influences how our child's differences are seen, absorbed, and understood by others, not because we care what they think about us or our child, but because we're doing the very important, paradigm-shifting work of challenging the stigmas that surround different ways of being.

Work Toward Goals with Patience and Support

Asher's close friend Sam lives on the other side of Vondelpark, a sprawling haven of greenery often referred to as Amsterdam's version of Central Park. With the exception of two city blocks, most of the twenty-minute trip (on foot) between their houses is spent loping through this car-free park. A few months ago, I realized that Vondelpark provided the perfect opportunity to start building Asher's independence, and so together we set a goal of having him be able to walk to Sam's house alone by the summer, a challenge he was ready for. To increase his chances of success, we built scaffolding—supports we could slowly pull away over time as he was ready.

First, I walked with him to Sam's while helping him recognize markers and pointing out areas where he needed to pay close attention to bicyclists. Next, I walked him to the edge of the park and set him free, following from about fifty feet behind, because knowing I was there allayed his anxiety. Today, we're at the point where I walk him to the edge of the park and he heads off on his own, Sam's mom, Donna, texting me when he arrives to allay *my* anxiety. The last step will be his getting safely to the park from our apartment fully on his own, which entails crossing several streets, including one teeming with cars, bikes, scooters, and the occasional tram. We're not there yet, but I know we will be soon. And when we are, it's going to feel good for Asher because he'll know he's ready for it.

It's fine to have goals for the things you'd like to work on with your child. In fact, it can

> **Start Now** Make a list of skills your child is struggling with, and commit to working *with* your child to improve on these skills with love, patience, and no preconceived time line.

be incredibly rewarding to work with your child to choose a few realistic goals for developing certain skills, habits, or abilities. The key is supporting their development with love and patience and not following any preconceived time line. Let them lead the way, and collaborate with them to determine what the scaffolding should look like and how and when they're ready to dismantle it.

Become Fluent in Your Child's Language

"Sometimes people are beautiful. Not in looks. Not in what they say. Just in what they are."
—Markus Zusak

Since moving to the Netherlands in 2013, I've devoted myself to learning Dutch, a language I had zero exposure to before arriving in Amsterdam. I have struggled to make sense of it, not to mention tried to reproduce the guttural "g" sound, ever since. Slowly but surely, I'm getting there, but true progress has depended upon my willingness to do two things: (1) accept that I'm going to make mistakes on a regular basis, and (2) become deeply curious about the idioms, peculiarities, and nuances of the language.

The same could be said for parenting—to be truly effective and understand our child, we must be fully committed and curious. Of course, this is the case with parenting any child, but becoming fluent in the unique language of an atypical child is like mastering an obscure dialect spoken in a remote region of the world without Google Translate. The only way it's going to happen is through complete immersion and devotion to discovering how our kids convey and process meaning and experience.

Through TiLT Parenting, I've heard about many incredible, beautiful ways in which people have dedicated themselves to becoming fluent in their child's language. Tia, mother to three unique children, including her twice-exceptional daughter who has a number of learning differences such as dyslexia, dyscalculia, and dysgraphia coupled with artistic giftedness, has learned to embrace and enlist her daughter's way of communicating through art. Tia encourages her daughter to grab paper and art supplies and draw it out when she's upset or dysregulated, which serves as a way for her to both self-calm and to express whatever tough emotion she's experiencing. That might seem like a small thing, but for a child who doesn't respond to the "usual" parenting techniques in difficult moments, honoring the way her daughter can be her best, most grounded self, is significant.

Lost in Translation

So often, especially when it comes to the more confounding behaviors differently wired kids may exhibit, we are missing the mark about what's really going on. Just like Bill Murray discovered, things get lost in translation. And when we're misinterpreting the ways in which our children are communicating with us, frustration only rises.

Anders Rønnau, the brilliant coach behind the Transforming ADHD movement, shared an example of how reframing the way we interpret our child's language in a difficult moment can literally change everything. As he tells it, during a big family dinner, a six-year-old boy with ADHD reached out and flipped over the milk carton, spilling the milk and garnering the ire of most everyone at the table, many of whom began to berate him. That is, until his aunt thought to ask him the following question: What were you *trying* to do?

Think about that question for a minute. She didn't ask him, Why did you do that? or What were you thinking? or What's wrong with you? Rather, by asking him, What were you *trying* to do?, she was really asking him, What was your positive intention? And of course he had one. As it turns out, this boy had noticed that his dad was about to need the butter, and he'd reached out to pass it over to him. Unfortunately, it didn't work out the way he intended. Yet, if his aunt hadn't been curious enough to ask him that simple question—What were you *trying* to do?—the whole incident would have been chalked up as just one more "annoying" action by a clearly misunderstood boy. As Anders explains, "If you can catch yourself and not just look at the behavior and what happens as a result of that behavior but pause for a second and go, *Wow, what was he trying to do?*, that will bring an end to a lot of conflicts for most parents."

It's not our child's job to publish a *Them to Us* dictionary. It's on us to become fluent in what our child is telling us through everything they do. Many of us assume the worst when our child is simply being who they are, especially when we're feeling stressed and their challenging behavior leaves us feeling under attack. But when we can calmly ask our child the simple question *What were you trying to do?* in such moments, we might not only prevent or lessen the intensity of a meltdown or negative emotional spiral, but give our child the gift of knowing themselves better.

The Gifts of Fluency

It helps to remember that "all behavior is communication" and that everything our child does—every action, every word or cry or yell expressed—is their way of conveying important information to us. Yet I'd venture to say that most of the time, we're not actually *listening*. We're too busy managing them, trying to problem solve in the moment . . . *parenting* them.

Communicating with our child in their unique language doesn't have to be that difficult—a little bit of translation goes a long way. It begins with noticing the ways in which they communicate with us. For instance, they communicate through many different ways

- body movements
- tears
- cries of frustration

- hugs
- laughter and joy
- how and when they reach for our hands and our laps
- the books, games, and other toys they choose to engage with

And we can express our fluency in their language through just as many ways:

- hugs and cuddles
- reading them a book they love
- anticipating their needs
- being a good listener when they're going on about an area of interest
- getting to know and anticipate their triggers

Here are a few examples of entries you might find were you to flip through an *Asher to Debbie Dictionary*:

My Behavior	How Asher Interprets It
Going on a long walk in the park and allowing Asher to talk to his heart's content about his area of interest	My mom is interested in me and what I have to say.
Bringing Asher a hot chocolate or croissant from the café as a surprise treat	My mom is always thinking of me and likes doing things to bring me joy.
Taking a break from work to play a game or read aloud a chapter from a favorite book	My mom will always make time for me.

Asher's Behavior	How I Interpret It
Increasingly loud grumbles of frustration	Asher's having a hard time and needs help moving away from the situation.
Getting into pajamas before dinner	He's had a difficult day and is looking for comfort and cuddles.
Asking me to spend a few minutes helping him set an intention for the next day after lights out	Asher wants to make positive changes in his behavior and attitude but needs my help and support.

Embracing the Tilt

Remember: There's Always a Reason

When her differently wired daughter was four years old, Whitney had an aha moment while reading Dr. Ross Greene's game-changing book *The Explosive Child* and taking to heart his widely shared notion that "kids do well if they can." As Whitney explains, "That idea completely shifted my thinking about how to approach the challenges I was having with my daughter. I could see every single struggle we were having as a matter of her 'lagging skills,' and that gave us more of a foothold into how to approach those struggles. It wasn't a magic cure," she continues, "but the way we now approach challenges together, as collaborative problem solvers, has dramatically shifted the dynamic. I'm so much better at listening to my daughter and really hearing what she's saying and what her needs are."

Reflect

What might my child be trying to communicate to me through their challenging behavior or unexpected emotional reactions?

. . .

How might becoming more fluent in my child's language support them in their journey?

. . .

How might true fluency positively affect my relationship with my child and their relationship with themselves?

I don't know about you, but there have been many, many, *many* times over the years when thoughts such as *Asher could have made a better choice if he'd really tried* or *If he'd* wanted *to, he could have been less disruptive in school* have crossed my mind, as if his behavior and actions were designed to make my life harder. In the throes of difficult moments, we may be convinced our child is a mastermind of emotional torture, set on injecting chaos into our world.

Sometimes, our kids are literally telling us everything we need to know about why they're behaving the way they are, but we're just not listening hard enough, or well enough. That was the case with Kathleen, the mother of a twice-exceptional son who was in elementary school; he clearly described how he was spending his time during daily recess. As she later explained, "I don't know exactly how it happened, but at some point we started listening to the actual words our son was saying and believing them, instead of accepting others' interpretation of events. So, when he'd tell us he was trying to keep track of all the movements and words of every kid on the playground in order to predict what they were going to do next (and failing miserably, of course), my husband and I imagined how frustrating that would be and realized his having a meltdown 'suddenly, for no reason' was the teacher's interpretation, not the reality. He was actually quite good at expressing why he was constantly falling apart at school, but pretty much everyone 'on his team' was dismissive of his reasons."

Let's clear things up: No matter how seemingly irrational, arbitrary, illogical, or flat-out absurd a child's behavior or reaction is to a situation, *there is always an underlying reason* for why they are behaving the way they are. Even if they *are* trying to push our buttons, they're doing so because some need isn't being met or because they don't have the necessary skills to act any differently. Remembering Dr. Greene's wise words—"kids do well if they can"—has the capacity to change everything.

> **Pro Tip** Personalize Dr. Greene's statement—"kids do well if they can"—and share it with educators and other adults in your child's world. For example, *Asher would do better if he could.*

When we fully embrace this idea, we can interpret our child's behavior with understanding and compassion. We can remind ourselves that (1) our child's behavior isn't about us, and (2) it *is* about our child lacking the skills necessary to do anything different right now.

Get to Know Your Baggage

We all have areas where our emotional baggage interferes with our ability to interpret the way our child is communicating his or her wants and needs. For instance, say you're frustrated in your job because your boss has a habit of disrespecting you in front of other people. Although your boss's treatment of you is deeply upsetting, you feel you have no option but to suck it up since you don't want to look for another job. Now imagine picking up your child from school only to become the recipient of even *more* disrespect, but this time it's coming at the hands of your seven-year-old, who boldly defies you in the grocery store in front of a mass of onlookers. You're now in one of your blind spots—it's difficult to respond objectively, because your emotions about an entirely different set of circumstances have been triggered and are getting in the way of calm, rational thinking. Instead of recognizing that your child's behavior is telling you she's overstimulated and needs to get out of there, pronto, you're caught up in your own experience and the message is getting misconstrued.

We all have these blind spots—thinking we're not good enough, feeling like others don't take us seriously, feeling unappreciated, feeling like a fraud, believing we're not smart enough, feeling misunderstood, feeling left out. After all, we're human, and our history invariably shapes how we see and experience the world. The goal then is to get to know our blind spots so we can better understand how they may be interfering with our ability to pick up on our child's communication signals in the moment.

Get to Know Your Child's Key Triggers

I used to think Asher could be triggered by just about anything—his explosions seemed random and perpetual. It wasn't until his therapist Julie George, after working with him for a few sessions, handed me a sheet of paper outlining Asher's biggest triggers—the things that invariably cause him to experience angst, anger, sadness, or any other big emotion—that I realized there wasn't anything random about his reactions at all. In fact, in that moment, Julie provided me with the beginning of my own translation key to understanding Asher. I now knew that above all else, the three things most likely to set him off were (1) unpredictability, (2) situations where things didn't go the way he expected, and (3) having people place demands on him.

Suddenly, I was able to see his behavior in context. Having that information helped me predict which situations would be difficult, which consequently allowed me to give him a heads-up, role-play, or discuss solutions in advance so things could unfold more smoothly. Even more, Asher now had the benefit of understanding himself better, which gave him a tool for managing his expectations. He understood better why certain things set him off, and worked on tempering his responses. We can reinforce this self-knowledge through the words we use—*What I know about you is that unpredictable outcomes can make you feel anxious*—and then use that awareness as a jumping-off point for moving through the situation with less angst and drama. *What do you think would help you feel okay with whatever the outcome is in this situation?*

Becoming fluent in our child's language involves getting to know their specific triggers, as well as the unique ways in which they communicate their physical, social, and emotional needs. When we start paying attention, we can build up our own child–parent dictionary. Get curious about the following language:

- How does your child express love?
- How does your child express fear?
- How does your child express anxiety?
- How does your child express anger?
- How does your child express happiness?
- How does your child express contentment?

Get Your Child Involved in the Learning

A primary goal of becoming fluent in our child's language is getting them involved in understanding themselves. Just as in the last Tilt, where we talked about making conversations about strengths, weaknesses, and time lines part of our family's everyday vernacular, we want to do the same here. That means talking out loud about our observations and bringing our child's attention to things we're noticing, asking questions of them, and working with them to make meaningful connections between behavior and intention.

Asher was five when he first articulated the way his body felt when he was having a particularly "off" day. He called it the "bubble head feeling," and through lots of curious questions, I learned more specifically that this feeling corresponded with feeling ramped-up or intense, strange energy throughout his body. The "bubble head feeling" not only earned a special spot in my Asher fluency dictionary, but provided Asher with deeper language to express something he was feeling but had a hard time describing.

Getting our child involved begins by asking them the kinds of questions that will help them reflect and get curious about themselves:

- What do you think is going on for you right now?
- How can I help you right now?
- What are you feeling in your body right now?

These are all nonjudgmental ways to ask about what our child is thinking and feeling in a way that builds their own self-awareness.

Adapt Your Language So They Can Understand *You*

Just as communication can work only if there's a sender and a receiver, fluency is a two-way street—we have to be able to communicate in a way that others will understand. Over the years, I learned that the key to Asher receiving my communication is doing things like putting my messages in writing, taking him for long walks out in nature where he's better able to tune in, reading aloud, letting him share something before I share my own thoughts, frequently verbally acknowledging his effort and growth, being silly, playing games with him, and showing genuine interest when he shares details galore about one of his areas of interest.

> **Pro Tip** Identify a handful of methods that are most effective in ensuring your child is able to receive the information you want to share.

I know many families who put their family "policies" in writing—family rules, daily schedules, screen-time guidelines, chore lists, routine schedules, and more. Some even type up "contracts" that are signed by all parties involved. Others use role playing, or tell elaborate

> **Start Now** When your child does something that elicits a strong, negative response in you, commit to respectfully asking them why they made that choice (or use the question Anders shared in his story, *What were you trying to do?*) and listen to their answer with an open mind. Add whatever you learn to your personal translation dictionary.

stories with stuffed animals, or make up adventures with Legos or dolls. Even media can be used as an effective communication method—in an essay for the *New York Times* Rasha Madkour writes about how the preschool show *Daniel Tiger's Neighborhood* helped her autistic son understand and learn valuable social skills. The possibilities are endless, because every child is different and what works for them will be unique, not to mention continue to change and evolve over time. Our job is to be a detective and learn how our child best interprets what we have to share, and then adapt our message accordingly.

For example, I spent weeks verbally prepping Asher on every detail of a family vacation only to realize halfway through the trip that he hadn't actually heard *any* of what I'd shared. So for our next holiday, I took a different approach—creating a fifteen-page illustrated itinerary breaking down every little detail of the trip, and then having him review it every night while we were on the vacation to ensure there'd be no surprises.

Create a World Where Your Child Can Be Secure

"Peace is a daily, a weekly, a monthly process, gradually changing opinions, slowly eroding old barriers, quietly building new structures."
—John F. Kennedy

Imagine being a child going through life in a constant state of stress, bracing yourself for the next assault of negativity (intense sensory information, intolerant teachers, other children who bully or make fun), being shamed by parents and other adults, feeling like you're constantly screwing up, not to mention hosting a running stream of negative self-talk in your head. Imagine being a child in an ongoing state of protecting yourself from the emotional and physical input you're flooded with as a result of living in an intense world.

This is a daily reality, not just for kids with anxiety disorders or sensory processing issues, but for many atypical kids who feel as though they're under constant attack. It's critical that we address this, because when we're in a stress response, our brains literally shut down. We can't regulate our emotions, we can't make good decisions... we can't settle. Studies show that to be effective learners and take the kind of risks necessary for healthy growth, children need to feel safe, secure, and supported. On top of that, operating at high levels of stress and anxiety can become a chronic condition, which can lead to a slew of mental health problems.

I don't think I realized how shut down Asher was until I started homeschooling him and had to guide him through a detox of sorts. In those first four months of our new reality, Asher and I worked hard to learn our new rhythms and routines, create respectful boundaries, and determine what our ideal school day should look and feel like, all while adjusting to a new home, new language, and new life. We experimented with a variety of schedules, trying to strike the perfect balance of work and breaks and projects and class time and screen time and field trips. Some days it would seem as if we'd figured it out, but then the next, and often for no apparent reason, everything would fall to pieces.

Looking back, I realize I was unwittingly contributing to Asher's sense of anxiety and defensiveness, because I wasn't sure how or when to be rigid about expectations and structure and when to reject them and do things our own way.

But after a few months of trial and error and playing with the balance of structure versus flexibility, I cobbled together a proposed schedule and pitched it to him like an ad exec trying to land a big new account. "What do you think of this plan?" I asked him. "We can move things around if you don't like the order, but whatever we decide on, we're going to stick with it. So you'll know exactly what's happening when, and there will be no surprises."

"It's awesome!" he yelled, jumping off the couch and sliding around the living room in his wool socks (his standard "I'm excited" reaction). "It's just like real school, except I'm the only kid!"

"And is that a *good* thing?" I asked, confused. I mean, the kid did not like school . . . never had.

"*Yes!*" he said.

And in that moment, I put it together. Asher craves predictability. He doesn't do well with last-minute changes or when things go differently from how he planned them in his head. And even though he can't help but push back and defy rules and regulations, he craves the structure. It makes him feel secure and calm and actually more in control. In those first few aimless months, I was feeding his anxiety by not supporting him in feeling safe. He was continually off balance and therefore dysregulated. A fertile ground for learning and growth? Yeah . . . *not so much.*

The Gifts of Security

Just as a child in a continual state of stress will be hard-pressed to make meaningful developmental and cognitive leaps, once they begin experiencing more peace and contentment in their daily life, they'll naturally be open to all kinds of learning, not to mention be happier and less reactive overall.

Kids are no different from us in this respect—we all need a soft place to land when going through a challenging time. We need spaces where we feel safe, where we can regroup, where we can be ourselves without worrying about others judging, mocking, or hurting us. Our security might come in the form of Netflix, a cozy throw, and a generous glass of wine. It might be reinforced by a compassionate partner or friend who, just as Mr. Darcy feels about Bridget Jones, likes us just as we are.

This is what our kids need from us. We want our home environment to be their safe, secure place—a place where they are seen and respected, and where they can express themselves without worry of being shamed or shunned or punished. We want our children to know we have their backs, even when they're lashing out at us or struggling.

When a child is moving through the world differently,

Reflect

In what environments and situations does my child regularly become anxious or stressed?

. . .

How might these stressful environments and responses be standing in the way of his or her learning and growth?

. . .

How might my child blossom if he or she felt more secure and grounded in everyday life?

they are often all too aware that they don't quite fit in, which frequently results in their being stuck in fight-or-flight mode. But when parents commit to creating an environment where their child can let down their defenses, there's no limit to their growth. No matter their school situation, we want to ensure their home environment is a place where they can feel safe, secure, seen, and accepted for who they are.

/////////////////////////// **Embracing the Tilt** ///////////////////////////

Identify Your Child's Stress Triggers

I first heard of the online education and information site Asperger Experts a few years ago when someone recommended a video by cofounder Danny Reade about "getting out of defense mode." As Danny, who himself has Asperger's, explains, defense mode is a "state in which someone with Asperger's is scared, frustrated, or angry, as well as shut down and withdrawn." According to Danny, when someone is in defense mode, they appear to be oppositional and unmotivated, which might be true, but only because of the underlying fact that they're in that state of fight-or-flight—on the defense—and so everything else stops.

What struck me most when I first saw this video was the fact that so much of the intervention for kids with Asperger's/high-functioning autism focuses on developing social skills, yet in reality, there's no room for that learning to occur, because the child's basic need to feel safe isn't being met. According to Danny, we're doing it all wrong. Intervention should focus on getting kids out of defense mode, because when we do, the rest of the learning can actually happen pretty easily.

So . . . how do we do that? Just as we work on becoming fluent in our child's language, we want to learn which situations and environments push them into a state where their learning shuts down, as well as what that anxiety looks like. As I wrote earlier, I learned that Asher's traditional school environment was resulting in a lot of stress, and I could tell just how stressed he was by the intensity with which he was gnawing at his fingernails. Since then, I've realized that situations with any element of time pressure are another surefire way to garner a stress response, which might look like his being short-tempered, snapping, or completely tuning out the rest of the world. I've learned that participating in activities where his need to fidget and express his excitement is met with disapproval is a one-way ticket to becoming closed off and defensive, which he'll express by storming away in frustration.

Understanding the specific situations that create anxiety or stress in your child, as well as the way that anxiety manifests itself, is the first step in helping them feel more secure. We may not be able to control what happens in the outside world, but we want to do everything in our power to mitigate those stressors at home.

Develop Stress-Coping Strategies

Sometimes an anxiety-inducer can't be avoided, especially when school is the cause of angst, so we want to work with our child to develop coping strategies ahead of time, as well as build in the scaffolding to help them integrate these strategies when the time comes. Many parents work with teachers to design positive behavioral systems where teachers can award "points" if a child remembers to use a coping strategy in a difficult moment. Anne, mother of a five-year-old on the spectrum, not only role-plays tough situations and how to handle them with her daughter in advance, but makes sure the educators in her daughter's classroom know how and when to verbally remind her daughter to take deep breaths. Anne also writes little notes as visual reminders, which she places in her daughter's school bag and binder.

A therapist or coach can help your child figure out a simple emotional-regulation coping routine made up of a few subtle actions he or she can do, even discreetly in a public situation, to calm down. Clasping hands together tightly, taking deep breaths, rubbing palms along the top of thighs, squeezing a stress ball, or sucking on a "chewy" (to avoid chewing on their shirt collar)—try different things and be curious with your child about what might work. Or look for clues in how your child already self-soothes or calms down—Legos, reading, hugging a stuffy, drawing—and help them recognize what they're doing and find ways to reinforce those choices, especially in emotionally charged situations. And if something that once worked stops working, get curious again and try something new.

Beyond helping our kids develop in-the-moment stress reduction strategies, perhaps the most useful thing we can do is be proactive in helping them anticipate situations that might trip them up and develop a plan *ahead of time.* The expert on planning ahead for tough situations is *The Explosive Child* author Dr. Ross Greene, who developed the Collaborative and Proactive Solutions model—or, as I like to call it, the best thing since sliced bread. In his model, Dr. Greene encourages us to identify situations that routinely create challenges for our kids and collaborate with them to develop a plan for responding when and if that situation arises.

For instance, say the annual Halloween parade creates stress for Jackson, a ten-year-old boy, in large part because people on floats randomly toss candy to bystanders and he may not get the type of candy he wants, whereas the kid next to him does. Or maybe Jackson is slow and misses out on getting any candy at all, which leaves him frantic, anxious, and unraveling. Jackson's parents have a few options. One, they can skip going to the parade altogether. There's no shame in sitting it out—we get to do what we need to do to help our child feel secure.

But say Jackson *really* wants to attend the parade. Then his parents can work with him to anticipate the possible scenarios and brainstorm ways to handle them. *What will you do if you end up only with candy you don't like? How will you handle it if you're standing next to a grabby kid who scoops up all the candy before you get any?*

What should our plan be if we start to notice that you're getting really upset? According to Dr. Greene, it's important to let our kids lead the way in coming up with possible solutions. This helps them "buy into" the plan and feel more in control of how they'll feel or experience the tough stuff that comes their way. But keep in mind that the agreed upon solution has to be acceptable to both parent and child.

Ensure That Home Is a Safe Space

Becca knew her six-year-old, twice-exceptional son was struggling—he was beginning to act out in a number of ways—and the whole family was feeling the weight of the misunderstanding they were facing from members of their school and local community. Becca and her husband realized that what was happening every day was negatively affecting not just them, but their son, who was ramping up the intensity.

At their wits' end, Becca and her family sold their house and moved to a more rural community where they could be free from the stress of nosy neighbors and other assorted critics. As she describes it, "Our new country lifestyle has been very healing. We've been here for two years now and have 'found' ourselves as a family. To support our son emotionally, we try to be here for him at all times and honor his needs. We keep up with his interests, and the three of us pretty much do everything as a family. He's ten years old now and doing great."

Although packing up and moving isn't something everybody can (or wants to) do, we can still make tangible changes at home to foster feelings of security, safety, and comfort. Kayte helps her neurodiverse daughter feel safe at home by encouraging her daughter to cry when she needs to cry and let her anger out when she's angry. Kayte has also worked hard to create a judgment-free atmosphere where her daughter can talk to her about anything. "Making myself available to listen no matter what personal daily stresses and distractions seem so important to me at the time," she says, "has created a strong bond and sense of security for my child."

One mother of a ten-year-old twice-exceptional boy told me she puts all her energy into accepting her son for who he is, supporting whatever interests and passions he has, and making sure he knows he's a good kid, since he hears so often at school that he's bad: "My priority is for him to feel safe and supported by me. Because school isn't a safe place, friends' houses aren't safe places, and even public spaces aren't really safe places for him. So our house has to be."

For Mary, mother of three differently wired kids, making home feel safe means striking the right balance between knowing when to push and when to back off: "I think the best way I've been able to make them feel safe is to not push them past their limits. When they're experiencing anxiety, they're not learning anything anyway. It's important to me that my kids know their parents are supportive and aren't going to push them over an emotional cliff for missing softball practice or skipping one night's homework."

Here are a few other ideas:

- Work with your child to create a cozy space in his or her bedroom or another room that will always be available. Their cozy space might include things like a pillow and a soft throw, a weighted blanket, some favorite stuffies, a pair of slippers, art that inspires or calms, access to music that soothes or boosts energy, favorite books, and so on.
- Create family rituals such as pizza night, movie night, and game night where the family is together for fun and bonding.
- Foster morning and bedtime routines that help your child begin and end their day feeling regulated, calm, and loved.

Reinforce with Love Every Single Day

In her groundbreaking 2011 children's book *My Princess Boy*, my friend and fellow author Cheryl Kilodavis shares the story of her son Dyson, a boy who bends traditional gender stereotypes by loving pink, wearing dresses and tiaras, and frequently dancing like a ballerina. After facing and coming to terms with her own discomfort with the way her son was expressing himself, Cheryl recognized how difficult her son's path could be if he didn't feel secure and embraced, and she wanted to take a bold step in creating a world where he would be accepted. As she explained in a 2011 interview on the *Today* show, "My turning point was when [my other son] Dkobe said to me, 'Why can't you just let him be happy, Mom?' I realized at that moment that this was my issue, not his, and not Dyson's or [her husband] Dean's." So Cheryl did some soul-searching and began journaling, ultimately printing out a mock-up of the book she wrote to express her feelings about the costs of exclusion and the power of true acceptance.

I'm not suggesting we all pen children's books like Cheryl did to let our child know they have a safe haven in us, but we do want to find our own ways to let our children know that we see and appreciate who they are ... *every single day* (even on, or perhaps *especially* on, the really bad days). We want to find opportunities to reinforce the idea that our child is loved. This might be as simple as a sweet little bedtime ritual, love notes slipped into a lunchbox, shared private jokes, or simply lighting up when we see them after school or when they stumble into our bedroom early in the morning still half asleep. Even in the midst of a tense interaction with Asher, I work hard to make the conversation safe as soon as I recognize he's getting defensive. I pause to remind him how loved he is and let him know that I respect his point of view and process for whatever we're working through.

> **Start Now** Make a list of situations that regularly create anxiety for your child, and work in collaboration with him or her to develop a plan for *proactively* addressing each one.

Give (Loud and Unapologetic) Voice to Your Reality

"It took me quite a long time to develop a voice, and now that I have it, I am not going to be silent."
—Madeleine Albright

One of my favorite things about hosting the *TiLT Parenting Podcast* is connecting with inspiring people on the front lines of changing the conversation about neurodiversity. People like Ann Douglas. The author of several parenting books, including her most recent, *Parenting Through the Storm*, Ann is a writer and speaker known for sparking conversations that matter. She sees one of her most pressing missions as helping lift the stigma surrounding neurodiversity and mental illness. And despite sometimes being criticized for openly speaking out about challenges faced by both herself and her four atypical kids, Ann presses on because she believes the cost of not talking openly is too high.

She explained that when she was interviewing parents of differently wired kids for her book, even anonymously, many were petrified someone would put two and two together and realize it was their child she was writing about. As Ann describes it, "There was this visceral level of terror which I thought was just so awful. Not only are families sometimes carrying the burden of a lot of stress and anxiety and trying to make systems work for their kids, but on top of that, they feel like they can't reach out for the support that would make that easier."

In "Tilt 2," I wrote about the importance of getting out of isolation and connecting, but in this chapter I want to take things a step farther. Because if we really want to change the way our children's neurodifferences are perceived by the world, we need to start honestly sharing what's real for us and for them. I'm convinced it's the only way to get rid of the stigmas and shame that silence so many of us, perpetuating misunderstanding.

The Cost of Not Speaking Up

When I Googled the definition of "stigma," this is the first thing that popped up: "a mark of disgrace associated with a particular circumstance, quality, or person." Wow. The word "disgrace" really says it all, doesn't it? No wonder no one wants to talk outside of their safe family unit about what's really going on.

Before I go any further, I think it's important to acknowledge that I recognize that stigma is a very real thing. People have certain beliefs about, and make associations with, different types of neurodiversity, largely based on negative stereotypes, isolated or out-of-context experiences, or just plain old misinformation. They will and often do treat our kids differently when they learn about a specific diagnosis. Our children might be excluded from things. Their qualities such as kindness and generosity and creativity might be overlooked or missed, because stigmas blanket everything in a shroud of negativity. In fact, Derin was initially concerned about letting Asher's teachers know what we knew for that very reason—he equated that disclosure with pinning a target on Asher's back, and was worried that teachers would be especially critical of him or look for problems that might not have been there. So, I get it.

But I still believe we need to get vocal. Because when we don't, our kids may begin believing they're not okay, no matter how loving or supportive we are at home. And as they grow up and increasingly find themselves in situations where self-advocacy will be a critical piece of their success, they may feel afraid, insecure, or embarrassed about speaking up. By not giving a voice to our experiences, we're perpetuating stigmas by "awfulizing" what is. We're staying in our lane. We're playing small. And our kids deserve much more.

Speaking Up (and Out) Changes Everything

I recently had a conversation about this very topic with my friend Melissa Wardy, creator of *Pigtail Pals & Ballcap Buddies*, author of *Redefining Girly*, and mother to a daughter with anxiety disorder. Melissa told me the story of a girl she met through her daughter's swim team. As she described it, she was watching the swimmers one day when one of the girls walked up to her, stuck out her hand, and introduced herself: "Hi! I have juvenile diabetes and a little bit of Asperger's, so when I get excited, these are the things that I do. But otherwise, it's all good." Melissa had to laugh at this girl's confidence—after all, Melissa didn't have *her* elevator pitch ready—but loved that this girl not only knew who she was and how to advocate for herself, but was unfazed by it all. *This is who I am and this is what I need. Thanks!*

That right there? That is what we're going for. We want to normalize difference so it becomes just another aspect of who someone is—a way to better understand their experience rather than a commentary on what's wrong with someone. We want our children to hear the assuredness in our voice every time we talk about them.

Reflect

Am I comfortable using the language surrounding my child's diagnosis if he or she has one?

. . .

What am I afraid will happen if I am open about what's happening in our world?

. . .

How might my experience, and that of my child, improve by giving a voice to our reality?

People always tell me that they love how open and confident Asher is, but he is this way because we talk openly about everything all the time—in our family, with friends and extended family, with doctors, with teachers. Asher's neurodifferences are a part of who he is, and there is absolutely no shame in that. (And why would there be?)

////////////////////// **Embracing the Tilt** //////////////////////

Get Honest with Yourself

How we parent—from the way we discipline to what kind of education we prioritize for our child—stems from our personal beliefs, thoughts, values, and ideas about life, regardless of a child's wiring. So it only makes sense that when a child is neurodiverse, these same beliefs, thoughts, values, and ideas play a *major* role. I believe that as parents raising differently wired kids, it's critical that we take the time to explore our personal feelings surrounding neurodiversity. Just because our kid is atypical doesn't mean we don't have our own hang-ups about it.

Maybe upon closer examination, you will realize that you harbor some ideas about gifted kids being doomed to experience a life of wasted potential. Or maybe, like I used to be, you're turned off by hyperactivity, so when your own ADHD kiddo is running around, you switch into instant annoyance mode. Some people struggle with the actual labels themselves, uncomfortable with words such as "autism" or "learning disability" or "slow processing speed."

Whatever those things are for us, we need to get honest about them, which means uncovering and naming any negative beliefs we may have surrounding our child's diagnoses. Even if you'd prefer to skip this step because you feel a tinge of guilt or shame about harboring negative thoughts, don't. Denial, even with the best of intentions, doesn't serve us or our kids. And once you've acknowledged those unhelpful thoughts and beliefs, you'll be able to reframe them in ways that are more positive, and true, for you and your child.

Notice Where You're Keeping Quiet

Derin and I were flabbergasted when Asher started reading just before his third birthday. Although he had a bookshelf stocked with toddler favorites, and Derin and I read together with him a lot, we hadn't been trying to teach him how to read. It wasn't even on our radar. Yet there we were, with this tiny little human, suddenly and unexpectedly literate. By the time he was three and a half, Asher was a reading machine, consuming any children's book within reach.

We knew from the experiences of friends with older kids that a child learning to read is a big deal, a leap into a whole new world of books and literature, and one worth excitedly sharing with others. Yet we quickly realized that Asher's reading wasn't necessarily something other parents wanted to hear about. From the disinterested or strange reactions we received, we got the sense that when we talked about Asher's reading with parents whose older children were just learning the skill, they felt it diminished their own child's accomplishment or took away from some of their joy. So we stopped talking about it, not saying anything unless someone witnessed Asher reading and brought it up themselves, and even then minimizing the whole thing lest they think we were bragging.

We all have topics we keep quiet about when our child is developing differently. Sometimes it's their gifts we downplay—those amazing talents or quirks or abilities that could make others feel uncomfortable. Other times we downplay their challenges because we don't want to make *ourselves* uncomfortable. To complicate things even further, many of us don't talk about our child's neurodifferences with them or in front of them. I find this to be especially true in the early years when we're still coming to terms with what we're learning and aren't ready to speak the words out loud. For instance, when we first got Asher's provisional diagnosis of PDD-NOS and ADHD, I asked the clinician for a copy of the assessment that omitted the actual diagnosis. I just wasn't ready to openly share that level of detail with the world (or possibly even with myself). My hunch is that you have your things, too—areas where you may be staying mum in an attempt to squash feelings of shame or embarrassment or fear or insecurity. I encourage you to reflect on areas where you're regularly keeping quiet, about both negative *and* positive aspects of your differently wired reality. Once you know what these areas are, make a deal with yourself to be honest and true to yourself and your child.

Speak Out on Social Media

In the spring of 2017, fidget spinners—little spinning devices that fit in the palm of a child's hand—became all the rage in classrooms around the world. Almost overnight, it seemed as if every child was bringing spinners into school, the idea being that the toys helped them relieve stress and stay focused. Because we're homeschoolers, Asher and I didn't even know fidget spinners were a thing until we saw a story about them on the Dutch youth news channel, *Jeudgjournal*. We watched the piece, incidentally, while Asher played with his own Fidget Cube, a small cube-shaped toy we'd backed through Kickstarter that had lots of features to keep his fingers busy so he could concentrate.

Something about the fidget spinners and their explosive popularity didn't sit well with me, but I wasn't sure exactly what it was until I found a post by Aiyana Bailin on the site *Thinking Person's Guide to Autism* that reflected my thoughts. She wrote, "Something that was considered entirely pathological and in dire need of correction when done by disabled people is now perfectly acceptable because it is being done by non-disabled people." For me, Aiyana nailed it—fidgeting is a problem when kids like Asher do it, but when it's adopted as "normal" behavior by neurotypical kids, suddenly it's perfectly acceptable. Of course, within weeks of emerging, fidget spinners had been largely banned by schools because they were too distracting, so we're right back where we started. (Or maybe we're even further behind?)

I shared Aiyana's post widely on Facebook and Twitter, because well-written posts like hers can be a powerful way of speaking up and saying, *Hey, something doesn't feel right here.* Through social media, we can speak up in big or little ways to spark important conversations about intolerance and acceptance and the experience of those different from us. Sharing posts like this is a simple and safe way to spread ideas and new perspectives, and, for the more outspoken among us, respectfully commenting or engaging in dialogues about controversial issues works well, too. Listen and look for threads, memes, and other items on your social media feeds that perpetuate negative stigmas surrounding neurodiversity, and then *use your voice* to speak out against them. The more kindly and consciously, the better.

Disclose in a Way That's Right for Your World

The idea of whom to tell and when came up in a group program I participated in with parent coach Margaret Webb many years ago. A mother on the call wondered if she should disclose her daughter's diagnosis to the parent of another child coming over for a playdate. I loved Margaret's answer, and I still follow her guidelines today. Margaret said who and what she tells about her son's autism is on a "need-to-know basis," meaning that if it's important in a situation that someone understand the specifics of her son's wiring, she discloses. If not and it's none of their business, she doesn't. So the meddlesome neighbor who has no relationship with us? Yeah, she doesn't need to know. But the soccer coach who regularly deals with our child's challenging behavior probably should.

Part of the challenge when it comes to unapologetically speaking our truth is that this is very personal stuff, and many of us get flustered or wound up when talking about it. Just as we came up with planned responses to people imposing their beliefs about our child's time line, you can do the same thing here and develop language around neuro-diversity, as well as create your own guidelines about what information you're comfortable disclosing, to whom, and in what way.

If it's the diagnosis itself that you're uncomfortable with and you feel safer talking in broader strokes, that works, too. *My daughter is incredibly energetic and never stops moving*, or *My son can get really upset when his schedule is disrupted*, or *My daughter is working way ahead of grade level*. That's one of the reasons why I love the term "differently wired" so much. It gives us a simple way to convey our child's atypical nature without going into details in situations where details aren't necessary.

Over the years, I've changed my policy about what, how, and to whom to disclose. These days, I tend to be fairly open about Asher's neurodifferences, especially in situations where he'll be interacting with new people and I know his way of being may be confusing without context. Even though many people don't fully understand what ADHD and Asperger's and giftedness entail, mentioning these things at least gives them a heads-up that they shouldn't expect Asher to participate in a typical way. And that is important for him to feel secure when trying new things.

Because Asher's wiring is such a part of who he is and my and our family's story, not talking openly would feel disingenuous. Disclosing has helped our family fully own our reality. This is who we are, and this is how we live our life.

So what's the right balance for you? Although it's clear by now that I don't recommend hiding a child's diagnosis from family, close friends, and teachers, I also believe there are ways to be open without grabbing a megaphone and announcing our truth to the world (or sharing your

> **Start Now** Commit to combating negative stigmas by honestly sharing what's happening in your world with one new person this week.

family's story to thousands of listeners in the form of a podcast, like I do). This is a personal choice, and you have to figure out where you're comfortable and what makes the most sense in your world.

My advice is to create a personal policy around sharing and make sure it's rooted in a place of love and possibility as opposed to fear.

Practice Relentless Self-Care

"Be there for others, but never leave yourself behind."
—Dodinsky

A little over a year ago, Asher and I realized we needed to begin each day more intentionally, so we decided to implement a new daily morning routine. We got the idea from Hal Elrod's book *The Miracle Morning*, which encourages people to consciously set aside time first thing for six different activities: exercise, meditating, writing, reading, visualizing, and affirming. We'd read that it takes thirty days to formulate a new habit, so we created daily check sheets, designed a schedule for our routine, and committed to trying it out for one month. More than a year later, we're still engaging in a semblance of our original routine, and continue to experience the benefits of taking the time to dream, scheme, and intentionally start our day on the right foot.

I love that our morning routine has helped Asher to become more deliberate about his goals and discover the power of reflection and sitting in stillness; but even more than that, I'm excited that it's teaching him the importance of doing something for no other reason than that it's good for him physically, intellectually, mentally, and emotionally.

Self-Care Isn't Optional

You know those people who put everyone else's needs—partner's, children's, friends', bosses'—ahead of their own? I am not one of those people. On the contrary, I am unapologetic about doing what I need to do to ensure my physical, emotional, and mental health, because in the past when I haven't been so self-interested, things tended to fall apart. For me, self-care is never selfish.

I realize that even contemplating the concept of self-care can result in a variety of reactions, including eye rolls from those who consider it a "new age" concept alongside "balance" and "self-interest," guilt from those who practice it but feel they shouldn't focus so much energy on themselves, and even shame from those who don't take care of themselves at all and recognize that neglecting their needs isn't doing them or their family any favors.

Me? I'm self-care positive. I believe in the benefits of self-care for everyone, but especially for parents raising atypical children. The way I see it, self-care isn't an optional "if and when I have time" kind of thing for us—it's an absolute *must*. It's what keeps our reserve tank full and enables us to be resilient even in the face of unexpected curve-balls, draining interactions, and the general emotional wear and tear that can accompany our experience. Self-care is about mental health. It's about modeling the importance of personal well-being. It's about taking care of ourselves so we have the greatest chance of staying present and dealing with the hard stuff in a way that best serves our child, ourselves, and our family.

I credit self-care for my ability to successfully homeschool a demanding twice-exceptional kid. I run or walk daily. I'm a frequent power napper. I call my sister anytime I need a pickup. I create opportunities for precious alone time. I move homeschool classes out to the park or onto our roof deck on beautiful days because sun and nature recharge me. I take a lunch break every day and spend it doing something that fills me up, whether that's listening to a podcast, catching up on the previous night's *Daily Show*, or blasting eighties music while folding laundry. Whatever it takes. *Self-care every single day.*

I'm a shameless advocate of self-care because the sentiment that we can't take care of our children if we're not taking care of ourselves is more than a cheesy quote in our Instagram feed. As one parent once wrote to me, "In order to help my son, I really need to be regulated myself. I can read any number of books and highlight tips, but I wouldn't be able to implement what I wanted to unless I invested the time to center and regulate myself. I realize now that self-care is not about pampering yourself, it is about spending the time to give yourself the tools to show up with awareness and compassion."

Getting Real About Self-Care

What do I mean by self-care? I'm not suggesting daily trips to the spa or gym or an hour of meditation each morning (unless of course that's your thing). Rather, I'm talking about taking daily actions that are two things: (1) intentional, meaning something you're consciously choosing to do because it's good for your mind, body, and/or soul; and (2) just for you.

Self-care doesn't have to happen alone. Sometimes my husband joins me for a run and I still consider it self-care, because it's intentional, and I'm doing it just for me. Sometimes Asher joins me in my midafternoon Michael Jackson dance break, and again—totally fine. Because I choose the tunes and dance my booty off intentionally and just for me. (If he joins in, that's just more fun to go around.)

It's the *intentionality* piece here that makes the difference. By embracing self-care every day, we are consciously choosing ourselves—we're giving ourselves the message that we are worthy and important . . . that we matter. And that kind of thinking pays major dividends, and not just for us. We're also modeling to our children that self-care is part of being a healthy, responsible adult. It shows kids that no matter how stressful things may get, there's always room for lightness and laughter.

I refer to self-care as a "practice," because it's not a once-and-done kind of thing. It's important that we foster a culture of self-care within ourselves and our families, actively creating daily pockets of joy and contentment every day, even when things are difficult. More than that, we want to establish true routines of self-care, because that makes it more likely that we'll continue engaging in those activities when we're facing unexpected regressions, school setbacks, or ramp-ups in difficult behavior. It's especially during those times that we'll need to find ways to recharge and reset.

///////////////////////// **Embracing the Tilt** /////////////////////////

Assess Your Current State of Self-Care

In her book *The Pie Life*, author and speaker Samantha Ettus offers parents a framework for creating a fulfilling life—one that sees life as a pie made up of seven different "slices": career, health, relationship, children, community, friends, and hobbies. Samantha encourages women to find ways to regularly be involved in multiple slices of their pie rather than just one or two, even when they're in the throes of the parenting years, when their role as a mother might feel all-consuming. "I'm not saying the slices will always be the same size right now," Samantha says. "Hobbies might only be a sliver and parenting might be forty percent of your pie and that's okay." Samantha believes it's especially important for parents raising differently wired kids to assess and rework their "pie" to make regular, planned self-care a part of daily life.

As Samantha explains, "It's so important that you are planning for essential things like leisure time because it's going to make you a better parent. You want to be looking at your pie and saying, 'Okay, today my hobby slice might only be a sliver. It's about being realistic about what you can fit in today.'"

Whether you are a mother or a father, one way to assess the current state of your self-care practice is to follow Samantha's suggestion of taking a good, hard look at your pie and considering the size of each slice. Another is to conduct a one-week self-audit in which you track your daily activities and get clear on how you actually spend your time. When you look back and reflect on the ebb and flow of your week, the gaps will become visible. You'll quickly see if you're all work and no play, or if your downtime is pretty much nonexistent. You've got to know where you stand in terms of self-care, as well as which other areas of your life are taking too large a role, to make the kind of changes that result in more balance.

Defend Against Your Self-Care Roadblocks

Asher is someone who has a lot of goals. On any given day, he has plans for things he wants to accomplish—complete a 3-D model render, build a new space plane for *Kerbal Space Program*, work on the font he's creating, make a new logo for his "brand." At the same time, he frequently gets sidetracked and finishes the day without ticking off any boxes, and then frustration ensues. Lately we've been working on identifying his personal roadblocks, aka those things that reliably result in his becoming distracted and squandering his valuable screen time, such as pop-up notifications from a forum, reading archives of his favorite comic strip *Pearls Before Swine*, or getting sucked into a game open in a different browser window. Now that he knows what typically gets in his way, he's learning to anticipate those roadblocks and defend against them. In his case, this means making sure notifications are turned off for his apps and programs, closing all windows and tabs that aren't related to what he's doing, and setting timers so that if he does get distracted, he won't go too far down the rabbit hole before being snapped back to reality.

This same strategy can be applied to safeguarding our own self-care. For instance, if someone were to explain to me why their self-care doesn't regularly happen, I'd venture to say their reasons relate to not having enough time, energy, or ideas about what to do, or some variation therein. Hidden within each of these "excuses" are roadblocks—thoughts or even tangible obstacles that regularly prevent them from practicing self-care. Any of these sound familiar?

- going to bed too late
- mindlessly wasting time on social media
- keeping your cell phone on at all times and responding to every notification
- constantly running behind schedule
- making commitments to everyone but yourself
- tying yourself up with volunteer obligations

Once we know what our roadblocks are, we can defend against them. We can turn off notifications on our phone. We can use online tools such as News Feed Eradicator to hide our Facebook news feed on our computer. We can banish our cell from the bedroom, and be vigilant about having lights out by eleven. We can gracefully extricate ourselves from committees and volunteer obligations that aren't nurturing to our soul.

In their book *Switch*, Chip and Dan Heath write about the importance of "shaping the path," which is essentially building your own personal "behavioral autopilot" as a defense against roadblocks. When he wants to ensure he'll have a good day, Asher does this by setting out the night before everything he needs to achieve it. I always know when he's shaping the path because he's laid out his slippers, lucky hat, favorite blanket, iPod cued to Hans Zimmer, journal and pen, book, and a sticky note reminding him of his goal. That way his self-care pile is the first thing he sees when he wakes up in the morning—he'd literally have to step over it to avoid engaging with the items. Instead, these items trigger the behavior he wants, in this case to be intentional about his day from the get-go. We can do the same with self-care. Lay out your workout clothes the night before, have your favorite yoga video cued up on YouTube, set your favorite journal and pen on your bedside table so you'll be triggered to write for a few minutes upon first waking.

How else can you shape your path?

Create Your Ideal Self-Care Practice

As a single mom completely immersed in raising her autistic daughter while finishing up her bachelor's degree, Brandi found that self-care was the last thing on her mind—until she realized her pace and lifestyle as a solo parent weren't sustainable. "A lot of people in my life were saying I had to take care of myself, because if I didn't, who would be around to take care of my little girl if something happened to me?" she explained. Brandi began building in a few daily self-care strategies that have made all the difference—an hour of reading, thirty minutes of meditation, and long walks, with her daughter sometimes joining her on the latter. And as Brandi describes it, incorporating daily self-care has been a game changer: "I feel totally different. I get the day started and I look at the world differently. And then I'm ready to go. I don't care if I don't accomplish anything else on that list."

No matter how busy we are, there is always a way to weave self-care into our lives. Part of that process might be as simple as redefining what self-care actually is. As I wrote earlier, self-care doesn't have to be big, expensive, or indulgent. The way I see it, a hot shower is self-care when done consciously, as is listening to a podcast or NPR during the morning commute or grabbing a cappuccino from the drive-through at Starbucks.

For instance, I work on TiLT Parenting almost every weekend, but I find ways to weave in self-care. I choose a café with a good vibe that's at least a fifteen-minute bike ride away so I can get exercise, upload a new podcast to my iPod so I can listen while I'm bicycling, plug in my headphones and chill with my Zen music list on Spotify while working, and imbibe a delicious mocha. Sometimes I even meet up with a friend for coworking so I can squeeze in a little girlfriend time. All of these things are intentional, they're just for me, and they make me happy. Self-care opportunities are truly everywhere once you start to look.

When I asked parents in the TiLT community to share how they practice daily self-care, I was flooded with creative, simple ideas (and a few that I've added to my own list): participating in a book club, getting enough sleep, writing in a journal, praying, closing the office door for ten minutes and meditating, turning the phone off an hour before bedtime, practicing yoga, gardening, drinking good coffee, playing the ukulele, doing needlepoint, and getting a closet or room organized, to name a few.

Pro Tip Brainstorm a list of self-care activities (from easy-to-implement to special occasion items) that you can commit to incorporating into your life.

What does self-care look like for you? Netflix nights? Drinks out with a friend? Curling up with a book? Five minutes of stillness? What kinds of things do you already do that you can tweak so that they qualify as proactive self-care? What kinds of new self-care activities would you like to build into your life?

Create a Plan with Support and Accountability

I'm a big believer in the power of accountability. Having someone or something to answer to can be highly effective, especially when forming new, healthy lifestyle habits. For example, if I arrange to meet up with a friend for a walk in the park, I wouldn't dream of being a no-show. Or if I know I need to squeeze in a run but I'm feeling too tired, I might post on social media and ask my online community to hold me accountable. When a half dozen Facebook friends have commented with words of encouragement, there's no way I'm *not* going to run. Both of these strategies help me follow through on what I want to do in the first place.

When I first began consciously building up my self-care habits, when Asher was around four years old, I created a chart for tracking the small self-care actions I took every day. The chart has a list of half a dozen different activities—from listening to music from *Rent* to taking a hot shower or going for a twenty-minute walk—and I set a personal goal of ticking off at least two items per day. I left that chart on my desk, where it served as a constant reminder of what I was working toward. That way, if I hadn't yet met that day's minimum when I checked in before dinner, I could choose an item from the list and get it done.

Of course, there are many different ways to be accountable. Some people like to report in to support groups such as Weight Watchers or the Whole Life Challenge or Facebook communities, whereas others prefer to be accountable only to themselves or their journal. People like me and my fellow lovers of structure and organization like being accountable to *charts*. Whatever works for you, works. Here are some ideas for ways to build in accountability as you develop healthy self-care habits:

Start Now Commit to doing at least one small act of self-care every single day moving forward. *You've got this.*

- Commit to recording your self-care activities in a journal (or spreadsheet or chart).
- Join up with a live or virtual "challenge" (à la the Whole Life Challenge) where community support and reporting in are part of the engagement.
- Tell a friend, partner, or family member about your self-care goals and ask them to hold you to them.
- Make firm plans to meet up with other people for exercise, social events, and more.
- Buy tickets in advance for activities you'd like to do (knowing you'd hate to throw the money away by not following through).
- Set a personal goal (for example, thirty days of consecutive exercise) and set your sights on a reward you can enjoy once you've reached your goal.
- Tell your partner and children of your intention and ask for their support in developing your new habits.

Let Go of Your Impossible Expectations for Who You "Should" Be as a Parent

///

"To free us from the expectations of others, to give us back to ourselves—there lies the great, the singular power of self-respect."
—Joan Didion

Lest you are under the impression that I've got it all figured out and always navigate bad days with grace and ease, I hereby present to you Exhibit A, an excerpt from my journal circa 2014, edited for length, language, and repetition:

What the bleep *is my problem? I would be furious if I heard someone else speaking to Asher the way I just spoke to him, in my ridiculously sarcastic, snippy way, "Always a pleasure to do business with you!" and "Oh, gee. That's so much clearer to me now that you've yelled at me.* Thanks*!" What the* bleep *do I think I'm accomplishing other than shaming him and telling him he's an idiot? I heard myself saying these words and watched myself do it, yet I did it anyway. I hate today. I hate myself as a mom. If I were on the outside looking in at my morning with Asher I would come to the conclusion that I was a horrible person. I know how to do better. But I can't seem to be able to do it. I know I'm not supposed to judge myself, but I'm doing such a lousy job. How can I feel like I don't even want to be around my son? Why can't I find the compassion I expect others to feel and show for him?*

Phew. And that was just one entry of too many to count, all saying pretty much the same thing. *I suck at parenting.*

No surprise here, but the most vocal critic of those of us raising atypical kids is often ourselves. Case in point, in the midst of my *own* meltdowns, I would frequently say to Derin something along the lines of, "But I'd be such a good mom if I had a typical child!" And then we'd both laugh, because we knew what I was saying was absurd. I *was* a good mom, but for some reason I believed I needed to be *better* or that I wasn't doing enough. I observed the way some friends remained calm and Zen when their children were pushing their buttons and self-criticized my inability to do the same. Most of the time, I felt like a walking contradiction, outraged at teachers and coaches and other parents who had no tolerance for Asher's behavior while demonstrating very little of my own.

When we parent from a place of guilt, frustration, and self-doubt, what we're really doing is telling ourselves that *we're not enough*. We're not patient enough. We're not loving enough. We're not resourceful enough. We're not good enough. Not only is harshly judging ourselves a waste of time and energy, but it results in our parenting from a place of weakness and fear. We pile on the self-blame when things are hard, and doubt our ability to provide our child with the kind of support they need, which can quickly spiral into feeling that familiar sense of being overwhelmed about future "what-ifs." When we're busy beating ourselves up, we just might forget how incredibly resourceful we are.

But there's an even higher cost of all this judging: Demanding perfection from ourselves inadvertently sends the message to our kids that perfection is what we expect from them. We miss out on opportunities to model flaws, failure, and growth.

Expecting Perfection

Cami, a mother of three kids, including one differently wired son, admits to seeing her successes as just barely meeting minimum expectations and her failures as much bigger than they actually are. "I'll look at other parents, especially if they're also parenting a differently wired child, and think, *How do they do it? How can I have more energy for my child like they do? Or advocate better for my child like they do?*" Luckily, Cami says her husband helps her reframe her thinking when she's comparing herself with other parents and demanding perfection. She explains, "When I'm feeling that way, he helps me see the bigger picture and recognize what I'm doing well, as well as what I can reasonably improve. But, yeah ... I tend to be pretty hard on myself."

Google "parenting perfectionism" and you'll get a half million results in less than a second. As it turns out, it seems that nothing less than perfect is what so many parents expect from themselves, as is evidenced by the millions of parents who don't allow themselves to miss one assembly or field trip, take time for themselves, or express human emotions such as anger or sadness in front of their child, even if those choices come at the cost of their own well-being. Parenting perfection is partly responsible for another harmful trend ... helicopter parenting, that state of being overly involved in every aspect of a child's life in an attempt to shield them from experiencing anything difficult or painful or challenging. In other words ... *life.*

Parents of differently wired kids aren't immune from this phenomenon, which is unfortunate, because we have so many more opportunities to butt up against imperfection, both in the way our children show up and in the way we respond to them. Most parents of atypical kids can't "tiger mom" them into being compliant, emotionally regulated overachievers, and if that's what we're trying to do, it won't feel good for anybody involved.

As psychoanalyst H. David Stein, MD, was quoted in Parents .com, our quest for perfectionism can have adverse effects on our kids, too. "Parents who cannot tolerate their imperfections often cannot tolerate their children's either. As a result, kids will feel that their parents are dissatisfied with them, even if it's not stated. They pick up on subtle cues." When you consider that quote in the context of differently wired kids who are already picking up on many *not-so-subtle* cues that there's something "wrong" with them, the implications of demanding perfection from ourselves need to be taken seriously.

When We Drop the Expectations

I'm all for working to become the best parent (and person) I can be—personal growth is one of my core values. But at the same time, it's critical that we let go of impossible expectations for how we should be raising our children, and treat ourselves with compassion. It's possible to strive for improvement while being gentle with ourselves about our faults. We want to replace sentiments such as *"I'm terrible at staying calm* when my kid is having a meltdown" with *"I'm working at staying calm* when my kid is having a meltdown."

When we can do this, we make room for something magical to happen in our families. We can be more relaxed during conflicts because we know the outcome isn't a reflection of how good a job we're doing. When we are gentle with ourselves and remember that we're doing the best we can in this moment, we can stop those downward emotional spirals grounded in the belief that we can't give our child what he or she needs. And most powerfully, we can model what healthy and beautiful imperfection looks like. We can let our kids see us fumble, recover, and try again.

I love what Momastery's Glennon Doyle Melton so aptly

Reflect

Where do I think I'm failing as a parent? In what areas do I experience guilt or shame?

· · ·

What do I regularly tell others I could be doing a better job at when it comes to my parenting?

· · ·

Where am I screwing up regularly in my relationship with my child, and what is perfect about that?

expressed in an essay for Oprah.com: "What if it has never been our job—or our right—to protect our children from every incoming bump and bruise? What if, instead, our obligation is to point them directly toward life's inevitable trials and tribulations and say, 'Honey, that challenge was made for you. It might hurt, but it will also nurture wisdom, courage, and character. I can see what you're going through, and it's big. But I can also see your strength, and that's even bigger. This won't be easy, but we can do hard things.'"

/////////////////////////// **Embracing the Tilt** ///////////////////////////

Unleash Your Inner Critic

As a life coach and author, Andrea Owen of Your Kick Ass Life helps people learn to manage their "inner critic," which is another term for that judgmental, negative voice in our head that gets in our business about everything from how we look to what we should or shouldn't have done or said. Our inner critic's favorite thing to do is rain on our parade and remind us that we're not good enough. Andrea says that our inner critic is loudest when it comes to our bodies (too fat, too skinny, too tall, too short), but that right up there in spot number two is the topic of *parenting*. Since our inner critic has an opinion about pretty much everything, it's important that we get to know him or her well so we can recognize when he or she is paying us a visit.

In describing a confrontation with her own inner critic, Andrea shared what this looks like in action. As Andrea describes it, she had just attended a not-so-great meeting about her second-grade son's IEP where she was reminded of all the ways in which he wasn't measuring up. In that same meeting, she also learned about advocacy organizations for parents like her in case she wanted to get more involved. Feeling beat-up and defeated, Andrea got into her car to drive home, highlights from the meeting playing over and over in her mind. As she sat at a red light, her inner critic decided to join in the fun: "My mind started to get away from me and I started saying things to myself like *I can't believe I haven't looked into that organization yet. I can't believe I didn't know about these organizations ahead of time. I should have been on top of this. I'm smarter than this. I haven't even done like a 5K for autism awareness! What kind of parent am I?!* It was like I picked up a bat and just beat myself up about all the ways I'm failing him as his mother. And then as the light turned green, I remember thinking to myself, *Okay, this isn't helpful at all. It doesn't help me become a better parent, it's not helping my son, and I need to give myself a break. I am doing the best I can. And I can do better and here are the ways.*" In just the space of a traffic light rotation, Andrea's inner critic had simmered down.

To be clear, unleashing and ultimately taming our inner critic like Andrea did requires conscious work and lots of practice, and can be difficult to do, especially mid–shame spiral. But the process Andrea described is what we want to work toward—recognizing that this voice in our head, the one telling us we're failing or not doing enough or screwing our kids up, is not the voice of truth.

As Andrea says, it's about catching ourselves in those moments, acknowledging what's happening, and then choosing to go in a different direction. And the more attuned we become to this critic, the easier it will be for us to lessen his or her effect on us. Become cognizant of times when you judge and shame yourself for parenting decisions, in-the-moment reactions, and other things that result in your feeling like a failure. And then tame your inner critic.

Stop Shoulding on Yourself

I must have just read Elizabeth Gilbert's *Eat, Pray, Love* or something—that's the only reason I can think of for why I'd convinced myself I should be more spiritually evolved than I was. Or maybe it was the fact that I know in my heart of hearts that Asher is perfect just as he is and we were meant to be on this mother-son journey together. Whatever the reason, it seemed as though I expected myself to have the patience, tranquility, and knowingness of the Dalai Lama at all times, even as Asher was a ball of raging intensity all around me. I mean, I was a certified life coach. I'd read the right books. I'd spent years working through my emotional baggage. I should have been able to do better.

At least that is the basic gist of what I dumped on Margaret Webb during a coaching call a few years ago. More than Asher's out-of-control behavior, it was becoming clear that the thing I was most upset about was my expectations for myself. I believed that if I were more evolved, I *should* be able to nip his regression in the bud, because my powerful, peaceful, and loving aura would be too hard for Asher to deny. And the fact that I couldn't do that meant I was a failure, plain and simple. Delusional? Perhaps. Yet these were my real thoughts. I was "shoulding" myself like nobody's business.

Back in my twenties, when I went into therapy at the Albert Ellis Institute, there was a T-shirt tacked to the wall behind the receptionist's desk that read, "Stop shoulding on yourself." I thought it was hilarious at the time, never imagining that twenty years later the sentiment would still be so relevant in my life. Generally speaking, the word "should" isn't super-helpful. It places demands and expectations and judgments where they don't need to exist. So my suggestion? Ban the word "should" and other self-judging language from your vocabulary for good. Really. You won't miss them ... I promise.

Give Yourself a Break

One of the things I hear most often from parents of atypical children is that they feel a sense of sadness for not realizing their child was struggling sooner. As one mother wrote me in an email about her profoundly gifted daughter, "My greatest regret is that I made her suffer because I couldn't own up to the fact that my kid is differently wired and needed a nontraditional education. Indeed, I had to change my life and plans to provide for her education myself, and I selfishly wanted to avoid that."

I realize all parents can be hard on themselves, but in my experience, parents of atypical kids feel like they're failing or aren't doing enough more so than other parents, in part because we get reminders every day that, in comparison with most families on our radar, things are not going well. I've been there, and I can tell you right now that that kind of thinking isn't healthy. More than that, it's not helpful. Just as I'm sure is true for you, I know my intention every single day is to do right by Asher. Holding on to that truth allows me to give myself room to screw up. Which, by the way, I do plenty of. Just two days ago, after managing to let Asher's snippy attitude roll off my back for most of the day, I completely lost my cool. It was ugly. As in, dropped-the-f-bomb ugly. Yet, in the end, two good things came out of it: (1) Asher was so shocked by my expletive that it snapped him out of his mood, and (2) I was so shocked by my expletive that I retreated to my room, took some breaths, and then returned to the scene of the crime, where I apologized and cracked a joke to lighten the mood, and we laughed and moved past it.

Have you ever been in my shoes? Snapped? Blown up? Yelled? Said the absolute wrong thing at the wrong time? Punished your child without thinking but then felt trapped into following through so they wouldn't see you "fold" under pressure? Or maybe you've even dropped a few f-bombs of your own. If so, remember that the same thing that goes for our kids goes for us—*we are not our behavior*. We are having a very human experience here, with all the rawness and imperfection that goes along with it. And that means we're going to have less-than-brilliant parenting moments. As my friend Courtney says, sometimes "life gets lifey." And when that happens, it's important to consciously give ourselves a break, take responsibility for our actions, and move on. Who knows, our kids might even learn something, too.

Take What Works and Let Go of the Rest

I love exploring different parenting philosophies and emerging parenting trends, devouring new books, and reading up on the latest research about what children need to thrive. At the same time, I recognize that the approach behind much of what I read—about things such as how to raise a resilient child, how to help them foster grit, how to help them fail, how to grow their critical-thinking skills—doesn't apply for us in the same way it does for parents with typical kids. As a result, there's an inherent disconnect that we have to recognize and accept.

Case in point. I'm fan of Jessica Lahey's work, especially her book *The Gift of Failure*, which explores why allowing our children to experience failure is a critical part of helping them eventually succeed. I strongly believe in the message and philosophy of Jessica's book. My goal is to parent Asher in a way that helps him develop the resilience Jessica writes about so that as he gets older, he has the wherewithal, ability, and confidence to handle whatever life throws at him. Yet, I can't apply all of the learning at face value. For instance, Jessica shares the story of her son forgetting to bring in a school project the day it was due. Despite the fact that she was driving to the school later that day, she decided not to bring it in for him. Jessica explains that although the urge to rescue her son, not just for his emotional sake but so his grade didn't suffer, was instinctual and almost overpowering, doing so would have meant that he would miss a powerful opportunity to learn about responsibility, consequences, and how to avoid that situation in the future. After all, getting a low grade for a missed school assignment may stink, but better to learn this lesson now while the stakes are relatively low than when her son is a grown-up and forgetting an important assignment may mean getting fired.

When I read that story, I thought to myself, *Yes* . . . and. *Yes* . . . I totally get Jessica's point and it deeply resonates with me, *and* I know that approach wouldn't work for a lot of differently wired kids, because many need scaffolding and support in the types of executive functions responsible for tracking and managing and remembering assignments. If this scenario played out in my world and Asher realized he was going to get a lower grade on a big project because he forgot it, the meltdown would be colossal. And that's not really an ideal launching point for meaningful learning.

So even though I strive toward helping Asher develop that resiliency Jessica talks about, it's important that I don't expect it to look the same in my family as it does in Jessica's. Rather than hold myself up to the parenting standards of those I admire, I can adjust my expectations based on the child I have and what's true in our world.

Heck, I don't want to be a "tiger mom," but I'll admit to feeling like Asher *needed* to learn an instrument after reading Amy Chua's controversial book. And reading Pamela Druckerman's *Bringing Up Bébé* made me question whether we were spoiling Asher by giving him "kid food" (aka food we knew he would eat) instead of expecting him to eat what everyone else was eating. These little micro-triggers happen every day—in our Facebook newsfeeds, in our Twitter feeds, on the blogs we read, and in the books we see on display at Barnes & Noble. Part of letting go of our expectations of who we should be as parents means understanding where our experience fits in with the noise around us. It's important to recognize when the media we're consuming are subconsciously sending the message that we're not doing a good job. Just like straining the pulp from the juice, we want to put parenting media through our own filter, hold on to only those things that feel positive and useful in relation to our circumstances, and simply let the rest go.

Start Now Write out an affirmation centered on your intention to parent your child in the best way you can right now. For instance, *I am doing the best I can with the information and resources I have available to me. And I'm working toward becoming an even better parent every day.*

Make a Ruckus When You Need To

"Please stop sitting around. We need you to make a ruckus."
—Seth Godin

Getting kicked out of aquarium summer camp was not what I had in mind when I signed Asher up for a week of maritime exploration at one of his favorite spots in the city. But on day one, the kids had been told to stay in a line. Asher's buttons were pushed by some other kids. He pushed back... literally. And that was the end of camp. It was a Monday. He was six. And I was furious. Primarily because I heard all about this at pickup, when I was not-so-inconspicuously singled out by the camp director and told in great detail exactly how inappropriate Asher's behavior had been, not only in front of other parents and kids, but in front of Asher. "Would you *please lower your voice?*" I hissed. "It is not okay for you to do this in front of him. He feels bad enough as it is."

This may have been her first rodeo, but it wasn't mine. I cut the conversation short, grabbed Asher's jacket and backpack, reached for his grubby hand, and made my way to the door. I was still shaking by the time we reached the car and Asher asked if he'd be going back tomorrow. I closed my eyes, braced myself for a rush of upset, and told him we'd be making other plans for the rest of the week. He was inconsolable. One of Asher's deep areas of interest at the time was the ocean, and he fancied himself a budding marine biologist, dreaming of being the first person to go to the bottom of the Mariana Trench (to say he was devastated when James Cameron got there before him, in 2012, would be a gross understatement). On top of that, he was thrilled to finally be old enough to attend the camp, and now here he was, shut down after one day.

But I wasn't okay with how the whole thing had gone down. There are ways to handle difficult conversations with parents, and that had not been one of them. So I called the camp director the next day and did what I was becoming increasingly comfortable doing—made a ruckus. The director invited me in for a conversation and we talked it out. When I explained that it was not so much Asher being expelled from camp that I found so upsetting but rather how poorly it had been handled, the camp staff heard me, promising to do better the next time they were in a similar situation with another camper. And when I described Asher's love of marine biology and how upset he was about losing this opportunity because of things that were beyond his control, they offered to make things right. And so, a few months later, Asher and I went to the aquarium for a private behind-the-tanks tour, where he was able to chat excitedly with a biologist about tides, algae, and sea life. The aquarium staff fixed things the best they could, and I was grateful.

Why We Need to Advocate

Forget thriving—many differently wired kids are simply trying to *exist* in environments that may as well have been designed specifically to speed up their descent into anxiety, stress, and unhappiness. Unfortunately, many atypical kids begin normalizing their negative experiences. Being teased or bullied becomes just another day at school. Being publicly shamed by teachers is just what happens. Hating school and everything about it becomes the new norm.

Zachary Morris, founder of the LEARN Inc. school in Missoula, Montana, which honors neurodiversity, encourages social collaboration, and fosters whole-person growth, sees this every day in the students who come to his school. The majority are differently wired, and many of them have transferred in after one or more negative experiences in traditional school settings. "I have students coming to me who are in elementary school having being diagnosed with PTSD from their previous educational experiences," Zach explains.

Elementary students with PTSD? These kids desperately need us. They need to see we're going to fight for them because they aren't in a position to fight for themselves (or at least not in a way deemed "acceptable"). Part of our job is teaching our kids how to advocate for themselves, but when they're younger, we need to be their voice, literally and figuratively.

As advocates for our children, we want to find the schools, resources, and people who will understand them, even when it's not easy or takes us outside our comfort zone. We need to be squeaky wheels, doing whatever it takes to be our child's steady support, as well as educate our families, our child's teachers, and any other adults who interact with him or her about who our child is. This is part of how we create that secure space for our child, and as such, making a ruckus is something we'll want to get really good at. I used to be an avoider of all things confrontation, but over the years I've slowly found my voice (in part because I was presented with many opportunities to practice!). Although it hasn't always felt comfortable, it does get easier. Trust me—if I can do it, so can you.

One last point: There is a difference between advocating for our child and being a helicopter parent. I've read plenty of articles about the preponderance of parents calling college professors and pressing for grade changes or attending job interviews with their child or doing a child's homework so their grades don't suffer. To all of that, I say *absolutely not.*

Rather, I'm proposing we figure out how to advocate for our children in a way that helps them more fully be themselves. I'm suggesting that we don't accept half-assed solutions to our children's challenges but rather push for meaningful resolutions—the kind that move the conversation forward and make things better for every differently wired kid who'll follow in our child's footsteps.

Get to Know the Advocate in You

Some people really struggle with the idea of speaking up. Not wanting to put people on the spot or ruffle feathers or risk offending someone, they avoid confrontation at all costs. In a quest to be liked, they avoid speaking up so the school staff or camp directors don't peg them as the pain-in-the-butt parent everyone avoids making eye contact with. For others, stepping into an advocacy mode may spark personal insecurities about not being taken seriously, or they may be afraid, plain and simple, of making a fool of themselves, of doing it wrong, of failing their kids. And still others may be already playing the role of an advocate, but are doing so reluctantly and without confidence. Whatever your experience, it's worth exploring those beliefs and attitudes about advocacy that may be holding you back or making you feel uncomfortable in the role.

Reflect

Have there been times in my child's life when I didn't advocate as powerfully as I could have?

. . .

What, if any, personal concerns or uncomfortable feelings do I have around the idea of making a ruckus?

. . .

How might my child benefit from my playing more of an advocacy role in his or her life, in school, activities, and among friends and family?

Although not everyone is born a natural advocate, I believe everyone has it within them to become one. After all, an advocate is just someone who publicly fights for or supports a specific cause. In our case, that cause is ensuring our children are valued, supported, and treated with respect. Could there be anything more important?

"It's never been my thing," says Mary, who, like many parents I talked with, admittedly hates confrontation. "It was definitely a learning curve to figure out how to best help my child, because what I actually wanted to do was tell the school how I *really* felt. But I knew that would defeat the purpose, because then they would ignore everything else I had to say." Mary had to acquire the ability to communicate with the school succinctly and kindly while also cc'ing a slew of people on any correspondence in order to get things done. "I think it's like anything else—the more you do it, the easier it gets."

A friend with a gifted daughter didn't realize she even knew how to advocate until she recognized that her daughter was losing her passion for learning. So my friend spoke up and pushed for the school to come up with a solution that would meet her daughter's intellectual needs. Though she was initially brushed off, with perseverance her daughter was eventually given permission to skip a grade, a solution that has worked out extremely well for all involved.

In an article for the online resource Understood.org, Amanda Morin, herself a parent to three children, two of whom are differently wired, shares her ten best tips for being an effective advocate for our children at school. My hunch is you've already got a bunch of these covered, so as you read through this list, consider some areas where you might be able to take your advocacy efforts to a new level. One thing I know for sure is that, just like any other aspect of parenting that makes us stretch outside our comfort zone, advocacy gets easier with practice. Here's a look at Amanda's list:

- Be informed.
- Keep and organize paperwork.

- Build relationships.
- Ask questions.
- Stay calm and collected.
- Remember that you're part of the decision-making team.
- Know your child's rights.
- Talk to your child.
- Learn the lingo.
- Communicate regularly.

You've Got to Ask to Get

Brandi knew something was different about the way her daughter Briana behaved and learned, but she was having trouble finding answers that fit. Even when her daughter received a diagnosis of ADHD, something still felt off. Brandi's gut said autism, but friends, family, teachers, and even a doctor disagreed, suggesting Briana was just misbehaving or being rebellious. Still, Brandi pushed for answers, both for herself and for her daughter: "I needed to have that other missing piece to help us congeal everything together so I could know how to approach her and talk to her. I knew something else was going on. And so finally I just went to this last place and I said, 'This is it.' And they said, 'You know, you're right. Your daughter has Asperger's.'" Brandi knew, and she didn't stop until she got the information and help she needed.

As my friend Tia once said about her own quest for answers regarding her twice-exceptional daughter, "I don't care how many letters are written after their name or how many years of experience they have in a specialized area—we are connected to our child in a way none of them will ever be. We know what we know about our child." And to that I say, *Truth.* We've got strong instincts, and our children benefit when we listen to them and ask for what we need.

This same idea holds true in the classroom. My former curriculum adviser Alison Bower, who spent years working as a teacher and a school administrator, as well as raising differently wired kids of her own, encourages parents to push for outside-the-box, alternative solutions to problems their child may be having in school, because educators are often open to trying anything as long as it's doable. "You're allowed to advocate for your child more than you probably realize," she said during an interview for my podcast. "Talk to an educator before you go in for your SIT meeting [the meeting to discuss a child's IEP] and find out what kinds of questions you should ask. Have a list and don't let them throw you off track. If something isn't acceptable to you, you're allowed to tell them that it's not going to work."

Securing the right diagnosis and lining up the right help, opportunities, or accommodations for our child ultimately fall on us. To get them, we've got to ask for what we want. Even when we do ask, we'll still need to show up with a combination of persistence and diligence, and keep our eyes on the prize—getting our child the support he or she needs to develop into his or her best self—to get results. If that's not motivating, I don't know what is.

Be Kind and Clear, Not Pushy

Bari, a powerful champion for neurodiverse learners at her children's school, compares her advocacy efforts with high-level school administrators to running for office: "I've called for meetings with the superintendents of the school district to say things like 'These are things we need to think about' or 'These are opportunities for our district to lead.' But it's been a struggle. You know, navigating at that level feels very political. There's a lot of smiling and head nodding and things like that."

Unfortunately, the parent-teacher relationship can sometimes feel adversarial, especially in circumstances where we realize our child isn't being successful and we're having a hard time figuring out how to improve things. But though it can sometimes seem as if educators are working against us, the vast majority do what they do because they love kids and truly want our children to thrive.

I asked Becca Wertheim, a second-grade teacher who is used to teaching differently wired kids in her inclusive classroom in a charter school, how parents can best navigate this sometimes tricky relationship with their child's teacher, especially in situations where the parent has to play a strong advocacy role. Becca suggests we commit to keeping the lines of communication open and work to foster a relationship based on respect and honesty. "We have to work together as a team in order for that child to show growth. And the only way for us to work successfully as a team is to build those relationships. There have been times where parents will have questions or maybe we'll both have a question about something, so I'll reach out to support staff at school to try to find the answer, while parents may try to find an answer outside of school by doing a different kind of research. And then we get back together and discuss what we found and find a common ground of what's best."

Though the parent-teacher dynamic isn't always as collaborative as Becca describes, it's an ideal worth striving for, and not just with teachers, but with coaches, counselors, and anyone else who works with our children. After all, these people want to do right by our kids, but they may not know how. Asking for what we know our children need in a way that's kind, clear, and respectful not only benefits our children, but educates others about how atypical kids can best be supported in general.

One last tip—if you find yourself feeling stuck (or too emotional) about how to communicate to your child's teacher about your concerns, I encourage you to visit Understood.org and read their helpful article titled "8 Sentence Starters to Use When Talking to Teachers."

Don't Take No for an Answer

One last short note on making a ruckus: When we ask for things such as support or accommodations or extra assignments for our child, we may initially be brushed off. Because, let's face it, our requests aren't always

> **Start Now** Identify at least one area of "least satisfaction" with regard to something happening with your child at school or in another institution/sport/group/organization. Put on your advocacy hat, and respectfully and intentionally speak up for the change or action you'd like to see.

easy or convenient. Sometimes what we're asking for costs money. Sometimes it translates into extra time or resources. And sometimes the powers that be would rather not put in the effort right now and so they may decline our request or provide "solutions" we immediately recognize as being inadequate.

When that happens, there's really only one thing to do: Don't take no for an answer. Because in my experience, there are very few situations in life where there isn't a little wiggle room. I like to think of a no as a "not yet," a challenge to get creative and see what kind of alternative solutions could be implemented. We can continue to gently, respectfully, and thoughtfully push for what our child needs, and more often than not, we'll make progress. (And if we can't, then it's time to figure out another plan.)

Cultural change-maker Jess Weiner likens her advocacy style to negotiating a car sale—she knows what she needs and her job is to get the other person to give it to her. She suggests language such as, "My goal in having this conversation with you is to come up with a solution for my child to be successful in this class. I'm asking you to work with me on that solution. Here's what I'm proposing. What do you propose?" This lets the other person know there is no other option in this scenario—we're going to get to a solution.

Align with Your Partner

"Love does not dominate; it cultivates."
—Johann Wolfgang von Goethe

I've gone through periods of time over the course of Asher's life when I've experienced a deep sense of guilt and responsibility for his neurodiversity. For instance, that study suggesting a correlation between high levels of Pitocin in a mother's system and ADHD was just one of several things I'd read that made me wonder if his attention issues were my fault. But it was Asher's diagnosis of "disruptive behavioral disorder not otherwise specified," which the assessor identified as a form of oppositional defiance disorder (ODD), when he was eight that really got the blame spiral going. ODD is a catchall diagnosis to encapsulate generally defiant, noncompliant, and often rude behavior toward parents, teachers, and other authority figures, but no one knows exactly what causes it. But according to the literature, parenting styles have a lot to do with it. The Johns Hopkins Medicine Health Library explains, "[Learning theory] suggests that the negativistic symptoms of ODD are learned attitudes. They reflect the effects of negative reinforcement methods used by parents and authority figures. The use of negative reinforcement by parents is viewed as increasing the rate and intensity of oppositional behaviors in the child."

Great. So through "accidental parenting," Derin and I had unwittingly created a highly obstinate person. If Derin and I had been more consistent or united, would Asher have had a more cooperative nature? Would he have respected authority instead of pushing back against pretty much *anything* asked of him? I know now that the answer to these questions is no. I also know that Asher doesn't have ODD—he's a complicated person who spent much of his early life in fight-or-flight mode and responded in the only way he knew how. But back then and with that diagnosis, all fingers were pointed at Derin and me, and my only thought at the time was *We did this*.

The Great Divide

There is no disputing that the uncertainty, financial strains, unexpected complications, and often unpredictable and intense behavior of our children can place an exorbitant amount of pressure on our relationships, even in cases where we may be, for the most part, on the same page.

Sometimes divides open up the moment it's clear there's something different in the way a child is developing, because it's not uncommon for one partner to drive the quest for answers while the other treats challenges as purely behavioral, relaying tales of their own outrageous behavior as a child. (*And, hey, I turned out just fine, right?*) This disconnect can lead to the equivalent of one parent lacing up their hiking boots and boldly forging ahead through the thicket while the other gently drifts down a long, windy river known as *denial*. It puts parents in a tough spot, since both may as well be parenting a different child—for instance, one bending over backward to accommodate a child's sensory processing issues with the other believing their child is just "touchy" and needs to toughen up, doing the exact opposite. Even when differing parenting styles aren't this cut-and-dried, feeling as though our partner isn't on the same page about things we deeply hold true can be incredibly alienating.

Other times, the great divide is the result of one parent not coping with *what is* as well as the other parent. For instance, one person may be diving in headfirst, fully committed to doing anything and everything a child needs to thrive, whereas the other one is emotionally (and sometimes physically) checking out, not ready, willing, or able to fully show up.

Whatever the reason and whatever it looks like, when partners aren't in alignment, everyone loses. Not only does the relationship suffer as resentment or disconnect builds, but our kids often find themselves caught up in an impossible situation. They hear the tense communication, feel the strained energy, pick up on those subtle cues that suggest trouble's brewing, and make sense of it in any way they can, sometimes even concluding that they themselves are to blame.

Closing the Gap

Luckily, we don't need to be in a perfect relationship with our partner to best support our atypical kids. But we do want to be in an honest and aligned one, one in which both parents share the same goals for themselves and for their child, are equally committed to helping their child thrive, and are willing to show up and do the work, even when the work is hard.

When a couple subscribes to these ideals, or even just commits to working toward achieving them, they are supporting their child as much as any other tool, intervention, or support ever could. It is part of helping children feel secure in their world and allows them to experience a deep bond with their family, secure in the knowledge that they are loved, safe, and seen. In a world where anxiety and dysregulation might be regular states for our kids, knowing that their family is solid and that together they can get through anything, even when parents are no longer living under the same roof, is a powerful thing.

What's more, when parents raising atypical children can get in true alignment with each other, the result can be a stronger, more connected relationship. Sigan Hartley, lead author of a 2010 study called "Marital Quality and Families of Children with Developmental

Disabilities," said in an interview in *Psychology Today*, "For some parents, the stress changes their relationship in a negative way, but based on our preliminary studies, the opposite can also be true. Some couples thrive—and comment that they have become closer as a result of their unique experiences related to having a child with an ASD [autism spectrum disorder]."

Maratea told me she and her husband put a lot of work into creating a strong foundation for their relationship before their kids even came along, and always saw their relationship as a team: "That kind of paradigm became even more critical as we realized things were happening with our son that were far beyond what we ever expected we would have to deal with as parents. Something that's really been important is keeping empathy as the guiding principle of how we interact with each other. It helps you to realize that they're not perfect and I'm not perfect and we're doing the best we can. Now that I think we're over the hump, I feel like my relationship with my husband is stronger than it's ever been. We have done this amazing thing together. We have helped our son be able to access his best self."

The same holds true even when two parents are no longer cohabitating or in a relationship together. It's still possible, and in fact crucial, for estranged parents to work together to foster a positive, healthy dynamic for the sake of their children. During a podcast interview, Dr. Jenna Flowers, author of *The Conscious Parent's Guide to Coparenting*, defined what this can look like for divorced or separated parents: "Conscious coparenting is two parents who

Reflect

Is the way my partner and I parent our child in alignment?

. . .

Do I feel like I'm carrying more of the weight of what's hard?

. . .

How might being more aligned with my partner benefit my relationship? How might it benefit my child?

are very intentional about listening with full attention and embracing a nonjudgmental and compassionate acceptance of yourself and your child, as well as your coparent." When Jenna first shared that definition with me, I remarked that although it sounded ideal, I had a hunch getting to that point isn't easy. She agreed, but added that this dynamic is what separated parents are increasingly striving for, because they recognize that it gives them a powerful opportunity to put their children first.

Because raising differently wired children can place high stress and demands on a relationship, it's critical that partners learn how to design an alliance, a true collaboration that honors each other's personal struggles and collectively and consistently works toward a more united, supportive family dynamic. Our children deserve no less.

////////////////////////////// **Embracing the Tilt** //////////////////////////////

Assess and Take Personal Responsibility

The first step toward fostering more alignment with our partner is to get honest about the current state of our relationship, as well as the role we ourselves are playing in supporting the status quo. And I'll just say up front that I am well aware of the fact that what I'm suggesting isn't necessarily easy, even in relationships where communication lines are open.

Even in the best of relationships, there's bound to be imbalance. For those of us raising atypical kids, that imbalance can be exacerbated because of the extreme nature of our daily reality. Typically, one parent holds most of the cards, because they're the one pushing for support, driving the child to appointments or activities, managing schedules, being the "public face" of the family, and leaving parenting books with dozens of earmarked pages lying around the house. Sometimes this is part of a shared division of labor—both parents are on the same page about who does what, and it works. Other times, the less-involved parent realizes they're not as engaged, but they're so relieved their partner has taken over that they happily retreat from the day-to-day.

That is what happened between Derin and me. The more enmeshed I grew in the demands of mothering Asher, the less involved Derin became. He threw himself into his role as the breadwinner, and I threw myself into managing our boy's world. Over time, frustration built up on both our parts—I felt like Derin wasn't doing enough, and Derin felt like I wasn't including him.

But as true as it was that I felt I was doing much of it alone, the controlling part of me was perfectly fine with that, I think because it somehow seemed "easier." So even as I was becoming increasingly frustrated with Derin's lack of engagement, I made the conscious choice to retreat, forming my own little fiefdom made up of Asher and me. I justified it by believing I was too tired to deal with tough conversations or what I knew would be Derin's defensive reaction. After all, I had enough on my plate as it was.

Years later, when Derin and I recognized that our relationship was in need of repair, the first thing we had to do was own our respective roles in getting us to that state of dysfunction. I'll level with you and say that it was *not* a particularly fun trip to go on—it involved lots of self-reflection and painful conversations, the kind that leave you feeling drained and raw. But without that honest look, it would have been impossible to move forward. We had to get things out in the open to know what wasn't working and why, in order to design something better.

So, are you willing to assess the state of your parenting dynamic and get real about areas that might be out of balance? Here are some suggested questions to honestly explore as a first step toward taking personal responsibility:

- Are you shouldering the bulk of the responsibilities that come with meeting your child's unique needs? (Or is your partner doing that?)

- Do you sometimes feel like your family is divided into two teams: you and your child against your partner?
- Are you regularly checking out instead of checking in?
- How might you be contributing (consciously or subconsciously) to a dysfunctional relationship with your partner?
- Do you have a need to maintain control that's putting your partner at a disadvantage?
- Do you and your partner work well together when tough stuff with your child arises?
- Do you regularly make the choice to not involve your partner?

See Your Partner with Compassion

I love the quote "Be kind, for everyone you meet is fighting a hard battle" (frequently attributed to Plato but more recently traced to Scottish theologian Ian Maclaren). To me, that quote beautifully reminds us that every one of us is going through our own experiences, frequently wrought with pain and sadness and the complex emotions that come from living a full life. It gently reminds us not to judge but rather to see things from another's perspective. But more than that, it promotes compassion and empathy.

Pro Tip If you're concerned about your ability to openly communicate with your partner in a fruitful way, consider working with a couples counselor who can be an objective mediator, one whose only goal is a stronger, more connected family unit.

Although many of us are good at seeing others—friends, extended family, colleagues, even complete strangers—with compassion, the person closest to us, our partner, doesn't always get the same treatment. We may feel fused with them and, as a result, struggle to see them as having their own separate experience. Or that resentment we talked about earlier may be overshadowing any compassion we may have for what they are going through.

When I was in a virtual class for my life coach training, my instructor Bridgette asked if I would be willing to be coached so she could demonstrate a coaching strategy. I didn't have to reach too far to identify a topic to offer up—just that morning I'd gotten upset with Derin because of the way he'd spoken with Asher, and my mama bear had not-so-tactfully emerged.

As I described the situation, it became clear that I believed I needed to "protect" Asher from Derin. Bridgette, prompting me to consider the situation differently, asked, "Doesn't Derin also need protecting from Asher?" Immediately I felt the goose bumps of truth, not because Derin actually needed "protection" but because he needed to know I truly and always had his back. I knew he was struggling and needed my help staying calm in the face of Asher's behavior. Yet, rather than seeing him with compassion and supporting him, I was judging and shaming him. (Add this to my list of not-so-great parenting/wife moments.)

As Dr. Jenna Flowers says, "When we're consciously coparenting, we're generous in our assumptions of how our coparent is trying to do the best they can in this partnership and in parenting the child." When we can recognize that our partner is experiencing parenting challenges through their own personal lens, and that their related emotions may look and feel different from ours, we can change the dynamic. Many of our relationship challenges stem from our partner not feeling seen or understood or as if their needs are being met. A little tweak—the conscious decision to be more kind, compassionate, and empathetic—can change everything.

> **Pro Tip** Commit to doing one thoughtful thing every day for your partner that lets them know that you see them.

Design Your Alliance

Andrea admits to going through a phase when her son Colton became her priority and her marriage took a backseat, especially when she recognized that in addition to having a diagnosis of high-functioning autism, her son showed signs of anxiety disorder. Andrea related to that, because she herself had gotten a diagnosis of severe anxiety disorder in her late twenties. She described the effect on her marriage: "I had to be really mindful about having reasonable and kind conversations with my husband, because my tendency was to let it build up and get resentful and then lash out over something that didn't have anything to do with our son, or I'd just kind of throw everything at him and blame him, which wasn't fair. I wasn't asking for what I needed in a kind way."

But Andrea and her husband eventually designed an alliance for best supporting Colton and each other. They set aside time for intentional conversations. Andrea consciously loosened her grip and let her husband in to become a more active, engaged partner. She surrendered and compromised. Ultimately, she says, "I had to push my ego aside and really look at us as a unit, which, being the selfish person that I am, and being the mama bear that I am, is not always easy. I sometimes make a mess. And I've learned the art of apologizing. It's been hard, but in the end it's been good for our marriage."

I first heard the term "designing an alliance" when I was working with my first coach, Courtney, the one who suggested I needed support when Asher was younger. I fell in love with the phrase, because to me it reflects exactly what we want to do with our partner, the person we're working in collaboration with to raise these unique humans. The word "design" feels creative, like there's boundless possibility and potential for what our dynamic can be, and the word "alliance" is positive, optimistic, and connected.

I asked relationship counselor Dr. Jennifer Finlayson-Fife what it takes for a couple to be in true alignment in parenting their differently wired child. Here's what she had to say: "In order to be an aligned or collaborative couple, you each have to be willing to deal with your own limitations and blind spots for how they impact your spouse and your child. It is often tempting to excuse your own imma-turities or indulgences given your partner's obvious immaturities and indulgences. For example, your spouse's zealous attempts to 'fix' your child may encourage your denial or minimization of his challenges. Or your partner's permissiveness may encourage and justify, in your mind, your harshness. This will always work against your child, as she will have two parents reacting against each other and unable to see their own shortcomings. And this will always undermine the larger goal of raising your child to be a healthy and happy adult."

My question for you is, How can you design an alliance with your partner to show up as your best, most united selves? What would your ideal alliance look like? What are your individual concerns and your shared goals for the family?

Take the time to do this admittedly deep and sometimes difficult work—because once it's begun, there is no turning back, and that's a very good thing. The whole family will reap the benefits.

Implement the Daily Check-In

We are creatures of habit in our house, and once we get into our rou-tines, they're very difficult to change. A few years ago, our routine looked something like this. Derin would get home from work around six, I'd head out for a run and then make dinner while Derin either hung out with Asher or retreated to his office. We'd eat dinner together at seven thirty, and Derin would clean up the kitchen and head back to his office while Asher and I watched an old episode of our favorite show, *The Amazing Race*. Then I'd pass the baton to Derin and work while Derin read to Ash and took over the bedtime routine. Derin and I would regroup around ten thirty for Netflix, and then we'd be off to bed. Repeat ad infinitum.

As we began working with a couples therapist to learn how to be a better team, we realized that the bulk of our communication about parenting was happening over Skype chat while Derin was at work and I was in the middle of my homeschool day. We'd sometimes go more than a week between conversations of importance, and half the time I'd just give him the top-line tidbits, because catching him up fully on everything going on seemed too daunting. Of course, over time this meant Derin was slipping more and more behind, the disconnect between the two of us widening like a crack in an aging wall.

So we instituted the ten-minute check-in every night—after Ash was in bed, before we watched anything—as a forum where we could both share, not even specifically about Asher but about what was happening in our individual worlds. The check-in helps us feel like we're emotionally in tune with each other—the highs and the lows—and even more important, it prevents all those little unspoken grievances from building up.

Start Now Make a date with your partner to talk about your desire to parent from a place of respect and partnership, and invite him or her to work with you to be a united team.

If you're not already regularly checking in with your partner, I encourage you to build a regular (ideally daily) meet-up into your schedule. As you can see from my example, it doesn't have to be long or a big deal. As with most things in parenting, the key is to be intentional about why you're doing it and what you see as an ideal shared outcome. Then just get started—somehow, some way—and adapt as necessary.

Find Your People (and Ditch the Rest)

"Stop planting flowers in people's yards who aren't going to water them."
—Anonymous

In one of my Facebook groups, a parent recently shared that, when prepping friends or relatives for being with her child, she invariably ends up apologizing for her child being so much work. This bothers her to no end, and she wanted to know if other parents have done the same thing. Dozens of us, including yours truly, chimed in with our nearly universal responses: *Yes, of course we have.* Because when our child's wiring results in their being more intense, wound up, loud, emotional, or socially awkward (or perhaps all of the above), many of us become conditioned to believe that asking others to care for or spend time with our kid is burdensome.

Before we dive into the complicated issues surrounding our relationships with others, let me just start by saying *this is messy stuff.* These issues are jumbled up with our own fragile egos, emotional baggage, and insecurities about our child not being okay. They also tie back to the fact that we're hardwired to crave acceptance. Since our child is in many ways an extension of ourselves, sensing that others find him or her "unacceptable" sparks our own vulnerability and defensiveness, and may lead to our reconsidering the people we let into our world.

We don't start out this way. When we first become parents, most of us feel a sudden and unexpected kinship with other parents because they, like us, are going through the life-changing experience of raising a child. Other parents are our *people*—they understand the torture of sleep deprivation and the joys of ditching diapers for good, and they're always up for an impromptu conversation at Water Babies or preschool pickup. We are part of the club and are grateful for the camaraderie.

But then things might change. For those of us with kids whose behavior is *bigger*, we might notice that invitations for playdates fizzle out over time, or that while some parents are more than happy to have their child come over to our house, hosting our child at theirs is treated like a "favor," often requiring a whole lot of planning and firm plans for pickup.

Since we know our child as well as we do, we may start feeling guilty about asking another to deal with behavior we know can be tough. We might project our insecurities and look for hidden meanings in others' words or actions even when none is there. See? *Messy*.

The People Who Get It and the People Who Don't

One of the hardest parts about raising atypical kids is dealing with people who just don't get it. Many of us, like the woman in my Facebook group, internalize this idea that our child is an inconvenience to others, someone we must apologize for. Sometimes we struggle to know how to deal with someone who is completely uninterested in getting to know who our child is or understand our experience. In still other cases, cultural or ethnic groups we're a part of may attach stigmas to certain diagnoses or disapprove of the idea of therapy. Whatever is at the root of the disconnect with another person, we know it's there because we can feel it. Something just seems "off" in the dynamic or we start to recognize we're not being our authentic self when we interact with them.

Here's the thing: Spending time with people who aren't *our people* is exhausting. And when we're raising kids who lie outside the window of "normal," we don't really have the time or energy to help people who are never gonna get it. On top of that, apologizing, not just for our children but *in front of* them, is definitely not how we want to operate. Not only do our kids recognize what we're doing (and I guarantee it doesn't feel good to them), but we're also reinforcing the idea that difference is bad—that it's something that needs to be apologized for—which is the exact opposite of what we want to do if our goal is to change perceptions and foster acceptance.

To complicate things even further, sometimes the people not getting it are family. I got an email from a parent last year looking for ideas on dealing with her intolerant sibling. This parent was expected to travel with her children and stay with her sibling over Christmas, yet she was feeling especially anxious because not only does her sibling get annoyed with the way her children behave, but the sibling's own children are equally turned off.

How do we balance familial obligation with protecting our kids? Is it possible to have a respectful relationship with our extended family even if they don't appreciate who our children are?

This is the question I posed to parent coach Margaret Webb when I had her on my podcast to talk about unsupportive friends and family. Margaret suggests that the majority of such family conflict stems from other people's misguided desire to be helpful or their being uncomfortable with what they don't understand. Whatever the reason, the challenge is knowing how to deal with it in the moment. I asked Margaret to describe her personal approach, and I love what she had to say: "I have this visual of a target with a ring in the middle and extending rings around that center. In any of these situations, we need to go to the center, which is us—the mom or the dad—and start there, doing whatever we need to do for self-care. Part of that self-care is taking care of those feelings like anger or sadness or grief that come up. And then from there, the next ring is your child and knowing, *Okay, this is who my child is. And I know that better than anybody else.* And I start there, because from there you can create a sort of 'shield.' The more comfortable and confident I am, the less I care about what other people think."

The Power of Our People

I love Margaret's visual of the target because it's such a simple reminder that we and our children always belong at the center of any interaction, whether we're talking about close family or the parents we see at the monthly PTA meeting. At the end of the day, our obligation is to the emotional, mental, and physical well-being of ourselves and our awesome kiddos, period. By acting from that foundation with love, kindness, and certainty, we set ourselves up for the very best possible outcome.

One of the ways we can bolster our foundation is to surround ourselves with people who fully support our family. When we do this, we relax, our kids relax, and we all get to go about our business from a place of confidence. Community changes everything. It lifts us up, it deepens our well of resources, it fuels our bravery, it allows us to be our authentic selves... it reminds me that we, and our children, are not alone. It's time we ditch the doubters, skeptics, and those who'll never "get it" and instead surround ourselves with *our people*.

///////////////////////// **Embracing the Tilt** /////////////////////////

Tightening Up the Circle

Have you ever joined an organization or community—a gym, a neighborhood book club, a co-op—shown up for an event, and immediately realized that you've made a huge mistake? You spend the rest of the time strategizing a graceful exit, practically leaving skid marks when you finally make a run for it.

Reflect

What are the signs my body gives me when I'm not with "my people"?

. . .

How do I, and my child, pay the price when I spend time with people who just don't get it?

. . .

How might my child feel more secure as the result of spending more time with people who see and appreciate him or her?

This happened to me once with a group I was hoping would be a core part of my homeschool community. From the very first meeting, I noticed myself slipping into "wanting to fit in" mode, not speaking my (and Asher's) truth, and definitely not showing up as my best self. I reacted that way because the community didn't feel safe . . . they weren't my people. And although that's okay, I'm glad I figured it out so quickly that I didn't waste time trying to force something that wasn't there.

There have been many unexpected gifts of starting from scratch in the Netherlands, but one of the greatest has been the chance to build new relationships. There were no obligatory social situations, and there was no context or knotty history to complicate things. It made tightening up our circle easy since the circle didn't exist in the first place. But you don't need to move halfway around the world to "declutter" your relationships like you would your bedroom closet and become clear on who gets to be in your inner circle. Here are some questions to ponder when considering the people in your life:

- Does this relationship bring meaning and joy to your life?
- Do you feel free to be your authentic self when hanging out with this person?
- Is this relationship reciprocal in that you're both benefiting from it and getting your needs met?
- Does this person accept and appreciate who your child is?

- Does this person acknowledge your personal challenges relating to parenting your child?

Make a list of people you regularly interact with who leave you feeling unsupported and/or unseen, and determine how you want to proceed with each relationship. For example, with family and others who will always be in your world, decide whether important conversations need to happen or if you can remove yourself from being emotionally triggered by things these people say and do. Remember that you get to decide what the rules and boundaries are for each relationship.

Be Okay with What You Feel

A mother in another Facebook parenting group recently started a controversial thread, one met with strong responses all around. The essence of her post was that she feels bad for not enjoying being around kids with neurodifferences whose behavior she finds annoying, stressful, or off-putting. Although she feels guilty about it, she doesn't know how to get past her own kneejerk reaction.

I opted not to join in the chorus of people commenting on the post, some in support of her willingness to be vulnerable and others offended by her posting it in the first place. But I will admit to feeling irked. And hurt. And sad. And I don't even *know* this woman. But I know that she's not alone in her thinking, and quite honestly, that bums me out.

Anybody who's ever been on the outs with a group of friends in middle school knows that being excluded can bring up all kinds of unpleasant emotions—embarrassment, disappointment, hurt, sadness. Just because we're all grown up and "evolved" doesn't mean we're immune to feeling the painful emotions that come with realizing some relationships aren't what we thought they were.

Just as we allowed ourselves the space to mourn the fact that our child's life doesn't look the way we expected, it's important to allow for uncomfortable emotions about how others relate to us and our children. Whether it's our kids not having a close friend yet or our family not including us in certain events because our child's behavior would be too disruptive, feeling like an outsider sucks, no matter how old we are. Be kind to the part of yourself that's feeling hurt or left out. It's okay and normal to feel this way. As with all tough emotions we face in our parenting journey, the key is to acknowledge the feeling, allow it to express itself, and then move on.

Find Your People

To hear my dear friend Simone tell the story, it was Asher's vigorous love of plums that led to his capturing a place in her heart. It was the summer of 2014, and a friend moving back to the United States from the Netherlands invited a handful of families for a late-June going-away picnic. The parents spread out on blankets with food and drinks while the kids—seven in total—roamed through the park. Suddenly, Asher ran up to the lot of us, spotted a bowl of juicy purple plums, and exclaimed with his usual infectious joy, "Plums! I *love* plums!"

I watched Simone, whom I'd met briefly once before at book club, look at Asher with a mix of love and amusement and say, "Wow... I love his enthusiasm! I want to hang out with *that* kid!" And that's when I knew Simone was one of my people. That she ended up becoming one of my closest friends was an added bonus. Today, though she's got two teens of her own and a busy job, Simone invites Asher out for lunch or midday walks just because she loves spending time with him. I know she can handle whatever comes up, and I never worry when they're together. Even better, their relationship has become an important one to him—I can tell by the way he responds to her that he feels respected and appreciated by Simone. And so do I. Sadly, there's not enough of Simone to go around, but the qualities that she embodies—respect, understanding, nonjudgment, love, and compassion—are what we are looking for in our people.

My biggest goal in creating TiLT Parenting was to let parents navigating this journey know they're not alone. Even more than that, I want parents to feel a sense of assuredness that they and their uniquely wired children *belong* and have value. I want them to know they are part of an extraordinary community made up of geniuses, creative thinkers, world changers, and sensitive philosophers. Children like ours live in every country around the world, and connecting as a community can be extraordinarily powerful because it provides for us an instant sense of belonging and the recognition of shared experiences that can't be understated.

But when I suggest that we "find our people," I'm thinking bigger than just other parents of differently wired kids. Our people are truly everywhere. They're teachers and camp counselors, tutors and mentors, coaches and school advisers. They're grandparents and neighbors, families in our homeschool co-op or baristas at Starbucks. They might even be a friend we met through book club who's tickled by our child's unabashed love of plums.

The only requirement for who "our people" are is that they love and appreciate our kids, full stop. We know them when we see them, because they light up when our child is around. We collect them over time, and they become the people we look back on with gratitude—a loving preschool teacher, a neighbor who goes out of their way to include our child, a gymnastic instructor who spends extra time after class to make sure our child masters a skill they didn't nail earlier.

Who are your people?

Create Safe Relationships for Your Child, Too

Melissa Wardy has worked hard to help her daughter Amelia develop safe and supportive relationships, not just with adults, but with the kids she spends time with. Part of that has been helping Amelia know that what other people think of her doesn't matter, and part of it has been empowering her to explain what's happening when she's struggling, not only so her peers will understand her, but so they can support her.

"We've been really open and honest with her friends, saying, you know, right now Amelia's having anxiety and we just need a few minutes to feel comfortable and then we'll come play. And once you've explained it, the giant majority of kids have been wonderful about it. They were really accepting of it once they had a word for it," explained Melissa. Today, some of the girls in Amelia's Girl Scout troop even stand up for Amelia when her anxiety sparks up in new situations and someone unknowingly handles it wrong. Once, on a recent outing, a tour guide pressured Amelia to speak up, saying, "What's wrong… cat got your tongue?" and one of her Girl Scout sisters explained, "This is Amelia and she has anxiety. She needs forty-five minutes to warm up."

This is what our children deserve—friends who understand their differences and accept them for who they are. Ash has friends like this, friends who've seen all sides of him and still respect and value the friend he is. When I asked Asher what happens when he loses his cool in front of, or even toward, a friend, he answered, "Usually, I feel a bit embarrassed and I apologize, because sometimes I take out my anger on things that aren't really related, such as friends." I used to worry about Asher losing his close friends because of his sometimes intense, big reactions, but he's got an excellent friend-ometer and has connected with wonderful kids who let Asher be Asher, whatever that entails.

Friends like these bring out the best in our children—even those who struggle with reading social cues—and give them opportunities to learn how to be a good friend. These are the friends our kids are emotionally safe around, and that's critical, especially as they get into the tween and teen years and social capital carries a lot of weight.

One last note: Your child may not have found his or her people yet, but give it time. They are out there, I promise, and once they find them, they will likely be friends for life. It wasn't until Alex's profoundly gifted twelve-year-old daughter participated in a summer STEM program run by a national organization for gifted children that she finally realized she wasn't an outlier at all: In those two weeks, she not only completely fit in with the other kids who shared her deep love of all things computer programming, but left the experience with a genuine friend. Many parents of differently wired kids find that as their kids get older and their personal interests deepen, those true connections happen naturally.

Find Your Water Holes

Recently we made our way through the BBC's excellent documentary series *Africa* for our weekly movie night. I was particularly struck by an episode about the Kalahari and Namib Deserts that included night footage of the Kalahari water hole, an oasis that attracts animals from far and wide, including the elusive black rhinos that, for the first time ever, were filmed being social with one another. It was a fascinating program, and I loved the visual of these unique, beautiful animals congregating for community and shared connection.

We have our water holes, too. Sometimes they're hard to find, and sometimes we may not realize our people are there until we spend a little time looking for them. But they exist in every community, virtual and in real life. Our job is to discover where these water holes are and figure out which ones feel like "fits" (not every community targeting kids like ours will resonate with us). Here are some ideas for places to begin your search:

- **Schools:** Even within mainstream public schools aimed at neurotypical kids, frequently you'll find small groups of parents raising atypical kids who connect regularly for advice, sharing, and/or bringing in experts to help parents navigate school-specific challenges. Sometimes these groups operate under the radar, but school administrators will likely know of their existence and point you in the right direction. (Of course, if such a group doesn't already exist at your school, you could start one yourself!)

- **Facebook:** Typing in search terms on Facebook relating to various neurodifferences such as "ADHD" or "gifted education" will result in hundreds of results for groups aimed at parents like you.

  Not every group is going to be a match for your needs and values, but chances are you will find at least a few whose philosophy, tone, and content provide you with the support and connection that you're looking for. Once you have found some ideal online communities, take the time to contribute and join in the conversation rather than just lurk—you will get much more out of your experience (and others will have the chance to benefit from your participation, too).

- **Organizations and community groups:** For every type of neurodifference, there are a plethora of organizations devoted to supporting parents raising kids with those differences. Many groups have online forums, while others send out weekly newsletters. Some host free webinars and Twitter chats, or post Facebook Live videos. Some, like TiLT Parenting, host weekly podcasts. Again, chances are not every organization that exists for a specific neurodifference is going to be a perfect fit for you and your sensibilities. Take the time to vet what exists to find the groups that give you what you need.

Start Now Reflect on the people with whom you most regularly interact, and identify relationships in which the other person doesn't respect or validate your parenting reality. Make a conscious plan for protecting yourself in that relationship.

Recognize How Your Energy Affects Your Child

"My doctors told me I would never walk again. My mother told me I would. I believed my mother."
—Wilma Rudolph

Asher was six when I first made the connection between my energy and his. It was spring of his kindergarten year, and he was going through what we had by then come to recognize as his annual "spring regression." (He also had a lengthy fall regression, a late-spring reprise, and a midsummer revival each year, but who's keeping track?) It seemed that as Asher grew older, his regressions were just getting worse. This particular one was a doozy. Just about any little thing—the wrong cereal at breakfast, an ill-timed reminder, his favorite pants not clean for the weekend—could set him off.

I had just spent a weekend in Phoenix with self-help guru Martha Beck as part of a life coach training where, among other things, we had explored the connection between our internal energy and our external reality. Through that work, something in me clicked. Enough so that when I flew home that Sunday, I was excited about my new insight and confident I could use it to make the thick cloud of toxicity hanging in our house dissipate.

When I walked through the front door that evening, I was one blissed-out mama, filled with the kind of tranquility that can only come from spending a weekend tuning in and getting grounded. My little guy had missed me and immediately showered me with enthusiastic, joyful hugs, but the feel-goods were short-lived. Less than an hour later, something set him off and Asher ramped up into another predictable rage. But this time, instead of emotionally checking out, bracing myself for the attack, or energetically matching his intensity, I tried something different. I *softened*.

I calmly walked over to Asher, crouched down to eye level, and silently folded him into my arms. I held him tight and breathed slowly, imagining with each exhale that I was infusing him with pure, unquestionable love. Within ten seconds, his rigid body loosened. The rage was over. And as though a circuit breaker had tripped unexpectedly, so was the months-long regression.

Energy Affects Our Kids, All the Time

As I experienced so profoundly in that moment, there is a clear connection between our energy and our child's emotional regulation. Why? Because one trait almost all differently wired kids share is emotional intensity or hypersensitivity to the world around them—physical, mental, emotional, and/or spiritual. In other words, they are incredibly responsive to "energy"—the invisible force or *chi* that can't be perceived through the five senses. The anecdotal evidence pointing to the relationship between our experience and external energy is overwhelming. It's one reason why professional organizing has grown to be a booming industry in recent years—as humans we are sensitive to our environment and what's happening with the people and spaces around us. But it's even truer for neurologically atypical kids.

Sure, this may sound a little "woo-woo" to some people, but for parents like us, this isn't breaking news. Ask anyone raising a child with sensory processing issues, and they'll tell you these kids can read a room better than a seasoned politician. They short-circuit over things like a pebble in their shoe or a tag in their shirt or a song from a movie soundtrack. Likewise, when kids with ADHD notice energy shifts, they often respond as if a switch has been flipped—instantaneously and full throttle. Capable of absorbing others' energy, they are excellent emotional barometers, not to mention mirrors for us as their parents and what we're feeling. And kids on the autism spectrum are not immune to energetic hypersensitivity. Despite the myth that autistic people lack empathy, research by Henry and Kamila Markram of the Swiss Federal Institute of Technology in Lausanne shows that the opposite may in fact be true. The Markrams recently theorized that people with autism spectrum disorders such as Asperger's don't lack empathy at all—in fact they "feel others' emotions too intensely to cope." As Kamila Markram, who herself is autistic, explains, "I can walk into a room and feel what everyone is feeling. The problem is that it all comes in faster than I can process it. There are those who say autistic people don't feel enough. We're saying the opposite: They feel too much."

Why does understanding the effect of energy on our children matter? Because we're frequently our children's first responders in challenging moments, our personal energy becomes a bona fide superpower. The only question is, Are we going to use our forces for good or evil?

When we're not consciously regulating our energy, we can unwittingly escalate situations, in part because of a type of brain cell called "mirror neurons"—cells that lead us to mimic behavior and feelings we see in others. For example, if we see a friend bump her head, our mirror neurons will fire up and we'll wince in sympathy. Likewise, if a lunch companion gets emotional talking about the loss of his parent, we'll feel a pang of empathy, sometimes even mimicking (or "mirroring") his tears.

In an interview for the website PsychAlive, Dr. Daniel Siegel, author of the must-read book *The Whole Brain Child*, explains, "The mirror neurons soak in like a sponge what you see in someone else, it takes it in, it resonates with your own internal bodily responses and emotional parts of your brain respond."

So when we get angry or yell or lose control during difficult moments with our kids, guess what's going to happen? Our child's mirror neurons rise up to meet ours. More anger ensues, the situation intensifies, and it takes us longer to get to a place of calm and resolution. Then we blame ourselves for not responding in the "perfect" way and for making the situation worse. Our kids experience post-conflict shame, and the cycle is complete. But it doesn't have to be that way.

Using Our Energy for Good

The good news is, mirror neurons can work in our favor and actually contribute to creating an environment of calmness, acceptance, and peace, even in tough moments. By learning how to manage our energy—an ability that can be developed with commitment and practice (okay, *a lot* of practice)—not only can we stop muddying the waters with our own energy, but we can defuse a conflict without saying a single word. And this, my friends, is what we want.

Even better, using our energy for good bonds us to our kids, since we will be their steady rock no matter what tough feelings they're working through. Likewise, we'll be modeling what healthy energy management looks like, which is a great way to reinforce the emotional regulation strategies we're trying to get our kids to embrace. Our kids will feel more secure and in control of themselves, and they'll see us as

Reflect

How in touch am I with my personal energy, especially in the midst of heightened situations?

. . .

What connections can I make between my energy reactions and my child's behavior?

. . .

How do I think my child might benefit if I were better able to manage my internal energy, especially during challenging situations?

a safe place to be themselves, which is exactly what we want, especially as they get into the teen years and we want those communication lines open and rooted in respect and trust.

Pinpoint Your Emotional Triggers

I recently received an email from a mother whose daughter has executive functioning challenges and dysgraphia, as well as, possibly, ADHD. For the last few years, this mother has struggled with anxiety about her daughter's struggles, specifically the potential effect on her daughter's social life. But then this mom noticed that the more anxious she was, the more anxious her daughter became. So she worked hard to focus on the present and recognize that her daughter would be fine in the long run, likely even stronger for her struggles. Once she did this, the mother was able to stop being so anxious, which she said directly affected the way her daughter experienced her life as well.

We've talked about triggers before, and this is yet another opportunity to get familiar with the situations that spark our own negative emotional responses. Many of us, like the mother I just wrote about, harbor anxiety about our present and future unknowns relating to our child. We might notice that our anxiety peaks during certain times of the year, such as high school graduation season, a time when our Facebook newsfeeds are filled with photos of happy students transitioning to bright futures. We see those images and suddenly we're showing up differently with our child—less patient, more intense, less trusting. Even if our behavior isn't markedly different, our energy will be. And our kids will feel it.

Or say you are someone who detests yelling or displays of anger. Maybe you're uncomfortable with conflict or were raised in a household or culture where expressing anger wasn't acceptable. If that's you, the sound of your child yelling might flip a switch in you and suddenly all bets are off—the behavior is unacceptable and *must stop now*. Of course, rigid reactions to an upset, dysregulated child are unlikely to result in peace and tranquility anytime soon.

Just as we identified our child's biggest triggers as a way of becoming fluent in their unique language, we want to get to know our own emotional triggers as well so we can recognize when they've been switched. I know mine like the back of my hand—feeling like I'm not being taken seriously, having someone be angry with me when I feel they have no right to be, and people not following through on their commitments. Being aware of these triggers keeps me honest about my reactions when something Asher does sparks a strong response in me. It helps me stay in my (emotional) business and out of his.

What are your buttons? Chances are they are the same things today that they were twenty years ago—our baggage runs deep. Get curious about what types of situations trigger those deep emotional responses and start recognizing that they're about you, not your child.

Answer the Big Question: What Am I Making This Mean?

In past chapters, we've talked about becoming familiar with our fears so we can separate out the ways in which our thoughts and emotions are interfering with the reality of any given situation. One way to get to the heart of things is to explore this simple question—*What am I making this mean?* This simple six-word phrase can be the key to shifting our painful thoughts or beliefs, the resulting negative emotions, and therefore, our energy. Here's what using this question as a prompt for further exploration looks like.

I have a friend with a teenage twice-exceptional child with high-functioning autism. He goes to a public high school, enjoys a bunch of extracurricular activities such as fencing and band, and has exactly zero friends. My friend is despondent over the state of his social life and racks her brain looking for ways to help him build a social circle, because his lack of connection with kids his age breaks her heart. Once, during a conversation in which she was explaining her most recent attempt to foster a friendship for him, I asked her what she was making it mean that her son didn't have a typical social circle. I happen to know her son is highly introverted and, similar to Asher, is quite happy doing his own thing and spending time alone. When my friend gave it some thought, she realized she had a lot of beliefs tied up in the idea that her son needed, at the very least, a small, tight-knit circle of friends to be happy, in part because she herself wouldn't have survived high school without two best friends. Making this connection didn't end the worries for my friend, but it did prompt her to consider that her son's needs were different from hers, and that he might be someone who spends a lot of time alone in his life. And that's okay. Remembering that helps her stay more relaxed and not be sparked as easily when another social situation triggers that same response.

Another powerful reframing question is the one parent coach Margaret Webb used to pose to me regularly when I was in an emotional spiral: *What's perfect about this?* Meaning, how might what's happening in this moment actually be exactly what needs to happen for my child, for me, or both of us? Quite often my initial response would be "I can't think of a single thing."

> **Pro Tip** Make a greatest-hits list of your negative emotional triggers.

But then she'd help me brainstorm and I'd discover there's always something. There is always a way to flip a situation around and consider the gifts that might be hidden within.

Reframes sparked by getting curious about what's going on in our mind can stop us from heading into an emotional spiral, preventing us from contributing not-so-helpful energy in any given situation.

Create Your Own Coping Routine

This is kind of embarrassing to say, but I was so focused on trying to get Asher to embrace a coping routine that for a long time it didn't occur to me that I should have one of my own. My standby strategy for dealing with intense situations with Asher used to be to pretend I was high. As in, Jeff Spicoli in *Fast Times at Ridgemont High* high. Seriously . . . that was my best strategy. Just chill, speak gently and slowly, and let everything roll off my back. That approach helped me get through some tough moments. But inside, I knew I was faking it. Because in reality, I wasn't chill at all—I was *really* upset. And our kids know the difference. They can smell disingenuous a mile away.

I don't remember exactly where things went wrong the morning everything changed for us, but I'm sure it had something to do with an iPad and Asher's refusal to turn it off. It was shortly after we had moved, and we were living in a tiny apartment with thin walls. Asher was yelling at me and, not wanting the neighbors to hear the horror show, I turned into a crazy mama and told him to stop yelling in a low, horror-flick-worthy voice. I should have just walked away then, but instead I ramped up, demanding that Asher use his coping skills that instant, an order he flat-out refused. (Gee, I wonder why?) I started dishing out threats like after-dinner mints, our back-and-forth escalating until eventually he stormed into his room.

Ten minutes later, a somewhat calmer me peeked in to check on him. Asher looked up gleefully and explained what he'd been doing in *Minecraft*, as if our fight hadn't even happened. I sat down on his bed.

"You know what's funny?" I asked.

"What?"

"The fact that we were just arguing about you using your coping skills, while *I'm* actually the one who needs them."

"Yeah, that is funny," he said.

"Do you think you could teach them to me and help me with them?"

"Sure! They're really easy!" Asher then proceeded to walk me through his routine, asking if I'd like to listen to his relaxation CD. (How could I say no?)

He gently laid a blanket on the cold marble floor, and as we sat down, I began to cry, apologizing for my less-than-perfect parenting: "I think I'm feeling a little overwhelmed right now, and I'm not behaving the way I want to. I don't ever want to speak to you in that tone of voice—I'm really sorry."

"It's okay, Mom." Asher gave me a squeeze and invited me to lie down next to him, where he taught me how to relax my body, take belly breaths, and empty my mind. I stared at the ceiling and breathed, turning to look at Asher five minutes later. His eyes were closed, his breathing slow, calm, and steady.

When we finished a few minutes later, I thanked him for teaching me his coping routine, and told him how much better I felt. He responded, "That's great! Now let's go get you a Diet Coke so you won't feel cranky anymore." (Turns out he really *did* know my coping routine.)

Pro Tip Take the time to come up with an actual plan for yourself when you are triggered. How many breaths will you take, where will you go, who will you call, how will you respond?

My personal coping routine no longer includes a Diet Coke, but it still involves me sitting or lying alone in stillness and taking deep belly breaths. Sometimes, if I'm really upset, I clasp my hands together and squeeze hard. A coping routine should be something you can do anywhere and anytime that doesn't require anyone else, and that can move you from upset to calm. I suggest trying out different strategies, or a combination of them, to discover what helps you most in the midst of difficult moments. Here are some ideas:

- squeezing a stress ball
- deeply inhaling, holding for a count of five, and slowly exhaling
- meditating
- disengaging from heightened situations by calmly leaving the room or walking away (if it's safe to do so)
- reading a book
- calling a lifeline
- listening to a favorite song (never underestimate the power of music to shift a mood)
- doing a burst of exercise to burn off energy (such as jumping jacks or sit-ups)

Design a Reset Ritual

When Asher was a little guy, around three or four, I developed a habit of going into his bedroom long after lights-out to catch a glimpse of him asleep. I did this not only because there is perhaps nothing as beautiful as a sleeping child, especially a high-energy ADHD one who rarely ever stops moving or talking when awake, but because it gave me a few minutes to push the "reset button." No matter how explosive our day had been, how shredded I was feeling, or how worried I was about the next day, in those moments I could find a stillness deep within myself that allowed me to see him as the perfect being he was. I'm not a religious or overly spiritual person, but during those night visits, I imagined our souls exchanging sentiments—*I see you. I appreciate you. I support you. You are perfect as you are. Thank you for choosing me to be on this journey with you. I'm so grateful.* Then I'd quietly slip out and gently close his bedroom door behind me.

It was such a simple, small thing, yet those few minutes each night had a profound effect on me. They allowed me to shed guilt about times when I hadn't shown up as my best self; gave me the space to consider Asher's unique journey in the context of life, the universe, and everything; and helped me tap into a sense of peace and trust, which I so desperately needed to start the next day with optimism.

I highly recommend creating your own energy reset ritual, for after good days or bad, for the transition between work and home, for the shift from being your child's homeschool teacher to their parent. Consciously resetting our energy helps us wipe the slate clean, lean in to a more trusting place, and ensure that we're not contributing to any emotional dysregulation in our child. Here are some suggestions for how you might spur an effective reset:

Start Now Create a personal energy management plan and commit to using it when interacting with your child during difficult moments and situations.

- a special nighttime ritual (reading a book or poem, a special hug, a special saying or phrase)
- listening to a specific song
- a nightly bath with candles and incense
- prayer of some kind
- starting the day with yoga or meditation
- daily journaling to reflect, process, and set intentions
- flipping back through baby pictures
- taking the dog for a walk

Show Up and Live in the Present

"Be messy and complicated and afraid and show up anyways."
—Glennon Doyle

Each week during our first year living in Amsterdam, Asher and I bicycled down to Amstelveen, a village about eight kilometers away, for a session with his therapist Kate Berger. One afternoon on the way home, we cut through the Amsterdamse Bos, a 2,500-acre man-made forest that's among my favorite spots in the city because it's big enough to get lost in and feels like a true nature retreat. It was a gorgeous spring day and we were in no hurry, so when Asher asked to stop for an ice cream in the park, I said, "Sure, why not?"

Asher picked out a rocket Popsicle while I parked the bike and looked for a spot in the sun, eventually settling on a rainbow-colored, oversize hammock. We climbed in and lay next to each other, his head cradled in the nook of my arm, and we swung slowly, gazing up at the giant sycamore trees, new green leaves silhouetted against the blue sky. It was the first time in recent memory that I'd stopped moving, thinking, planning, working, or teaching and done nothing but *be in that moment*. A moment, I might add, in which Asher stopped talking about *Minecraft* and *Plants vs. Zombies*. Instead, as we lay there gently swaying, we talked about spring. And homeschooling. And beauty. And peace and contentedness. And how nature can be a kind of church. And how important it is to notice and appreciate it. And about how sticky hands get when Popsicle juice drips on them.

Twenty minutes later, the frozen treat was gone, hands were wiped off, our bicycle was mounted, and we were headed for home. The moment was gone. But Asher's openness stayed for the rest of the day. And I learned a lesson about the gifts of being in the moment.

The Problem with Not Being Present

I remember listening to a story on NPR many years ago about a theory for why time seems to speed up as we get older. One of the explanations was that as we age, things we do regularly—commute, take a shower, make our coffee, load the dishwasher, brush our teeth—are so routine that we do them on autopilot. We may not even remember doing them at all, because we weren't paying any attention—our body knew what was involved and went about its business, and our brain was otherwise engaged.

By the time many of us are raising kids, large portions of our lives are spent on autopilot, which is a shame, because that state is the exact opposite of being in presence. And presence is where we want to be as often as possible when we're with our children.

Remember when I talked about the perils of living life in fear and spinning out over worries about future unknowns? Neglecting to be fully present for our kids and showing up for them every single day is a one-way ticket to this vortex. Beyond that, when we're not present, we miss out on *so very much*. Our kids know when we're not showing up—when we're distracted or not really tuning in. When we're not living in the present, we forget that everything is changing all the time. A monthlong regression might end, but instead of enjoying it, we worry about when the next one will start. When we're not living in the present, we forget to stop and enjoy our children right now. We miss out on so much, and we'll never get this time back.

This right-now—the hard days, the challenges, the tense parent-teacher conferences, the conversations wrapped up with tears and a hug—is *life*. This is what we're doing right now. This is why we're here. Cue my favorite line from the musical *Rent*: "There is no future. There is no past. I live this moment as my last." When we're not living in presence, we miss the little things—the bright spots that are there, even when we have to search hard to find them. The tiny growth spurts. The moments of brilliance. The sparks of joy. To experience these things we have to fully be here, open, and present.

Present Moment Awareness

In addition to helping expat kids adapt to their new lives, Asher's therapist Kate is an expert in mindfulness. When I brought her on to my podcast last year to talk about the benefits of mindfulness for children, I asked her what our goals are for being present, as well as how learning to do it benefits our kids. Kate answered, "What we're really looking for is present moment awareness—paying attention on purpose to the present moment . . . what's happening right now. If you think about it, many of the stresses and difficulties we experience in life have a lot to do with what's happened in the past or what's going to happen in the future. And so we get pulled into those two directions with our thoughts and with our mind and aren't present for what's happening right now. We miss the opportunity to be able to respond to what's happening in the moment, and

Reflect

How connected to my child (in a meaningful way) do I feel on a daily basis?

. . .

What obstacles are preventing me from more fully living in the present?

. . .

How would my child benefit from my being more present in day-to-day life?

instead we get caught up in some sort of an autopilot mode, reacting to what's happened in the past or what we think might happen."

When we're in a state of presence, not only can we respond better to difficult situations, but our child feels it, too. If you've ever made conscious efforts to stay present with your child, you've likely experienced what I have with Asher—more positive and connected interactions, and more peace all around. Just being in the moment with Asher is the thing that's made the biggest difference in my life, not only for how I personally feel day to day in being his teacher and mother, but for how he experiences our relationship as well. Every day for the past few years, I've set an intention to be present, calm, and patient when I'm with Asher. He deserves that. And so do I.

///////////////////////////// **Embracing the Tilt** /////////////////////////////

Intentionally Show Up Every Day

Intention is one of my favorite words. Because when we apply it to any aspect of our lives, it ensures we're doing it *consciously*. We are choosing how we want to experience our life, actively striving toward an outcome that feels positive and right for us. And that is how we want to show up for our child each and every day.

Being intentional in the way you parent is as simple and straightforward as *setting an intention*. Seriously... that's it. And setting an intention is as simple as taking a moment to consider how you *intend* to feel, think, and experience your day with your child. For example, do you want to have infinite patience? Do you want to take deep breaths in tough moments? Do you want to make sure your child feels seen and heard every time you interact with him?

Here's what this looks like for me. Every morning I take a moment and write out my intention for the day. Sometimes my intention changes daily, and other times, like in the past few months, I go through phases where I set the same intention every single morning. At the moment, my intention reads as follows: *I am calm, patient, and present when I'm with Asher, and focused and productive when I'm working.* I write it in the present tense, as if it's already a done deal, because that makes it feel truer, which in turn helps it *become* true as the day unfolds.

Asher has recently gotten into the intention-setting business as well. These days, when I come into his bedroom for a good-night hug, he'll ask me to join him in setting an intention for the following day. Inspired by Hal Elrod's suggestion in his book *The Miracle Morning*, Asher likes to intend to feel well rested in the morning, even when it's late and he knows he has to wake up early. Beyond that, he declares his intention for being focused or in a great mood and super-productive in school. It's become part of his nighttime ritual, and it has made a big difference in how our mornings unfold.

I encourage you to take a moment to consider what *your* intention is right now, in this moment, with regard to how you want to show up as a parent, and think about ways to build daily intention-setting into your morning or evening routine. I always get inspired by hearing about the intentions other parents set for themselves. Here are a few that parents have shared with me to get you thinking about ideas for yours:

- Take deep breaths in difficult moments.
- Respond with peace and love, not anger.
- Notice the little things.
- Be compassionate and curious.
- Set firm personal boundaries.
- Have more patience and understanding.
- Remember that my child has a right to feel overwhelmed.
- Listen and connect more.
- Practice empathy.

Create Your Own Rituals

By now we've all heard about the many benefits of the whole family sitting down to meals together. Research shows that regularly dining together does everything from building vocabulary and improving kids' grades to boosting a child's physical and mental health. That's because when we put the smartphones away, turn off the TV, and share a meal together for which we're showing up with warmth and presence, we create the space for honest sharing, laughter, and meaningful conversations. Our children feel secure and know they have a venue for connecting with their parents, whether they had a good day or a bad one.

Having meals together is just one ritual that builds in regular opportunities for presence and connection with our kids. Brandi has created her own rituals to spend time in presence with her autistic daughter, Briana, which she finds especially beneficial if she senses that Briana is having a hard time. "We do puzzles whenever I feel like she's getting ready to have a meltdown. And we also color a lot in inspirational coloring books that have positive affirmations in them. So while she's coloring, she's seeing these positive words. She's taking them in, and then I'll ask her about them, too," Brandi explains.

Recently, because I've been doing a few too many work things, I recognized that I wasn't spending as much time in presence with Asher, and it was affecting his mood and energy. I resurrected one of our favorite rituals—listening to the *Radiolab* podcast while doing a ridiculously complicated jigsaw puzzle. Every evening after dinner, we've been cuing up another episode and piecing together an Italian landscape, pausing the episode to comment on something or, as is often the case with Asher, launch into a tangent sparked by what we just heard. However it unfolds, it is our time, and we're not doing anything other than what we're doing. And that feels special.

What (screen-free) rituals can you design to do together with your child that focus on fostering closeness and the bonding that comes from shared experiences? Here are some ideas to get you started:

- long walks or runs in nature
- stopping for a croissant or bagel on the way to school one morning a week
- weekly hot chocolate or dessert dates
- coloring or drawing while listening to music
- living room dance parties
- baking or cooking together
- volunteering together
- cozying up under a shared blanket and reading together

Look for the Bright Spots Every Day

I'm a writer who doesn't regularly keep a journal, but I do like the act of *reflection*. A few years ago, I started using something called the *Five Minute Journal*, a simple guided daily journal published by Intelligent Change that prompts users to write an affirmation and goals each morning and then, at the end of the day, not only contemplate what could have made the day better, but also highlight three amazing things that happened. This last part is my favorite piece of the ritual because it encourages me to consciously reflect on what I call the "bright spots," even on days when I have to dig deep to find one, let alone three.

I suggest you build in a regular practice of recognizing the bright spots with your child. And when I say bright spots, I mean just what it sounds like: positive things in relation to your child. One of my favorite memories of a bright spot with Asher was the day he stood on the front porch of our house in Seattle and, when his friend Brodie came over to say hello, asked him, "How was *your* day?" That was the first time I'd ever heard Asher, six years old at the time, show interest in someone or something outside of himself. It brought tears to my eyes, and was a bright spot that kept shining in my mind for weeks. A favorite bright spot in recent memory is Asher putting on and tying my shoes for me after I threw my back out and couldn't lean over. Even though I was in incredible pain, his act of kindness and placing my needs before his own overshadowed any pain or despair I was feeling.

The great thing is that when we actively look for the bright spots, we start seeing them everywhere. Your bright spot might be your child brushing their teeth without a battle or noticing they had a positive interaction with another child at school. Maybe it's realizing your child's meltdown recovery time has decreased in recent weeks. These are all things we might miss if we're not paying attention. And we *want* to notice these little flashes of growth and joy and connection, not just because they feel good for us, but because we want to point them out to our child so they can experience the sense of pride that comes with being recognized.

Pro Tip Create an end-of-day check-in ritual for yourself that involves time for reflecting on the bright spots.

Give Your Child All of You

Years ago I wrote a book for young women called *In Their Shoes* in which I interviewed fifty women about their jobs as a way to give readers a picture of what different careers entailed. One of the women I interviewed was a human resources recruiter, and I'll never forget what she said when I asked her how she deals with the high stress of her job. She told me she keeps things in perspective by reminding herself that "there's no heart in the cooler," meaning she's not involved in life-and-death decisions in the way a surgeon prepping for an organ transplant would be.

The same goes for us. *There's no heart in the cooler.* Very few things happen in our lives that preclude us from setting aside time each day to be fully present, and playful, with our child. And in case you're wondering, yes, that means ditching the iPhone. It means sometimes doing things you may not love, such as getting down on the floor with a tub of Legos or engaging in a seemingly endless conversation about creepers and mobs and the Nether. It means breaking the rules every now and then to have breakfast for dinner in pajamas while camped out on the living room floor or embracing reckless spontaneity by jumping into the car after dark to go get a better view of a meteor shower.

Recently, Asher had a really bad day. And since really bad days have been few and far between for some time now, this one made me sit up and take notice, as well as recognize that I'd been so caught up in my own work that I'd been neglecting to give Asher what he needed from me. Trying to get things back on track, I went up to his room with sneakers and a jacket in hand and asked him to go for a walk with me. Despite the fact that it was past his bedtime and he'd spent the past hour fuming on his top bunk, he stepped down and did as I asked. And then we walked and walked and walked. He explained to me the intricacies of anisotropic properties, and I gave him my undivided attention. We stopped at a park and took turns balancing along the rim of a fountain. We marveled at the sunset and clouds and tried (and failed) to capture their beauty with my iPhone camera. And two hours later, all was right again in his world, and with us. That night, Asher needed all of me, and I'm glad I recognized that and gave it to him. Our kids deserve no less. And when we can give ourselves to them, magic can happen.

Start Now Create a routine for setting your parenting intention every single morning and reflecting on three bright spots at the end of each day.

Help Your Kids Embrace Self-Discovery

"I was built this way for a reason, so I'm going to use it."
—Simone Biles

As I am writing this, Asher is a few weeks away from attending Space Camp at the U.S. Space & Rocket Center in Huntsville, Alabama. This is kind of a big deal, because he has wanted to attend ever since a retired NASA employee he met when he was five suggested it to him. When I told Asher I had called the camp and discovered that they supported differently wired campers, he immediately began bouncing off the walls with excitement, but quickly turned more serious. "I am going to have to do *a lot* of work to get ready to go to camp, Mom," he said earnestly.

"Oh yeah? What kinds of things do you think you'll need to know how to do?"

"You know, teamwork and stuff. I *really* want this to go well! Maybe I could start seeing Kate again to work on things?" On the outside, I was calm and cool. "That's a good idea. . . . I'm sure Kate would love to help you do that. I'll shoot her an email." On the inside I was freaking out. *Holy crap! He wants to work on himself!* My boy had recognized an area of future challenge, advocated for himself, and was now committed to improving his group work and collaboration skills . . . *all on his own.*

The Gifts of Self-Knowledge

I'm convinced that the greatest gift we can give our differently wired kids is the knowledge of who they are, how their brain works, and what they need to do to create the life they want. Because when we guide our children along the path of self-discovery, they can feel good about themselves, develop self-advocacy skills, and ultimately grow up to be self-realized adults.

Many parents shy away from talking openly with their child about the way they're wired, because they want to protect them. They don't want their child to feel "different" or flawed. I hear this all the time, and I totally understand the thinking. Many of these kids are already hearing every day and from multiple sources that they don't fit in or that something's wrong with them. It only makes sense that their parents would want to shield them from knowledge that might crush them or make them feel odder than they already do.

Yet most of the time, these kids know something is up— they just don't know exactly what. And so they develop their own theories for why they're always getting in trouble or bombing in math or not connecting with other kids their age. They try to make sense of snippets of conversation they overhear between their parents or wonder why none of their other friends goes to occupational therapy. Without context or information, they might conclude they're defective or broken, disappointing their parents, and/or aren't as smart as everyone else.

One night when Asher was six years old, we lay together in bed reading before lights-out. I don't remember the name of the book, but I do remember it included a character with ADHD whose behavior was described as energetic, impulsive, and distracted. Asher stopped me midsentence to ask a question. "Do I have that?"

"Actually, yes ... ADHD is one of the things we think might be going on with you," I replied. "Why? Do you see a bit of yourself in this character?"

"Yes," he answered.

He knew. He was six and he knew.

Years later, when we got the diagnosis of autism spectrum disorder, we sat him down and told him what we'd learned. His immediate thought when he found out was *Yeah, that makes sense.* And his immediate emotion? *Relief.* He wasn't broken or bad or screwing up. He was wired differently. (Actually, wired *better*, in his opinion.)

Why Getting Kids Invested Matters

The adage *knowledge is power* couldn't be truer than it is for our kids. Because the kind of knowledge we're talking about here? It has the capacity to empower our kids to not only feel good about their differences, but fully own and embrace every aspect of who they are. David Flink, founder of Eye to Eye (the mentoring organization for kids with learning and attention differences) and author of the book *Thinking Differently*, is a firm believer in the importance of empowering kids to understand and embrace their differences. As someone with ADHD and dyslexia, he recognizes how everything changed for him when he hit high school and learned how to self-advocate. "I got really comfortable going to my teachers and saying, 'I'm going to fidget like crazy. Can I sit in the back of the room so I can fidget and not distract other students and not get myself in trouble?' And they were like,

Reflect

Am I actively fostering and modeling a culture of self-discovery in our family?

. . .

Am I regularly sharing insights for my child about his or her neurodifferences in a way that encourages reflection and self-awareness?

. . .

Do I handle difficult situations or challenges in a way that focuses on helping my child learn more about who they are rather than punishing them or addressing only the behavior?

'We don't care—you can stand in the hallway as long as you can hear the lesson,'" he explained.

Through David's organization, middle school students are connected with older mentors wired in the same way they are, so the kids not only see what's possible, but are led by people who accept and love themselves just as they are. David's organization also sells T-shirts with bold expressions like "This is what dyslexia looks like" and "ADHD proud to be." Creating a community where neurodiverse kids are encouraged to proudly own their differences sets them up for growth galore, buoyed by confidence, belonging, and the belief that anything's possible.

This is what can happen when our kids feel invested in themselves. They become their own greatest champions. Over time and with steady support and positive messaging, they develop a keen awareness of both their challenges and their gifts, and gain confidence in their ability to overcome whatever obstacles they're facing. When our kids are personally invested in their self-discovery, they're already halfway to anywhere they want to go.

//////////////////////////// **Embracing the Tilt** ////////////////////////////

Nurture a Culture of Openness and Honesty

One mother I talked with says it was her openness and decision to regularly loop her 2e son into conversations about his neurodiversity when he was younger that ultimately helped him become the independent young adult he is today: "It was important to me that I was honest with him, because he needed to recognize what he needed personally to succeed. And I don't think that makes him different from a neurotypical kid. Everybody has limits. I believe that knowing yourself is the number one most important thing."

If you were to rate the way you communicate with your child on a scale of one to ten when it comes to transparency and honesty (ten being very transparent and honest), what would your score be? Consider these questions:

- Do you avoid talking about current events in age-appropriate ways to "protect" your child?
- Do you bend the truth to avoid challenges and disappointment?
- Do you minimize or downplay things that are difficult?

If you're already at a ten, nicely done. And if you're not, know that a ten is what we're after, and also know that it's possible to get there. Here's how to do it:

- Check yourself. If you believe your child's challenges will always negatively disrupt their life, your child will feel it, no matter what you actually say to them. Differently wired kids are wildly perceptive—it's critical to acknowledge and deal with thoughts or beliefs that could cloud your message.
- Make open and honest communication a core value for your family, and work toward it every single day. It's okay if you're not there yet—just get started now. Call a family meeting, talk about the importance of honesty, take responsibility for times you haven't prioritized honesty in the past, and ask everyone to commit to it moving forward.
- Make conversations about strengths and challenges a part of your family's every day. A great way to do this is by creating a mealtime ritual where everyone answers the following question: What went well today and what was hard today? Then, find ways to connect each person's highs and lows to their individual strengths and challenges.
- Don't shy away from difficult conversations. Whether you're talking about current events or the meaning of life, be honest

with your child (tell them as much as is age appropriate) and talk to them in a way that helps them feel respected and seen. When you do this, they'll feel secure in knowing nothing is off-limits and that your word is gold.

Explore Brain Science with Your Kids

One way to engage our kids in conversations about neurodifferences and personal growth is to get into the brain science behind it. After all, that's really what being differently wired is about—variations in brain functions. Luckily there are many kid-friendly resources out there to introduce brain science concepts in a way that captures children's interest and imagination. Using brain science as a launching point for exploring neurodiversity and personal growth works well because it's not personal—it's *science*. It encourages curiosity while allowing kids to objectively explore why they are the way they are.

And the payoff can be big. Not only does exploring brain science provide a neutral way to consider different ways of being, but research shows that teaching all kids (atypical and typical) about concepts such as neuroplasticity can positively affect the way they learn. According to a 2014 article in *Edutopia* called "Engaging Brains: How to Enhance Learning by Teaching Kids About Neuroplasticity," "lessons on discoveries that learning changes the structure and function of the brain can engage students, especially when combined with explicit instruction on the use of cognitive and metacognitive strategies that guide them to learn how to learn."

The conversation Asher and I have had about brain science that has made the greatest impression on him centered on researcher Carol Dweck's work surrounding fixed and growth mindsets. According to Dweck, fixed-mindset people believe traits such as intelligence are "fixed" and can't grow (i.e., you're either smart or you're not), and growth-mindset people believe intelligence and other traits can be developed (i.e., if you work hard, you can get better at something).

Since first introducing this idea to Asher through Dweck's TED Talk, it's become an integral part of how we process challenges with assignments or especially rigid thinking when facing new or uncomfortable tasks. Asher understands that in those moments he's embracing a fixed mindset, and since he *really* wants to be a growth-mindset guy, he's open to working toward that.

Whatever your point of entry, regularly talking about and exploring brain science concepts can, over time, lead to increased curiosity and self-knowledge.

Use Language That Supports, Not Shames

Alison Bower, my brilliant friend, educator, and coach, has advised hundreds of parents on how to talk about difference with their child. I love the language she suggests, such as this wording when talking with a younger child: *Because of the way your brain is wired, you experience things in a way others might consider unusual or unexpected. That doesn't mean the way you experience them is wrong, but your behavior is likely to cause you lots of frustration and get in your way. So we're going to work together to figure out ways to help you so it doesn't feel so frustrating for you.*

Boom. It's honest, it's respectful, it's logical, it emphasizes that there's nothing "wrong," and it leads to a child-focused solution. Here's another example from ADHD coach Yafa Crane Luria: *There's nothing wrong with you that we need to* take away—*there are just a few additional skills for you to work on.*

Victoria and her husband were worried that their ten-year-old son would feel dejected, inferior, or sorry for himself if he knew about his ADHD, but they ultimately decided they needed to fill him in so he would understand why he was working on certain things. But rather than just focus on their son, they decided to make it a family affair: "At a family meeting, we talked about how Daddy is good at understanding nutrition, but he's not good at remembering things. We discussed how his sister is good at sports, but she's prone to being moody. And I said that I'm good at planning events, but I often lose my temper. Then, we pointed out how he has a big heart, is a very sensitive person, and is great at making new friends, but he has difficulty controlling his impulses. We reinforced the idea that we *all* have things to work on—his ADHD challenges are just one of those things for him. He responded very well, because it not only kept him from feeling like a failure, but actually made him bond more with us as a family because he knows we're all working on something."

Of course there are kids who might resent your shining a spotlight on their differences when they really just want to be like everyone else. Because of the negative way others have responded to them, some kids may be stuck in a cycle of embarrassment or shame. But these kids still need and deserve open and honest communication from us about their challenges and what they're working on, done with special care and consideration, such as:

- **Validating their emotions and empathizing:** You're feeling embarrassed by this conversation. I know how it feels to be embarrassed, and it can be a pretty uncomfortable feeling. That's really hard.
- **Giving them space and not forcing the issue:** I can tell you're not in the mood to talk about this right now, and that's okay. Let's talk about it later when you're ready. My only request is that you keep an open mind about talking with me about this again. Can you do that?
- **Avoiding bringing up challenges in difficult moments:** Wait until the storm has blown over and look for opportunities to debrief when you can more calmly explore what went wrong (and what went right).
- **Being aware of self-shaming language:** When "I'm sorry" becomes a child's default response to anything that goes wrong, there's a good chance they're internalizing their challenges and

turning them into faults about who they inherently are. *There's no need to apologize ... you didn't do anything wrong. We're all just learning. And learning is great, because it will help us come up with a plan to make this situation easier in the future.*

The consistent message we want our kids to hear—in every conversation that touches upon their challenges—is this: *There is nothing wrong with you. We are all working on things. The great thing is, once we know how our brains operate, we can support ourselves in making things easier for us.*

> **Pro Tip** Supplement your positive messages at home with some of the many helpful books aimed at helping children better understand and appreciate their unique wiring. *All Cats Have Asperger Syndrome* and *All Dogs Have ADHD* by Kathy Hoopman are two of our favorites.

Remember That *Everything* Is an Opportunity for Growth

The best part about making self-discovery and personal growth a core value of our family is that literally *everything* is an opportunity to get curious, learn, and grow. We want to notice, reflect, ask questions, and help our children make meaningful connections. Here's what it might sound like in a variety of situations:

- I noticed you turned off your computer without any yelling today. How did you do that? What do you think was different about today compared with yesterday?
- Have you noticed that getting out the door for school at the end of the week is much harder than at the beginning of the week? Do you have any ideas about why that might be?
- It seems like when you're listening to soft classical music, you're able to better focus on your homework. Have you noticed a connection?

- You had no trouble getting to sleep last night compared with most nights. I wonder why. Do you have any ideas?
- Did you notice any difference in the way your body felt after you ate that cupcake? What did it feel like?

Embracing these questions also offers a helpful reframe for us in the midst of particularly difficult moments. If we adopt a mindset of curiosity and consider tough moments as opportunities for our child to learn more about themselves, our experience of them can feel completely different (and better). *Everything* is information: When we are willing to *use* that information to expand our knowledge of what our child needs, and share those insights with him or her, even the hardest days can lead to true growth.

The key is looking for opportunities to help your child make connections between their thoughts, feelings, and action by regularly asking questions in a nonjudgmental way. By our doing so, our kids will recognize the value in reflecting and identifying their personal roadblocks and successful strategies. With every connection they make, they'll become that much better prepared to tackle whatever comes up next. At the same time, we want to generously tell them where we see growth—not through empty praise but by recognition of effort and progress. *I can tell you're trying to be more patient with your brother, even when he's really pushing your buttons. I know it's not easy, and it's wonderful to see. Nice work!* Words like these not only make our kids beam with pride, but serve as positive reinforcement to inspire even *more* growth.

Pro Tip Embrace the question *What can I help my child learn in this moment?* and ask it anytime you're facing a challenging or frustrating situation.

Make Self-Discovery a Priority for You, Too

Self-discovery work doesn't have to stop with our kids. In fact, when we embrace our own self-discovery, we're not only modeling important skills for our kids, but strengthening our families. This idea is a big piece of Giselle Marzo Segura's work through her business Strength Clusters, and I love the way she talks about how we can experience profound personal growth when we lean in to who our children are and recognize the gifts that come with the challenges. As Giselle says, "Our differently wired children are here to teach us to remember our strengths and to rediscover 'who we are.' As adults, we may have forgotten our strengths and settled for a life far away from meaning and purpose. When we work on strengths with our children, we have the opportunity to also connect with our strengths, our gifts— that which we were meant to do, and to be. It's a journey that is not just focused on the child, but on growth toward a life of wholeness, meaning, and purpose for all involved."

Start Now Introduce your child to Carol Dweck's theory of mindset and work together with them to identify where they land on the map of growth mindset versus fixed mindset.

This kind of personal development won't just happen—we have to actually do the work. Who are your favorite gurus? What kinds of writers or bloggers or podcasters inspire you to reflect? How can you set aside time to do your own work?

If It Doesn't Exist, Create It

"If it's a good idea, go ahead and do it."
—Grace Hopper

Dr. Debra Caudy and her husband, Dr. Clay Heighten, of Dallas recognized the lack of services for young adults with autism, such as their son, who was aging out of the school system and facing a future without the support that had helped him make meaningful progress. So they joined together with other families in their same situation to create 29 Acres, a "safe and dynamic housing development where adults with autism will live and be offered enriched, evidence-based programming that will allow them to build relationships and feel value, success and happiness in their lives." The nonprofit, in development mode as of this writing, hopes to secure the funding to bring their brilliant vision to life—building a twenty-nine-acre community featuring sustainable, simply designed housing for up to sixty people, 24-7 security, and custom programs for residents focusing on career readiness, independent living, emotional well-being, and more. Debra and Clay and the families joining them saw a need and took matters into their own hands. I can't wait to watch their vision come to life.

Being in Choice

There's a single-panel cartoon, I believe from an old issue of the *New Yorker*, that I absolutely love. The black-and-white illustration features a person clinging to and looking out between two jail bars. Only as it turns out, he's not in jail at all—he's just holding two foot-long bars in front of his face. To me this cartoon says a lot about how we can think ourselves into a corner and forget about the fact that we're in choice in every aspect of our lives. That's right—*choice.*

When I interviewed Zachary Morris, founder of the LEARN Inc. school, for my podcast, we got into a lengthy conversation about this idea of *choice,* and I love his perspective on it, which is rooted in Marshall Rosenberg's model of nonviolent communication. Zach told me, "I would say there's never anything we *have* to do. We always have choice. We might base those choices on certain perceived repercussions in relation to what our needs and intentions are, and so we get directed by our experience and what we're trying to manifest for ourselves and for our children. But ultimately, we always get to choose. So I would encourage parents to really question that 'have-to' mindset that we can so easily slip into. Parents are the best advocates for their children. We can stand up to the existing structures if they're not working for us, and figure out other options."

So far we've talked about getting out of our limited thinking and envisioning how we'd design our ideal day if we knew we would be successful. We explored letting go of our own emotional baggage, recognizing when our personal triggers have been provoked, and committing to parenting our children from a place of possibility instead of fear. But for this last Tilt, I want to talk explicitly about fully leaning in to the power of our personal choice and using it as a foundation for creating what our child needs. Because the truth is, what our child needs may not exist yet. But why should that stop us?

Doing whatever is necessary to support our child takes guts. Chances are other people will question our choices, doubt our chances of success, and judge our willingness to take a different path. We've got to be willing to ditch the fear and lean in to our courage. On rough days, I still question what I'm doing… what our nontraditional education and life choices will look like down the road. And that's when I draw upon the work of author and thought leader Simon Sinek, who, in his book *Start with Why*, explains the benefits of focusing on the *why* before getting caught up in the *how* and the *what*. Although his message is geared toward leaders, I've found that this same idea applies to every aspect of life. When we home in on our personal *why* for doing anything... including *why* we're making the bold choices and creating what our atypical child needs... the *how* and the *what* become not only easier, but doable. Instead of feeling trapped and powerless, we can embrace a mindset of freedom and the belief that anything is possible. (Because it is.)

There Are No Dead Ends

Parents like us trying to fit our child into what exists frequently find ourselves in an uphill battle with seemingly very few options for getting to the other side. We have to be scrappy, resilient, and relentless, even in the midst of our own personal crises of thinking we don't have what it takes to do this most important job of our life. But despite the fact that we may not have unlimited time or resources, and we're more or less making it up as we go along, I believe every one of us has what it takes to create what our child needs to help them thrive.

Let me paint a picture of how we want this to look and feel. Because like everything else in life, it starts with our thoughts and beliefs. We want to model possibility and creative problem-solving for our kids, because when we do, they'll grow up knowing there is no such thing as a closed door or a dead end—there are just opportunities for new ideas. We want our kids to know what bravery looks like because they'll see it on our faces every day. These are lessons that can't be taught, but rather are felt and experienced. When our child knows we're willing to create what doesn't exist to ensure their success, they'll know there's no limit to what's possible for them. And what better gift could we give to them?

Get Inspired

In many ways, this last Tilt is the culmination of all the work we've tackled throughout the rest of this book. We have committed to questioning everything we thought we knew about parenting to uncover what could be. We have spent ample time exploring areas where we may be engaging in limited thinking and staying stuck. We have exposed our baggage and recurring fear triggers so they no longer hold sway over us. And we have built a foundation for ourselves in which we are in touch with our intuition, have activated our inner advocate, and let go of things that are no longer serving us and our children. Now we are ready to embrace all this learning and step into what is possible by THINKING BIG and considering what we want to create for our children.

There are many great examples from which to glean inspiration and learn—people who followed the tug in their soul to create what they wish existed for their own child. People such as Carissa Tozzi and Gena Mann, who created Wolf + Friends, an inclusive online shopping and lifestyle destination designed to highlight toys, playroom decor, thoughtful style ideas, and inspiring advice for typical and atypical kids. Carissa and Gena created it because they were tired of shopping experiences for products aimed at special-needs kids embodying an overriding feeling of doom and gloom. As Gena, mother of several differently wired kids, said in an interview with the *New York Times* about why she felt so passionately about bringing Wolf + Friends to life, "You know what I really wanted? A space online where autism didn't suck all the time."

There are numerous examples of parents of differently wired kids who, finding the educational options available to be lacking, created their own. No, I'm not talking about homeschooling—I mean they created their own schools. This is the case for the Quad Preparatory

Reflect

What one thing would I change right now if I could that would have a positive, tangible effect on my child's immediate experience?

. . .

Am I willing to take a risk and/or get uncomfortable to help my child be fully seen and embraced?

. . .

What is the biggest hurdle I need to overcome when it comes to embracing my brave self?

School in New York City, a school designed to support 2e learners that was founded by Kimberly Busi after she watched her twice-exceptional son become increasingly sad and anxious in a traditional school setting. Another school for 2e kids, Bridges Academy in Los Angeles, began as a private tutoring arrangement for three students by educator Carolyn McWilliams in 1994. Educator Dr. Kirsten Stein, who was homeschooling her own gifted children, ultimately founded Athena's Advanced Academy as a virtual online learning experience for gifted learners from around the world. I even interviewed one woman, Devon MacEachron, who went back to school to get her PhD in school psychology because she wanted to better understand her differently wired kids. Today she specializes in assessing and supporting twice-exceptional learners.

Of course, there's inspiration to be found all around us, in people just like you and me. People like Sherry, mother of a twelve-year-old with ADHD, who partnered with another mom to create a small neighborhood support group for parents raising differently wired kids; or Brooke, who runs a group at her daughter's public school for those with 2e kids; or the hundreds of parents who start and moderate private Facebook groups for parents who are seeking comfort, camaraderie, and advice.

My advice? Make inspiration a part of your daily routine. Just as we are what we eat, we are what we think about. And if we want to lean in to the belief that we have the power to do big things, we want to fuel ourselves with stories and words that strengthen that belief. Here are a few ideas for getting your daily inspiration fix:

- Follow people who inspire you on Pinterest or Instagram.
- Listen to an interview with a change maker on Jonathan Fields's podcast *Good Life Project*.
- Read Chris Guillebeau's excellent blog, *The Art of Non-Conformity*.
- Dive into a few pages of a memoir or autobiography of someone who has changed the world by following their big (crazy) ideas.
- Start your day by watching a TED or TEDx Talk.
- Dream and scheme in your journal each morning by exploring your ideas for what you want to create to better your child's life.

Create Your Own Cheering Squad

When Julie Neale launched her online movement and podcast, *Mother's Quest*, she did so because she wanted to create a community to inspire mothers to live what she calls their E.P.I.C. lives (Engaged, Passionate, Invested, Connected) and recognize that we're all the hero of our own life's journey. But she also created this community in large part because she wanted to meet her *own* needs. In addition to generously sharing with her audience, Julie brings guests on to her podcast who are mothers she can learn from, as a way for her to get the support she craves as she strives to live her own E.P.I.C. life.

We don't have to start podcasts or online communities to feel buoyed by support and inspiration, but we can follow Julie's lead and actively surround ourselves with people who not only inspire us, but wholeheartedly believe in us and will cheer us on as we do the brave work of creating the circumstances, opportunities, and life that will allow our kids to thrive. Our cheering squad might be made up of family members, friends, or mentors. We may even have people we consider to be in our corner whom we've never met—authors or podcasters or high-profile thought leaders whose life's work inspires us to tap into the power within.

Whatever it looks like, the purpose of our cheering squad is to form a foundation on which we feel confident about creating what we want to create for our children and our family. Just as a good cheerleader never loses faith in his or her team, our cheering squad will always be a source of motivation, inspiration, confidence, and strength.

Remember That You Are More Powerful Than You Know

Melissa Wardy, who put her successful solopreneur business on hold when she began homeschooling her differently wired kids two years ago, was challenged to build the kind of school and social situation that her children needed, especially for her daughter Amelia. Because Melissa and her kids are frequently out in nature climbing and hiking near their home in Texas, she uses the metaphor of mountain climbing when talking about her personal journey of creating what didn't exist to help her children thrive.

"You know, there are times where I'm looking at this forty-foot-high rock and I'm just thinking, *There is no way up this thing. I will fall to my death and then my children are going to watch me die from a broken neck and it's going to be awful.* But then I'm like, *Oh wait— there's a toehold. Okay, if I put my hand like this and wedge my knee like that, I can get up.* And next thing I know, I'm ten feet higher. Then I'm like, *Okay, now I'm ten feet off the ground and there's no way out of this.* But I just keep looking. And like I always tell my kids," she continues, "when we're bouldering, the rock has the answers. Just look at the rock for your answers and they'll come out to you. And it always comes true. There's always a path."

I love this story because it reminds us that even when we're afraid, even when we don't know how we'll get to where we need to go, we can find a way if we're willing to take those first steps. When we're motivated by love and committed to doing what it takes to help our children thrive, only a fool would underestimate what we're capable of.

Sometimes it's helpful to remind ourselves of just how powerful we are by reflecting on times when we accomplished something we didn't think was possible.

For me, it is the memory of crossing the finish line after my first marathon, in 1996. I hadn't properly trained for the race, but after getting an entry at the last minute, I felt I couldn't pass up the opportunity. I will never forget hobbling across the finish line in just under five hours, smiling through tears of relief, disbelief, and pride. I can still muster up those emotions when I reflect on that moment more than twenty years later, and it serves as a reminder of how strong I am and what's possible when I believe in myself and when I tap into my power.

We all have those moments, and I encourage you to call on them as a way to remind yourself of just how capable you are. Think about a time when you did something you didn't think was possible, when you felt your strongest and most empowered, when you defied all odds. That same person who did all those things is part of who you are. And he or she is waiting for you to give the signal that it's time to get busy and take bold action.

Start Somewhere, Start Now

Of the books I've written for young women, my favorite is *Doable: The Girls' Guide to Accomplishing Just About Anything*. I wrote it to give young women the tools and information they need to take any idea, no matter how small or how epic, and plot a viable path to bring it to life. Perhaps the most important step in the Doable process is to break down the big vision into small tasks so that what initially feels like a big, overwhelming, jumbled mess of ideas can be transformed into manageable, doable steps.

This is what we can do in our parenting lives, too. As we consider what we want to create in support of our child, we can look at the big vision and think about small baby steps that can propel us forward. Parenting these differently wired kids is a day-by-day (sometimes minute-by-minute) kind of thing anyway—no need to try to tackle everything at once. The important thing is to give yourself permission to take it slow and steady, and *just start.* Think about what small change you can make today to start creating more of that ideal world in your life for tomorrow and beyond. Once you know what you need to do, get busy doing it.

Join the Revolution

At the start of this book, I asked you to imagine a world where you could ditch the worry, fear, and guilt; where you could talk openly about who your child is without worry of stigma; where you could bring empathy and respect to your parenting; where you could feel present, secure, confident, and, yes, even joyful in knowing that you are exactly the parent your child needs.

Because, this vision right here? This is how we work toward that larger goal of making the world a more accepting and supportive place for neurodiverse people. As parents and caregivers and educators of differently wired children everywhere, we must make this goal our critical contribution to sparking the inevitable sea change to come.

I hope that what I've shared in this book has helped you grow closer to that vision. I hope it inspires you to start—and stick with—game-changing conversations with friends, family members, educators, and other parents.

And I hope you feel the power in our numbers and know that we are right there with you as you move boldly forward. Because what I know for sure is that *you are not alone* in this. At TiLT Parenting, we're building a passionate community of parents just like you, and together we are going to do some epic stuff. Just visit www.tiltparenting.com to join us.

Thank you for being in this revolution with me. I'll see you on the front line.

Acknowledgments

Writing *Differently Wired* was one of the most challenging projects I've ever embarked upon. Luckily, I was buoyed by an incredible community of friends, family, colleagues, and the bravest parents you'll ever meet.

I am deeply grateful for the wise team at Workman Publishing. The best editorial team—Maisie Tivnan (my person), Page Edmunds, Suzie Bolotin, Beth Levy, and Danny Cooper; an incredible design team—Galen Smith and Janet Vicario; and my dream team in PR and marketing—Selina Meere, Chloe Puton, Rebecca Carlisle, Zelina Bennett, Lathea Williams, and Cindy Lee. This truly was a match made in heaven. Thank you for your deep commitment to bringing this book to life.

To Maria Provok—thank you for sharing my podcast with Page and getting the ball rolling in the first place!

To my wonderful agent, Susan Schulman—I love that you knew this book was an inevitability way back when. Thank you for your friendship, your belief in my vision, and your dedication to this project, to my career as a writer, and to my role as a mother over the past eighteen years. I'm so grateful.

I was fortunate enough to tap into the wisdom of sage mentors at every stage of the journey in creating TiLT Parenting and writing *Differently Wired*, including Jonathan Fields, Pamela Slim, Elizabeth Marshall, Theo Nestor, and Jessika Lynch. I can't imagine a more kick-ass team!

To the incredible people who helped me meet Asher's needs while not losing sight of my own—Alison Bower, Julie George, Margaret Webb, Courtney Macavinta, Deborah Sweet, and Jennifer Finnlayson-Fife. And the educators who truly saw and embraced my boy—Kerry McMannis, Sarah Graham, Pamela Hobart Carter, Marissa Baratian, Siri Miller, and Rachel Donnelly Smith.

To my research assistant, Maddie Kroll—thank you for helping me with the big and little stuff and caring so much about this book!

To the lovely humans who work at my favorite Amsterdam writing spots, Anne&Max, Dignita, and Drovers Dog—thanks for the caffeine, the great atmosphere, and the friendly smiles.

To Angela Santomero—thank you for your friendship and for the opportunity to collaborate on your brilliant book *Preschool Clues*. I love that we spent 2017 supporting each other in bringing our messages to the world!

To my Amsterdam bestie and work and retreat partner, Simone Davies—every single day I'm grateful for your friendship, your love of my boy, your beautiful children, your wisdom, and your endless supply of good ideas (how do you do that?).

To my sister, Michele Reber—thank you for reading early (and late) drafts and being there for me anytime I needed to talk, vent, brainstorm, and freak out (not to mention being the best auntie my boy could hope for).

To my soul sister Alice Wilder, who saw the possibility for the journey Asher would take me on long before I did. Your friendship and belief in me and in the change I hope to bring to the world is a constant source of fuel.

To AnneMarie Kane and Ed and Renee Adams—having you as "my people" is a gift I am forever grateful for. Thank you for loving me and my family so deeply.

A special thanks to the friends who invited me for coffees and kept me sane during deadlines—Donna Bardsley, Emmy McCarthy, Gia Duke, Lee Davis, and Daniel Afonso; and dear friends far and wide who have been part of my parent support team over the years—Alison Bower, Gina McManus, Sara Gersten-Rothenberg, Mardi Douglas, Elizabeth Kiyasu, Bridget Perry, Tip Blish, and Judy Aks.

Thank you to my parents, Dale and MaryLou—I feel your encouragement and love every day. And to my in-laws, Barbara and David—thank you for always cheering me on!

To Derin, my partner in all things in parenting and life—*you're my rock*, now and always. Also, thank you for watching Netflix with me late into the night, for the generous foot rubs, for your endless belief in me, and for your love.

To Asher—you are pretty much my absolute favorite person on the planet, not to mention my heart, my inspiration, and my teacher. I love you fiercely.

To the incredible parents who told me their personal stories for inclusion in this book—thank you for your trust in me and for sharing your experiences so others could see their own lives reflected. I am inspired by each and every one of you for the love, advocacy, and boldness you bring to your parenting.

To the wise coaches, parenting experts, scientists, therapists, educators, and authors who generously shared their wisdom with me for the *TiLT Parenting* podcast and for this book—thank you for what you do. You are guiding lights for parents like me and, plainly put, you make our lives better.

Lastly, to everyone in the TiLT community—knowing you are in this with me, raising your incredible children, doing the difficult work of moving society forward, and embracing the chaos and messiness that can come with the territory, is something for which I will forever be grateful. *Our village rocks.*

Selected Sources

Bright Kids Who Can't Keep Up: Help Your Child Overcome Slow Processing Speed and Succeed in a Fast-Paced World by Ellen Braaten, PhD, and Brian Willoughby, PhD (The Guilford Press, 2014)

The Explosive Child: A New Approach for Understanding and Parenting Easily Frustrated, Chronically Inflexible Children by Ross W. Greene, PhD (HarperCollins, 2014)

Far from the Tree: Parents, Children, and the Search for Identity by Andrew Solomon (Scribner, 2012)

The Gift of Failure: How the Best Parents Learn to Let Go So Their Children Can Succeed by Jessica Lahey (HarperCollins, 2015)

The Gift of Maybe: Finding Hope and Possibility in Uncertain Times by Allison Carmen (TarcherPerigee, 2014)

Mindset: The New Psychology of Success by Carol S. Dweck (Ballantine Books, 2006)

My Life with Asperger's (blog)

NeuroTribes: The Legacy of Autism and the Future of Neurodiversity by Steve Silberman (Avery, 2015)

Not What I Expected: Help and Hope for Parents of Atypical Children by Rita Eichenstein, PhD (TarcherPerigee, 2015)

The Out-of-Sync Child: Recognizing and Coping with Sensory Processing Disorder by Carol Stock Kranowitz, MA (TarcherPerigee, 2005)

Parenting Through the Storm: Find Help, Hope, and Strength When Your Child Has Psychological Problems by Ann Douglas (The Guilford Press, 2016)

Quiet: The Power of Introverts in a World That Can't Stop Talking by Susan Cain (Crown, 2012)

Thinking Differently: An Inspiring Guide for Parents of Children with Learning Disabilities by David Flink (William Morrow, 2014)

Unconditional Parenting: Moving from Rewards and Punishments to Love and Reason by Alfie Kohn (Atria, 2005)

The Whole-Brain Child: 12 Revolutionary Strategies to Nurture Your Child's Developing Mind by Daniel J. Siegel, MD, and Tina Payne Bryson, PhD (Delacorte Press, 2011)

Favorite Resources

ADHD

Faster Than Normal: Turbocharge Your Focus, Productivity, and Success with the Secrets of the ADHD Brain by Peter Shankman (TarcherPerigee, 2017)
Learning to Slow Down and Pay Attention: A Book for Kids About ADHD by Kathleen G. Nadeau, PhD, and Ellen B. Dixon, PhD (Magination Press, 2004)
The Survival Guide for Kids with ADHD by John F. Taylor, PhD (Free Spirit Publishing, 2013)
ADDitude (magazine)
ADHD Kids Rock (website)
Eye to Eye (mentoring organization)
Faster Than Normal (podcast)
Transforming ADHD (website and coach)
Understood (organization)

Anxiety

Freeing Your Child from Anxiety: Practical Strategies to Overcome Fears, Worries, and Phobias and Be Prepared for Life—from Toddlers to Teens by Tamar E. Chansky, PhD (Harmony Books, 2014)
Helping Your Anxious Child: A Step-by-Step Guide for Parents by Ronald M. Rapee, PhD, et al. (New Harbinger Publications, 2008)
Hey Warrior by Karen Young (Little Steps Publishing, 2016)
What to Do When You Worry Too Much: A Kid's Guide to Overcoming Anxiety by Dawn Huebner, PhD (Magination Press, 2006)
Hey Sigmund (website)

Asperger's/Autism

Asperger's Rules! How to Make Sense of School and Friends by Blythe Grossberg, PsyD (Magination Press, 2012)
The Asperkid's (Secret) Book of Social Rules: The Handbook of Not-So-Obvious Social Guidelines for Tweens and Teens with Asperger Syndrome by Jennifer Cook O'Toole (Jessica Kingsley Publishers, 2013)
Look Me in the Eye: My Life with Asperger's by John Elder Robison (Three Rivers Press, 2008)
NeuroTribes: The Legacy of Autism and the Future of Neurodiversity by Steve Silberman (Avery, 2015)
Asperger Experts (website)
My Life with Asperger's (blog)

Gifted and Twice-Exceptional

Bright Not Broken: Gifted Kids, ADHD, and Autism by Diane M. Kennedy and Rebecca S. Banks (Jossey-Bass, 2011)

Misdiagnosis and Dual Diagnoses of Gifted Children and Adults: ADHD, Bipolar, OCD, Asperger's, Depression, and Other Disorders by James T. Webb, PhD, et al. (Great Potential Press, 2005)

Parenting Gifted Kids: Tips for Raising Happy and Successful Gifted Children by James Delisle PhD (Prufrock Press, 2006)

A Parent's Guide to Gifted Children by James T. Webb, PhD, et al. (Great Potential Press, 2007)

The Davidson Institute for Talent Development (organization)

Dr. Devon MacEachron (blog and diagnostician)

Gifted Homeschoolers Forum (website and online classes)

Hoagies' Gifted Education Page (hoagiesgifted.org) (website)

Johns Hopkins Center for Talented Youth (organization)

Supporting the Emotional Needs of the Gifted (SENG) (organization)

Twice Exceptional Children's Advocacy (TECA) (organization)

2e Newsletter

2e: Twice Exceptional (film)

2e2: Teaching the Twice-Exceptional (film)

Learning Differences

The Dyslexia Empowerment Plan: A Blueprint for Renewing Your Child's Confidence and Love of Learning by Ben Foss (Ballantine Books, 2016)

The Dyslexic Advantage: Unlocking the Hidden Potential of the Dyslexic Brain by Brock L. Eide, MD, MA, and Fernette F. Eide, MD (Hudson Street Press, 2011)

If You're So Smart, How Come You Can't Spell Mississippi? by Barbara Esham (Mainstream Connections, 2013)

Overcoming Dyslexia: A New and Complete Science-Based Program for Reading Problems at Any Level by Sally Shaywitz, MD (Vintage Books, 2005)

Thinking Differently: An Inspiring Guide for Parents of Children with Learning Disabilities by David Flink (William Morrow, 2014)

Eye to Eye (mentoring organization)

National Association of Learning Disabilities (organization)

Understood (organization)

Processing Disorders and Executive Functioning

Bright Kids Who Can't Keep Up: Help Your Child Overcome Slow Processing Speed and Succeed in a Fast-Paced World by Ellen Braaten, PhD, and Brian Willoughby, PhD (The Guilford Press, 2014)

The Out-of-Sync Child Has Fun: Activities for Kids with Sensory Integration Dysfunction by Carol Stock Kranowitz, MA (TarcherPerigee, 2003)

The Out-of-Sync Child: Recognizing and Coping with Sensory Processing Disorder by Carol Stock Kranowitz, MA (TarcherPerigee, 2005)

Smart but Scattered: The Revolutionary "Executive Skills" Approach to Helping Kids Reach Their Potential by Peg Dawson, EdD, and Richard Guare, PhD (The Guilford Press, 2009)

Seth Perler (website and coach)

General Parenting

The Explosive Child: A New Approach for Understanding and Parenting Easily Frustrated, Chronically Inflexible Children by Ross W. Greene, PhD (HarperCollins, 2014)

Far from the Tree: Parents, Children, and the Search for Identity by Andrew Solomon (Scribner, 2012)

The Gift of Failure: How the Best Parents Learn to Let Go So Their Children Can Succeed by Jessica Lahey (HarperCollins, 2015)

No-Drama Discipline: The Whole-Brain Way to Calm the Chaos and Nurture Your Child's Developing Mind by Daniel J. Siegel, MD, and Tina Payne Bryson, PhD (Bantam Books, 2014)

Positive Discipline: The Classic Guide to Helping Children Develop Self-Discipline, Responsibility,Cooperation, and Problem-Solving Skills by Jane Nelsen Ed.D. (Ballantine Books, 2011)

Unconditional Parenting: Moving from Rewards and Punishments to Love and Reason by Alfie Kohn (Atria, 2005)

The Whole-Brain Child: 12 Revolutionary Strategies to Nurture Your Child's Developing Mind by Daniel J. Siegel, MD, and Tina Payne Bryson, PhD (Delacorte Press, 2011)

The Child Mind Institute (website and organization)

How to Talk to Kids About Anything (podcast)

Lives in the Balance (website and organization)

Margaret Webb (parent coaching)

Homeschooling

Creative Homeschooling: A Resource Guide for Smart Families by Lisa Rivero (Great Potential Press, 2002)

Educating Your Gifted Child: How One Public School Teacher Embraced Homeschooling by Celi Trépanier (GHF Press, 2015)

Athena's Advanced Academy (online learning)

Crushing Tall Poppies (blog)

Gifted Homeschooler's Forum (online learning and resource)

Book Club Discussion Questions

As Debbie writes in *Differently Wired*, we can *all* play a role in changing the way neurodifference is experienced in the world. Here are some questions to get people thinking—and talking—about how we can best move forward together.

1. Debbie suggests society embrace a new paradigm where neurodifference is supported in every aspect of life. Are you in alignment with this vision? Why or why not? What do you think it will take for this shift to occur?

2. Debbie identifies four factors keeping the current paradigm in place: parents of neurotypical children, the current educational model, the "broken system," and parents raising atypical kids. Do you agree with her? Which one do you believe is the most powerful contributor? How can it best be addressed?

3. Debbie suggests that "difference is difference" and encourages people to embrace neurodiversity as a broad spectrum rather than fitting people into individual diagnostic buckets. Do you agree? Why or why not?

4. Debbie prefers the term "differently wired" over terms like "disorder." What are your thoughts? Do you think it helps or hurts the movement?

5. In reading *Differently Wired*, did you recognize any negative beliefs or prejudices you hold regarding neurodiversity and/or specific diagnostic labels? If so, what are they? Have they changed since reading this book?

6. What do you believe is the key to eliminating the negative stigmas associated with diagnoses such as ADHD, autism, giftedness, and anxiety?

7. Debbie believes that transparency by families raising atypical kids is an important step in shifting the paradigm, recognizing that stigma is real and that disclosure is a personal decision. Where do you stand on this issue?

8. What do you see as the biggest roadblocks schools face in supporting atypical students? What changes would you like to see so all kids can be embraced?

9. Which of the eighteen Tilts resonated most with you? Which ones do you feel have the most potential to effect meaningful change, both within individual families and within society at large?

10. What role can you play in shifting the experience for neurodiverse kids, and the families raising them? What are you willing to do differently moving forward?

Index

A

Ableism, 61

Acceptance, hard-wired craving for, 105–6, 214

Accepting who child is, 114–23; appreciating child's unique wiring and, 122–23; homeschooling and, 114–16; leaning in and, 117–18; mourning who child isn't and, 118–20; reframing what is and, 121–22. *See also* Arguing with reality

ADHD, 25–28, 38, 40, 52, 57, 62, 66, 117, 146, 168, 203, 224; dealing with interruptions and, 116; energy shifts and, 227–28; myths and untruths about, 25–26; number of children with diagnosis of, 26–27, 41; school options and, 51

Advocating, 194–202; by children for themselves, 166–67, 246, 247–48; creating what doesn't exist and, 256–64; need for, 195–97; for outside-the-box, alternative solutions, 199–200; with teachers and school administrators, 196, 199–202; tips for, 197–99

Aggression toward others, 46–47

Aligning with your partner, 203–13. *See also* Partner

Anxiety disorders, 38–39, 63, 91, 156, 211

Anxiety or stress, 106, 153, 222; about unknowns in future, 55–57, 125–26, 229, 238; atypical child's state of, 156–59, 195, 205; developing strategies for coping with, 160–62, 164; giftedness and, 30–31; home as safe space and, 158–59, 162–63; responses to, 47–48; your child's triggers and, 159–60; your own triggers and, 229–30

Apologizing: by child for who they are, vi–vii, 252–53; for your child, 214, 215, 216

Arguing with reality, 114–23; homeschooling and, 114–16; ignoring child's needs and, 116–17; leaning in as alternative to, 117–18; making difference a bad thing and, 116, 117; mourning who child isn't and, 118–20; recognizing in yourself, 120–21; reframing what is and, 121–22; "should" and "shouldn't" statements and, 120–21

Asperger's/high-functioning autism, 34–36, 38, 56; controversy over terminology for, 35–36; defense mode and, 159. *See also* Autism

Assessments, 73; developmental milestones and, 135–36; expense of, 54; parent's resistance to, 78; waiting lists for, 74, 75. *See also* Diagnoses

Autism, 27, 34–36, 38, 44, 64, 66, 70, 73, 206; effect of energy on, 227; housing development for, 256; increases in diagnoses of, 41; mild or high-functioning (Asperger's), 34–36, 38, 56, 159; parents' narratives of suffering and, 44; unsafe behaviors and, 47–48

B

Behavior: as communication, 147–49, 150; helping child connect intention and, 153–54; interpreting the underlying reason for, 149–51; routinely "correcting," 121–22; unsafe, 47–48

Behavioral challenges. *See* Challenges

Being in the moment, 236–39

Berger, Kate, 127, 236, 238–39, 245

Blind spots, parents' own emotional baggage and, 151–52

Brain science, exploring, 250–51

Bravery, 132–33

Bright spots in every day, 242–43